JESUS KING OF LOVE

Jesus
King of Love

by
FATHER MATEO CRAWLEY-BOEVEY, SS.CC.

Sixth Edition
Revised and Updated

FRANCISCAN PUBLISHERS
Pulaski, Wisconsin

NIHIL OBSTAT:
  Francis Larkin, SS.CC.
  Censor Delegatus

IMPRIMI POTEST:
  Fintan D. Sheeran, SS.CC.
  Provincial

NIHIL OBSTAT:
  Nicholas L. Gross
  Censor

IMPRIMATUR:
  † Aloysius J. Wycislo
  Bishop of Green Bay
  February 4, 1970

Library of Congress Catalog Number: 79 - 119756

This edition was revised by the Fathers of the Sacred Hearts, National Center of the Enthronement, Washington, D.C.

FOREWORD

A book such as this, written by a recognized master of the spiritual life, and one who at the same time has given such clear indication of successful personal application of his teachings merits more than passing attention. When the history of Christian spirituality is extended in years to come to the period in which we are living, Father Mateo will unquestionably be singled out as the leader of a most helpful and inspiring movement for the sanctification of the family, and thus for the restoration of all things in Christ. The Enthronement of the Sacred Heart in the home has been the means of arousing and sustaining within thousands of families throughout the world the love of God and the loyalty to Christ our Lord, which must be the focal points of genuine domestic happiness and peace.

The homes of the mid-twentieth century, compared to those of even a quarter of a century ago, present an environment as revolutionary and unprecedented as that of the larger society in which they are situated. From the crowded apartment areas of large cities to the newly plotted townships of modern suburbia, the circumstances of the home have felt the impact of a positivistic and sensate philosophy of life. What was once an impregnable fortress has been brought into direct contact with an unbelievable complexity of social activity and achievement. The family of today no longer lives in isolation; its members are face to face with the world, even as they associate with one another around the fireside.

It is still true, however, that Christ our Lord must be the unseen head of every Christian home. It is He who strengthens the authority of parents; it is by His grace alone that fathers and mothers can rise to the dedication and self-sacrifice which are so necessary for the faithful discharge of their duties. And it is still true that Christ is the Model of obedience and filial love for sons and daughters who must learn in the home the lessons of adjustment to the demands of social life which are so important for their subsequent careers.

In "Jesus the King of Love," Father Mateo has written forcefully and practically of the blessings which are realized through the holy union of the members of families with our blessed Lord in His Sacred Heart. Father Mateo's zeal for spread of devotion to the Enthronement reflects his own conviction of the psychological value of its simple ritual. The home in which the Sacred Heart is enthroned, and whose members follow faithfully and perseveringly the implications of the Enthronement, will be a happy home, a God-fearing home and a peaceful home. May God continue to bless the efforts of all who work to promote devotion to the Sacred Heart of our Lord according to the teachings of this book.

† *Richard Cardinal Cushing*
ARCHBISHOP OF BOSTON

DEDICATION

This book is dedicated to all those who have shared with me the responsibility and the glory of the crusade of the Enthronement of the Sacred Heart. Read it and ponder it lovingly, for I have written it with love for the friends and apostles of the divine Heart of Jesus.

May these simple pages, by the grace of the King of Love, bring light and love into your interior life and your apostolate in hours of difficulty and trial. The book claims no literary value; it seeks only to make Jesus better known and better loved, for as St. Bernard says, "His Name is joy unspeakable, honey to the lips and music to the heart."

Love Him and make Him loved!

If you find these pages helpful, after reading them pass on the book to a friend.

Most Sacred Heart of Jesus, Thy Kingdom come!

Father Mateo Crawley-Boevey, SS.CC.

CONTENTS

Foreword --- 5
Dedication --- 7
Sketch of Father Mateo's Life --------------------------- 11
Origin of This Book ------------------------------------- 22
Introduction -- 25

Part I
IN THE SCHOOL OF THE SACRED HEART

Chapter 1: Life of Faith ------------------------------- 31
Chapter 2: Spirit of Faith ----------------------------- 37
Chapter 3: Life of Love -------------------------------- 44
Chapter 4: Loving Confidence --------------------------- 54
Chapter 5: Humility ------------------------------------ 69
Chapter 6: Into Thy Hands ------------------------------ 76
Chapter 7: Be Saints ----------------------------------- 79
Chapter 8: How To Become a Saint ----------------------- 88
Chapter 9: Generous Giving ---------------------------- 107
Chapter 10: Jesus in the Gospel ----------------------- 115
Chapter 11: The Holy Sacrifice of the Mass ------------ 125
Chapter 12: Jesus in the Blessed Sacrament ------------ 142
Chapter 13: Apostles Through Love --------------------- 148
Chapter 14: Apostolate of the Sacred Heart ------------ 160
Chapter 15: Catholic Action --------------------------- 168
Chapter 16: The Sin of Friends ------------------------ 176
Chapter 17: Mother and Queen -------------------------- 183
Chapter 18: The Prime Minister of the King of Love --- 191

Part II
AT HOME WITH THE SACRED HEART

Chapter 19: The Enthronement of the Sacred Heart
in the Home --- 199
Chapter 20: Behold, the Great King Is Coming! ------ 216
Chapter 21: Christian Family Living ----------------- 225
Chapter 22: The Feast of the Kingship of Our Lord
Jesus Christ --- 232

Part III
"WATCH ONE HOUR WITH ME"

Chapter 23: Night Adoration in the Home ------------ 239
Chapter 24: A Message to Night Adorers ------------- 252
Chapter 25: Two Holy Hours ----------------------- 256
Chapter 26: In the Sanctuary of the Home ----------- 272

APPENDICES

Appendix 1: How to Enthrone the Sacred Heart ------ 281
Appendix 2: The Ceremony of the Enthronement ----- 296
Appendix 3: Night Adoration — How It Works -------- 304
Appendix 4: The Popes Speak — Papal Approval ------ 311

SKETCH OF FATHER MATEO'S LIFE

Edward Crawley-Boevey Y Murga, the future Father Mateo, was born in Tingo, Peru, November 18, 1875, of an English father and a Peruvian mother. Toward the end of 1884, his parents moved to Valparaiso, Chile, where they placed young Edward in the college conducted by the Fathers of the Sacred Hearts. Here he showed a great aptitude for study and at the same time distinguished himself by deep piety and a remarkably apostolic spirit. The future apostle of the Sacred Heart began very early to exercise his zeal in his family circle, thanks especially to a precocious oratorical talent. No one was surprised when, as soon as his studies were finished, he entered the novitiate of the Fathers of the Sacred Hearts. He received the religious habit February 2, 1891, and was professed September 11, 1892.

During his philosophical and theological studies he was entrusted with the teaching of little children, and he devoted himself to this charge with remarkable success. On December 17, 1898, he was ordained a priest. Although, after ordination, Father Mateo assumed the professorship of a number of classes at the college, he devoted himself with great zeal to the sacred ministry, especially as director of the "Extern Association of the Sacred Hearts" and among the men. He had a particular attraction for the social apostolate, and with the aid of a generous benefactor he had a law school built beside the college. In 1906 its construction was completed, but on August 16 of the same year, a terrible earthquake demolished the beautiful building. Far from being discouraged, Father Mateo began reconstruction of the law school for the furtherance of Catholic education in Chile.

Despite these cares and the labors of teaching, he did not neglect his preaching nor his apostolate of spreading devotion to the Sacred Heart, the practice and propagation of which is one of the ends of the Congregation of the Sacred Hearts of Jesus and Mary. Having discovered in the room of his Provincial the celebrated picture of the Sacred Heart which had been used at the consecration of Ecuador to the King of Love, by its President, Garcia Moreno, in 1873, Father Mateo had it framed and installed in the place of honor in the main room of the law school.

FIRST IDEAS OF THE ENTHRONEMENT IN FAMILIES

Meditation on the eloquent symbolism of this truly royal picture resulted in his preparing to undertake the work of bringing families closer to the Sacred Heart. The thought of installing the image of the Sacred Heart in the place of honor in the home, that is to say, of *enthroning* it, persistently occupied his mind. The project was still very vague and became definite only later. He wrote down some notes and composed a sample "Ceremonial." But he was to learn his providential mission in the sanctuary of Paray-le-Monial, where the Sacred Heart was waiting for him.

The combined works of teaching and priestly ministry, joined to the shocks occasioned by the earthquakes of 1906, had seriously impaired the health of Father Mateo, which had always been poor. On the advice of the doctors, it was decided to send him on a trip to Europe. Father Mateo left Chile in March, 1907. While he was in Rome, he submitted his project and the outline for the ceremonial of the Enthronement to His Eminence, Cardinal Vives, a friend of his family. Visibly moved and gratified, this Prince of the Church blessed and encouraged Father Mateo, saying to him, "It is a magnificent work. You must consecrate your life to it!"

INAUGURATION OF HIS CRUSADE OF LOVE

Encouraged by the eulogistic approbation of the Cardinal, Father Mateo solicited and obtained an audience with the gloriously reigning Pontiff, Pope St. Pius X, to whom he exposed the outline of his projected apostolate, at the same time imploring His Holiness to bless the project. The latter answered, "Not only do I permit you, but I *command* you to give your life for this work of social salvation." These words resounded like a command from heaven in the soul of the zealous priest, and he decided to go to Paray-le-Monial. There in the sanctuary of the apparitions of the Sacred Heart on August 24, 1907, he suddenly felt his whole being strangely moved, and not only did he find himself cured and ready to undertake his apostolic campaign, but by a sudden illumination he clearly saw the methodic plan of the work he was to do for the Christian regeneration of families and society. He determined to take up the work which had been barely outlined by St. Margaret Mary, to organize the practice of the Enthronement, and in a crusade of love truly worldwide, to make the Heart of Jesus the King of the family, and thus extend His reign over the entire world.

On his knees that memorable evening, Father Mateo definitely revised the plan and ceremonial of his crusade. Immediately after, from September 5 to October 15, he made a pilgrimage to the Holy Land, during which, according to the testimony of his companions, he inaugurated his apostolate for the Enthronement.

In 1907, Father Mateo arrived at the motherhouse of his congregation, in Braine-le-Comte, Belgium, and there received from his Superior General the same blessing and encouragement as he had received at Rome. He then returned to Valparaiso, Chile, where in 1908, he launched his campaign of love, continuing at the same time his course in the Faculty of Law.

WONDERFUL SUCCESS

Father Mateo's work in South America was crowned with startling success. Not only did he win to the Sacred Heart ordinarily devout Catholic families, but even bitter enemies of the Church. The Bishops of South America, highly enthusiastic about the results of Father Mateo's campaign, wrote glowing accounts of his work to Pope St. Pius X. The latter was pleased to bless the work especially and to grant special indulgences for the families of Chile.

The first World War was at its height when Father Mateo undertook to preach the reign of the Sacred Heart in France. At first he was told to wait until peace had been restored, but to the bishop who suggested this, the ardent apostle replied, "Did Noe build the ark *after* the deluge?" Such language as this showed the indomitable purpose of Father Mateo, and won for him the signal triumph of restoring to Christ's kingdom many families of war-torn France, so sorely in need of the Sacred Heart. Crowds thronged to hear him, and a great renewal of piety resulted everywhere. Many families solemnly enthroned the Sacred Heart, and diocese after diocese felt the effects of his apostolic zeal. The indifference and tepidity of the people gave way to the reign of love, and miracles of grace were daily recorded.

From France the mission of Father Mateo took him to Holland. He was told that the Dutch were not so easily aroused to enthusiasm as their southern neighbors, and that he could not hope for so fervent a response from them. Nothing daunted, the apostle of love replied that the love of the Sacred Heart is for *all nations* and that the Savior yearns to draw *all* to His Divine embrace. Although Father Mateo was not versed in the Dutch language, crowds came to hear him preach in French. His success was more marked than it had been in warmer climes, for even Protestants flocked to his lectures.

POPE BENEDICT XV BLESSED THE WORK

Impelled by invincible faith and zeal, Father Mateo next took up his crusade in Italy. Here he was received in audience by Pope Benedict XV, who requested him to preach and organize the work throughout the country. Two weeks later the Holy Father presented him with a letter written by his own hand in which he imparted his apostolic benediction on the crusade of love.

Conferences breathing a deep supernatural spirit and love for the Sacred Heart were delivered to spell-bound audiences. Retreats and triduums were arranged, all of which brought forth abundant fruits and left profound impressions. In all, Father Mateo preached in 103 dioceses of Italy. In reply to the Holy Father's question as to how he succeeded in winning the hearts of the people as he did, Father Mateo declared that he acted merely as the instrument of the Sacred Heart, whose own grace-giving words were the cause of his wonderful success. For the language of the Sacred Heart is a language of divine love and is understood by all, the unlearned as well as those in the highest positions.

The work of Father Mateo in central Europe was also carried on in Switzerland and the Grand Duchy of Luxemburg. His arrival was given small attention by the Catholic press, but in spite of this, the burning words of the apostle of the Enthronement soon found their way to the hearts of the people, with the result that the Sacred Heart found His rightful place in the home of many a family. Father Mateo then returned to Spain, where he was welcomed with the same enthusiasm as before. Wherever he went enthusiasm was enkindled. Everyone seemed eager to pledge allegiance to Christ the King, and to help in the inauguration and spread of His social reign. On May 30, 1919, the feast of St. Ferdinand, king of Spain, Father Mateo officially enthroned the Sacred Heart at the national monument of the Sacred Heart in Spain, with King Alfonso XIII presiding at the ceremony, and the two Queens, the Royal Family and all the government officials assisting.

THE CRUSADE CONTINUES TO EXTEND

In the early months of 1920 Father Mateo made a memorable tour through Belgium, preaching the Enthronement in crowded cathedrals and well-filled churches. Wherever he went he met with the warmest response. Bishops and clergy extended to him a kindly welcome both in towns and country districts. No one encouraged him more than did the renowned Prince of the Church, Cardinal Mercier. The latter urged him to visit King Albert, assuring him that the sincere, upright character and noble Catholic principles of the great Belgian monarch would lead him to appreciate the work of the Enthronement. At first Father Mateo hesitated, but he finally yielded. Cardinal Mercier wrote on his behalf to the soldier-king. The answer was an invitation for a private audience at the royal palace. King Albert expressed his delight at the visit and asked the zealous apostle to tell him of his mission and preaching. The audience lasted three-quarters of an hour. The King listened attentively to his visitor and joined him in prayer to the Sacred Heart. Father Mateo presented him with a beautiful bronze medallion of the Sacred Heart as a reminder of his pledge to the King of Love in behalf of Belgium. When Father Mateo was leaving, the King asked him to pray for him and for Belgium and to come again.

Father Mateo also made his first visit to Great Britain in 1920. Arriving in June, he made a rapid tour during his five-month stay. He visited Edinburgh, Glasgow, Dumfries, Manchester, Leeds, York, Bristol, London and many other cities. In every place where he preached, the churches were filled to overflowing and the people listened with great interest. The time was too short to satisfy all the requests for sermons and conferences both for the laity and religious.

In July, 1923, Father Mateo returned to England for a more extensive tour. Centers for the Work of the Enthronement were established everywhere, and the fire of his preaching spread to all districts. Everyone felt inspired by his intense earnestness, as well as his conviction of the truth of his mission. He was followed with the closest attention and all were sorry when his sermons came to an end. Not only did Father Mateo address adults; children also benefited by special talks arranged for them. On the occasion of his Silver Jubilee of priesthood, December 17, 1923, which was spent at the Convent of the Sacred Hearts in Weymouth, Father Mateo received over eight hundred letters, besides numerous telegrams and cards. His greatest joy was occasioned by a letter from His Holiness, Pope Pius XI.

January, 1925, found him again in Italy, where he worked incessantly. He visited almost every city and town of importance. On this return to Italy, Father Mateo had the great satisfaction of receiving the full approbation and gracious encouragement of Pope Pius XI. This Italian tour was followed by another visit to Belgium, and, a little later, by a return to Spain in October, 1925. Families who had already enthroned the Sacred Heart in their homes renewed allegiance to Christ the King.

Local newspapers gave considerable publicity to Father Mateo. "After an absence of four years," wrote one editor, "Spain welcomes once more the apostle of the Social Reign of the Sacred Heart, that religious aflame with love for our divine King, the founder and propagator of the Enthronement in the Home." Wherever he went, enthusiasm was enkindled anew. His year of apostolate in Spain (1925-1926), during which he traveled the length and breadth of the country, was extraordinarily fruitful.

The latter part of 1927 and the first months of 1928 (a period of about nine months) Father Mateo spent preaching his crusade in Portugal. He had but scanty knowledge of Portuguese at that time, and the work was little known before his arrival, but so deep was the impression made by his preaching that it seemed as if the miracle of Pentecost had been renewed. The sight of the assembled crowds made the Apostle of the Sacred Heart realize more than ever the invincible power of the doctrine of love.

A little later Father Mateo set out for another tour of Italy, where he spent the year of 1929 and the first seven months of 1930. Pope Pius XI graciously accorded him two private audiences shortly before he left Rome. The Holy Father manifested great interest in the Work of the Enthronement and repeatedly blessed Father Mateo and his apostolate. From Italy, Father Mateo journeyed to Switzerland.

A new crusade was made in Portugal in 1931. Father Mateo's 1928 tour had left indelible impressions and he was welcomed wholeheartedly. His campaign included twenty-four retreats for the clergy, and his time was so fully taken up that the only period of rest he found was the short space of Holy Week. As was to be expected, his untiring devotedness reaped abundant fruit. In the latter part of 1931, the itinerary of the zealous preacher took him once more to France. Crowds had thronged to hear him ten years before, and the echoes of that visit still reverberated throughout the country. Long-standing invitations for conferences, retreats and triduums were everywhere tendered to him. In spite of the fatigue of his incessant labors, Father Mateo experienced the greatest pleasure in beholding the fervor of the French nation and the eagerness of the people to make reparation to the King of Love. The crusade in France continued throughout the years of 1932, 1933 and 1934.

THE HOLY FATHER SENDS HIM TO THE FAR EAST

On October 19, 1934, Pope Pius XI commissioned Father Mateo to carry his crusade to the Far East, saying, "Go, and preach sanctity to the priests." On January 25 of the following year he embarked at Marseilles for Japan, and on March 4, 1935, he reached the land sanctified by the blood of so many martyred missionaries of later times. Five years of zealous and fruitful apostolate were spent in the regions of Japan and China (1935 and 1936), in the Pacific islands, the Philippines and Hawaii (1937-1938), and lastly in French Indo-China, Malacca, Macao, India and Ceylon (1939-1940). In India and Ceylon alone, Father Mateo preached twenty-three retreats to the European and Native clergy. One of the most touching was given to a group of formerly schismatic Jacobite priests who had been received into the Catholic Church. Though it was impossible to visit the interior of China on account of the war, Hong-Kong, Canton and Swatow were evangelized by Father Mateo. In January, 1940, he left Ceylon for the Philippines and Honolulu.

After sojourning some months in the Hawaiian Islands, the renowned preacher set out for the United States, and arrived in San Francisco, California, in October, 1940. His coming to this country had long been awaited with great eagerness, and his arrival was hailed as a most auspicious event by the lovers of the Sacred Heart. In a letter written before his arrival, Father Mateo gave expression to the joy and determination with which he was ready to give himself "in this promising land in order to make souls love the Adorable Lover, and to spread and strengthen the Social Reign of the Sacred Heart in the home, the sanctuary of the family, the family, the rock upon which the Church builds the present and future of society."

Except for a brief period of inactivity occasioned by illness, an uninterrupted succession of engagements filled Father Mateo's time. The four years he stayed in the United States, he devoted with intensive self-sacrificing labor to preaching in the cities of San Francisco, Los Angeles, San Diego, Tuscon, Louisville, Chicago, Milwaukee, Indianapolis, New York, Rochester (N.Y.), St. Paul, Washington, D.C., Springfield (Ill.), Dubuque, LaCrosse, Rochester (Minn.), and in Arkansas and Nebraska, where retreats for the clergy, days of recollection, triduums, conferences and lectures followed one another in quick succession.

In 1944 Father Mateo left for Canada where he preached almost without interruption for two years until illness forced him into a hospital. Here he continued his work by prayer, suffering and writing. Finally, in February, 1956, he recovered sufficiently to fly back to Valparaiso, Chile. Since then he has carried on his apostolate by his many articles and letters, written in various languages and sent to all parts of the world. He died on May 4, 1961, in the College of the Sacred Hearts, where his apostolate began.

In concluding this summary outline of Father Mateo's apostolate, let us add a few words on the characteristics of this great "Preacher of Love." It can be easily appreciated that his extensive travels, his close acquaintance with every class of people from popes and kings to the most lowly peasants, his command of six languages (Latin, Italian, Spanish, Portuguese, French and English), and many other cultural factors, admirably fit him for the work he had undertaken. His vast experience of extraordinary and miraculous incidents and striking conversions provided him likewise with an inexhaustible resource for conferences and sermons. His hearers testify that he preached with authority, force, clearness, and above all with zeal and sanctity. The divine unction in the preacher's words captured his audience. One priest writes of him: "I fail to find suitable words to express the sweet and lasting impression Father Mateo's preaching has made upon his listeners. His saintly demeanor, the clear and candid expositions of doctrines and events in a style peculiar to himself, the narration of innumerable miracles of conversion which the Sacred Heart of Jesus has wrought through his instrumentality, his timely, witty remarks, and bold but correct assertions on spirituality, but above all, his overflowing zeal while speaking about the immense love of the Sacred Heart, keep his audience spellbound. . . ."

On the occasion of Father Mateo's death, His Holiness, Pope John XXIII sent the following message to Father Henry Systermans, Superior General of the Fathers of the Sacred Hearts in Rome:

Segretaria di Stato
di Sua Santita

Dal Vaticano, li 16 Mai, 1960

N. 37637

Very Reverend Father:

His Holiness received your recent letter in which you apprised him of the death of Father Mateo Crawley-Boevey.

He wishes me to transmit to you his paternal and heartfelt condolences, and to assure you of his prayers for the repose of the soul of the illustrious religious.

The Holy Father is quite familiar with the role played by Father Mateo in the diffusion of the cult of the Sacred Heart, Whose tireless apostle he had been during his entire life. Moreover, he is pleased to think that the sorrowful loss undergone by your religious family will be compensated by the presence in Heaven — it is permitted to believe this — of a new and effective protector.

The Holy Father was also edified by the attitude manifested by the regretted deceased in his last moments. He has no doubt that your Congregation, following the example of Father Mateo, will continue to labor for the greater glory of the Sacred Heart. For this intention he most willingly imparts to you and to all the members of your institute a special Apostolic Blessing.

Kindly accept, Very Rev. Father, the assurances of my devotion in Our Lord.

A. Dell Acqua, Sust.

PRAYER
For the beatification of Father Mateo

Sacred Heart of Jesus, King of Love, mindful of all Father Mateo accomplished during his life to make You known, loved and served, if it be Your adorable Will, deign to manifest the sanctity of Your faithful apostle by granting us the grace we humbly ask through his intercession.

In return, we promise to become apostles of the family and social reign of Your Sacred Heart. Amen.

Most Sacred Heart of Jesus, Thy Kingdom Come! (5 times)
Immaculate Heart of Mary, Pray for us! (3 times)
St. Joseph, Pray for us!
St. Margaret Mary, Pray for us!
St. Therese of the Child Jesus, Pray for us!

(Fr. Mateo's favorite aspirations)

21

ORIGIN OF THIS BOOK

Father Mateo preached most of what this book contains; he did not write it. Monks, priests, nuns and laymen for their own personal satisfaction and profit made notes of whatever most attracted and pleased them in the conferences of Father Mateo. Little by little, these manuscripts were made public, passing from the notebook to the printing press, and this in general without the knowledge of the author.

Here is an instance which, interesting in itself, will give a graphic explanation of the origin of most of these publications. About the year 1917, Father Mateo was in Paray-le-Monial, where he had gone to seek rest, worn out as he was, mentally and physically. But if he went in search of repose to that "holy land" as he called it, he made a great mistake. Without consideration for his exhausted state, pilgrims besieged and importuned him in his hotel, in the street, even in the very chapel of the Visitation Convent where the Sacred Heart had appeared to St. Margaret Mary. He resolved to go elsewhere, but where? A priest suggested the Trappist Monastery at Sept-Fons. The tired missionary, convinced that no one there was acquainted with him or he with them, asked for a lodging where he could have the seclusion of a fortnight or so, and by return mail received a favorable answer.

But the proposed rest lasted some three hours! In the evening of the very day of his arrival, the Father Abbot, after some hesitation, asked him how many times a day and at what hours he would like to preach to his eighty Trappists. Imagine Father Mateo's surprise when, on urging his weariness and the spiritual necessity of seclusion and prayer, he was met with this answer from the Father Abbot: "That's all right, you can make your meditations out loud. We do not ask for more." It was impossible to refuse the task. Moreover the community insisted with such simplicity and affection that he had to begin a kind of retreat for the monks that very evening. Father Mateo said afterwards, playing on the word *La Trappe* (the French name of the Monastery), "I was caught in *the trap*."

The monks took notes of the two daily conferences; then at various times they invited Father Mateo to come again, and thus completed their notes; shortly afterwards they published all that they had taken down. In about six years, more than 30,000 copies of this booklet had been sold. Father Mateo first heard of this publication when the Trappists wanted to correct the third or fourth edition. The same thing happened, with slight variations, in the three convents of the Visitation nuns at Lyons, Le Puy and Orleans, where the nuns made three other pamphlets containing the conferences he gave in these convents. Soon after the Secretariate of Fribourg, Switzerland, published the notes of a retreat preached to the promoters of the Enthronement in that country. Others did the same thing.

A little later the idea arose of combining all these different pamphlets in one book, especially since all of them contained substantially the same doctrine of love: the Gospel of the Sacred Heart. This task was carried out at the Convent of the Visitation at Lyons, a pious and learned priest aiding in the work. This compendium was first published under the title of *Vers le Roi d'Amour* (Towards the King of Love).

One might ask the reason for this eagerness to publish these notes of Father Mateo's conferences, and the answer would be that in all his sermons and talks on the Reign of the Sacred Heart, three outstanding qualities always attracted attention.

First, the absolute simplicity of exposition and the unaffected style which is such an attraction in the Gospel, and which, as a vehicle for divine grace and the conviction of the preacher, is a thousand times better than any literary or rhetorical skill.

23

Second, the doctrine of the love of the Sacred Heart for us and His desire to be loved in return; not a new one assuredly — God preserve us from thinking such a thing! — but in general so little understood even among devout Catholics that Father Mateo says: "There is no lack of *devout* people, but there is of those who are *lovers* in spirit and truth." And who would dare to say there is no difference between the two? "To make that Love loved, to make It very much more loved," that is Father Mateo's one ardent desire, his one obsession, whether he be talking to an immense congregation in a cathedral or to religious in a monastery or convent. And the extraordinarily early canonization of the Little Flower set the desired seal on this pleasing and powerful doctrine, as well grounded as it is consoling.

Third, the truth of this doctrine was brought home to his listeners by a great number of striking examples, most of them remarkable conversions, told by one who had witnessed most of them and even had a hand in bringing them about.

Such as it was, the French edition of this book has passed through innumerable editions and has been translated into eighteen foreign languages and dialects, for the Sacred Heart has willed to bless the endeavors of the generous souls who sought in its publication nothing but His glory and the good of souls. This is the only just and reasonable explanation, in the supernatural order, of the amazing success of this little book, which has all the merits and defects of notes jotted down during a sermon that impresses us: merits, because it contains what was most vivid, most spontaneous, in the apostle's words; defects, because a series of notes thus taken down cannot have the literary style and the logical sequence of a book meditated and written according to a fixed plan.

May Jesus, King of Love, bless the enterprise undertaken solely and exclusively for His glory and the extension of His reign throughout the world. Thy Kingdom Come!

INTRODUCTION

"Lord, what wilt Thou have me do?"[1]
"Give Me a free hand."
(Our Lord to St. Margaret Mary)

IN OUR DESIRE TO SANCTIFY OURSELVES we are only too apt to cling to some comfortable system of our own devising. We want to be saints, but in our own way. Let us resolutely choose the divine Way, Jesus Christ, who is also the Truth and the Life.[2] We have thought at times to attain perfection through our own moods or fancies, which we imagine spiritual, and, of course, we failed. What is to be done? "Leave Me a free hand," Jesus replied to St. Margaret Mary; and to St. Teresa of Avila He said, "Thou shalt be holy in My way, not according to thy fancy." Examine your conscience, therefore, to see of what you must empty and dispossess yourselves in order to fill your soul with that Jesus whom you wish to make known and loved.

But make this examination simply, without that exaggerated fear which often comes from self-love, without any uneasy feelings. Humility in self-knowledge yields as its fruit much peace, which in its turn gives us a better knowledge of ourselves, a greater light.

Say to Jesus, quite simply, as a little child would to its mother: "Jesus, look! here is a stain, and here is another, and another still. Thou knowest all my shortcomings better than I, and Thou canst best correct them." This loving King will at once reply to you as He did to St. Margaret Mary, when her superior bade her ask for a cure as a proof of the mission He was entrusting to her: "Now thou art confided to My

---

1 Acts 9: 6   2 John 14: 6

care, it is My will to return thee perfectly cured to her who committed thee into My hands." This is exactly what will happen to you. You are now entirely committed to His care. You have come to Him ailing, but fear not, He will heal you, if you give Him a free hand. Do not forget this indispensable condition. He will perform the divine work, not you, and He asks of you only docility. Let Him empty and amend you, and afterwards fill the chalice of your hearts to the brim, that you, in your turn, may give of your abundance.

Since an apostle must necessarily be a teacher, you must acquire a great wisdom, that of God and His saints. And if, in His mercy, the Lord has enriched you with intellectual gifts and talents, praise Him for this, and use these gifts to His glory. But place not your trust in that human culture. Seek first and above everything the divine wisdom, that science to which St. Paul referred when he said, "For I determined not to know anything among you, except Jesus Christ and him crucified."[3] This is the only true and profitable knowledge: *To know Jesus Christ.*

Seek Him fervently; seek Him in the Tabernacle. Here, you are but a step from the Master; fix your eyes on Him who is the Light: bring your hearts close to His divine Heart, ask Him to grant you the inestimable grace of knowing Him.

From this knowledge will blossom the spirit of faith and the spirit of love; not of a sentimental love, which so many seek, but of that "love... strong as death,"[4] which leads necessarily to self immolation and brings forth the spirit of sacrifice, both in matters touching our own personal sanctification and our apostolate.

Love Jesus firmly, unswervingly, conforming yourselves in all things to His Holy Will. Love Jesus generously and then in your turn you will make others love Him as they ought to do. Love Him trustfully, that is without looking back, without those misgivings and fears which destroy love and confidence in His mercy.

---

3 I Cor. 2: 2 '   4 Cant. 8: 6

26

Confide yourselves to a God who is all charity. He will use you to accomplish great things on the condition that you believe much more in His love than in your weakness. Believe in Him, trust in Him, with blind and absolute confidence because He is Jesus. Believe that Jesus, and Jesus alone, is life! And sanctity is nothing but that same Jesus intimately living in you. Live with Him, unite yourselves to Him.

He Himself said to St. Margaret Mary: "I wish thee to be a docile instrument to draw hearts to My love." "My divine Heart is so impassioned with love for man and for thee in particular that, being unable to contain within itself the flames of Its ardent charity, It must needs spread them abroad by thy means . . . I have chosen thee in spite of thy unworthiness and ignorance, for the accomplishment of this great design, so that all may be done by Me. Thou shalt never lack help until My Heart lacks power . . . Thou shalt always be the beloved disciple of My divine Heart."

Friends of the Sacred Heart who read this, you who are continuing the mission of the great Saint of Paray-le-Monial, apply these delightful, inspiring words to yourselves!

But that you may be like Margaret Mary, "docile instruments," you must live close to the Master, so that His Heart and yours form but one. As this is very difficult and indeed altogether impossible, given our fallen state, ask Him to do with you what He did with His servant: to take your heart and place in its stead His own adorable Heart. With courageous love say to Him that, since His divine Heart and your proud, susceptible, sensual nature cannot fraternize, He must burn up your nature, reduce it to ashes, so that you may say with the great apostle St. Paul, *"to me to live is Christ."*[5]

A generosity, proof against every trial, must be the necessary preamble to this transformation. Give yourselves unsparingly and our Lord will sanctify you and make you sowers of life and sanctity.

And here I may make an observation on the spirit of the

---

5 Phil. 1: 21

love which I preach to you: Serve the King of Glory with joy and gladness of spirit, casting aside and forgetting all that troubles and worries you. Meditate on the wonderful revelation of the Heart of Jesus. Dwell upon the burning words, the yearnings of that adorable Heart, His petitions, His promises, but *peacefully* and *joyously*.

Reflective reading of the life of St. Margaret Mary will be of great help to you. The Little Flower, too, affords deep and entrancing spiritual reading. With the skill of a doctor and the language of a child she tells stupendous things, shows depths still unexplored and gives us a second revelation of the Heart of Jesus. During days of prayer and recollection, I also recommend to you the works of St. Gertrude who is called the theologian of the Heart of Jesus. Above all, penetrate your minds with the Gospel which breathes forth God's infinite love and mercy. Let Jesus Himself be your book, your Gospel. How often the fruit is lost, at least in part, because too great an attention is given to a thousand details of minor importance and not to the living substance, which is the meditation and knowledge of Jesus.

I need hardly tell you to offer up constant, simple and trusting prayer. Pray *lovingly*, like children, with an earnest desire to love much and make loved the Love that is not loved.

PART I

IN THE SCHOOL
OF THE SACRED HEART

*Especially dedicated to Friends and
Families of the Sacred Heart*

Chapter 1

LIFE OF FAITH

"I do believe; help my unbelief,"[1]

FAITH IS THE FOUNDATION of all spiritual and apostolic life. In fact it is impossible to persuade or convince others unless we are ourselves persuaded. And where shall we find this persuasion and this conviction except in a living faith? Who will bring to souls that profound and victorious conviction?

Only those who draw near to Jesus to be taught and enlightened by Him; who approach Jesus simply and trustingly, succeed in knowing Him not superficially but fully and deeply. In return, these intimate friends of the Sacred Heart receive as a gift the revelation of His love and His secrets. A living faith and a strong conviction are given to those who live by that light which is the Master Himself: "I am the light of the world," He said, "He who follows me does not walk in the darkness, but will have the light of life."[2]

Jesus is Light incarnate, because He alone is the Wisdom of God. What we creatures call wisdom is but folly and ignorance, unless it be — as in the saints — a light kindled at the divine Sun, Jesus Christ. Unfortunately our wisdom is generally too worldly, and therefore we reason and calculate to excess in matters we ought not to examine. Let us never forget that the one sublime wisdom is that of our faith. No one is more keen-sighted and enlightened than the saint. He sees and understands everything in God who is indefectible Light.

---

2 John 8: 12   1 Mark 9: 23

Too many pride themselves on being cultured and intellectual but because of their weak faith they are unable to find the weighty and urgent solutions which society today requires. To bring the modern world back to a holier and happier life we have less need of learned men than of souls possessed of a strong and simple faith. A Cure of Ars, a Saint Therese of the Child Jesus, have done more good for humanity than all the intellectuals that have ever lived, because they shared intimately in the light of God, Jesus Christ, and radiated it around in a miraculous manner. Without Jesus Christ there is nothing but error, ignorance and falsehood, with all their fatal consequences. This is my intimate conviction; so I never discuss, I simply assert leaning upon Jesus the cornerstone,[3] the Supreme Truth. I insist: *What we lack is an ardent, a practical faith shown by good works.* The apostle must not only cultivate his faith, but live by a great spirit of faith. Through it we can see and know God; Jesus Christ Himself reveals Him to us, according to those words of His: "Nor does anyone know the Father except the Son, and him to whom the Son chooses to reveal him."[4]

This spirit of faith is indispensable to us if we are to attain to a true intimacy with the Heart of Jesus. There are too many souls who stop on the threshold of this divine Heart and do not know the real Jesus of the Gospel, nor the "magnificence of His Love," only because they lack that lively faith which is the key to that sanctuary, that "Holy of Holies." If our sins, like the spear of Longinus, have pierced the adorable breast let us now penetrate by faith into the depths of that wound and make reparation. Apostles of the King of Love, let us make the world great and happy by drawing it to His divine feet conquered and converted. "To serve Him is to reign,"[5] said St. Paul, and I add "to reign happily."

But, before conquering the world, we must first conquer the Master's Heart with all Its treasures, and this we shall never do except in so far as we believe and live by faith. In

---

3 Matt. 21: 42   4 Matt. 11: 27
5 Postcommunion of the *Mass for Peace.*

proportion as we advance along that road, faith will go on transforming our lives. How different our sufferings and the ups and downs of our daily life become when we see them in the lights of God. Then the troubling enigma of life vanishes, all things stand out clear, necessary and divinely ordered, and despite the bitterness of exile we enjoy an unalterable peace.

The revelation of God and of the mystery of life is made to us by Jesus Christ in the measure in which we are transformed into Him by prayer. He who knows how to pray certainly knows more in the divine order — though he be a child or a simple peasant — than the most learned men. Such a one may be ignorant of the secrets of science, but he will know with marvelous penetration the secrets of God and of souls, and that is something infinitely greater.

I listened one day at Lourdes to a poor peasant commenting on a sermon of mine on the King of Love and the Friend of Bethany. He discoursed with a sureness of doctrine, with a penetration such as I have never heard from any doctor of divinity; yet he was but a poor peasant. There he stood, shod in rough sabots, clothed in a smock; but for several hours I heard him hold forth on the adorable Person of our Lord with a profundity of dogma, and as sure a mastery of his subject, as if he were a great preacher.

I was amazed and sought in vain to catch him in a trap by making him write his wonderful thought. I cultivated his friendship and one day I suggested that we should correspond with one another. I begged him to write to me often and at length, but to treat of no other subject than the King of Love, and the Friend of the home. When at last I tried to extort a formal promise that he would do so, he broke into a laugh and said, "I write to you, Father? Why, I can neither read nor write!"

Seeing that I looked skeptical he continued, "You wonder where I have learned all this, Father? Why, I can tell you easily. You celebrate Holy Mass every morning. I receive Holy Communion every day. So you see, Father, we both have the same Sun, the same Master, Jesus!"

Note his words: We all have "the same Sun" near us, the same Master to turn to; if that poor illiterate peasant knew and understood the great mysteries of divine Love and we, with our culture and education, neither see nor penetrate into the Heart of Jesus, it is not the fault of the Sun but of our lack of intimacy with the Master. Again, I repeat, it is not the most learned or the deepest thinkers that know Him best, but His true friends, those to whom Jesus Himself speaks in secret, teaching them what no books can ever tell.

HOW TO PRAY

But how must we pray in order to induce the King of the Tabernacle to tell us His secrets? *We must pray as we love,* as a child speaks to his mother, lovingly and simply. Jesus is far more accessible, simpler and tenderer than a mother. Do not forget that prayer is the secret of the great light which fills an apostle's heart. The best prayer is the spontaneous raising up of a soul that seeks truth and love in their primary and eternal source. Prayer, like love, on which religion is based, is within reach of all. That is why I say, we pray as we love.

When we draw near God by prayer and lively faith, we are given another light essential to our sanctification, that of self-knowledge. But to know our virtues without being tempted to pride, or our faults without falling into discouragement, we must look at them with the Master's eyes which mirror unfailing truth and light. The gifts received from God must be used for His greater Glory and turned to a good account. Jesus alone can teach us this exquisite lesson. He alone can point out our shortcomings and defects without disheartening us who are so weak, inconstant and ready to desert.

This life of faith is of the utmost importance if we are to fulfill our mission as apostles for without it we shall be but tinkling cymbals,[6] or voices in the wilderness! The right understanding and appreciation of our sublime vocation, and the holy and indomitable energy we need to carry it on —

6 I Cor. 13: 1

in spite of a thousand difficulties — must come to us exclusively from a lively and unshaken spirit of faith.

Let us live by faith, and then we shall never say that we would work if we had health, money and influence. These are human excuses which too often mar the designs of God. When Jesus willed to conquer the world He did not reason in this way. His method was ever to make use of the lowly, poor and ignorant, and with these weak instruments He overcame the world. St. Paul alludes to this, saying that it pleased God to choose "things that are not, to bring to naught the things that are" and to turn to foolishness "the wisdom of this world ... by the foolishness of our preaching ... a crucified Christ."[7] Seen by the light of faith, this is a clear and radiant truth on which every apostle should base his work. When impotent and abject instruments glorify the Lord, they can attribute nothing to themselves, and the work blazes out in a magnificent way as being not that of men, but truly the work of God. Thus, for instance, the conversion of souls is a miracle that can only be brought about by a merciful and omnipotent God. However, we have so little true knowledge of supernatural things that we often attribute the transformations achieved by divine grace to a visible instrument — as would be the eloquence of some great preacher. It is a grave error to dwell principally on the exterior means for, though it undoubtedly has a share in the work, we must never ascribe to it a power which God has reserved to Himself, that of touching the heart.

Great conversions are frequently brought about by the prayers, generous sacrifices and loving immolations of some hidden, unknown soul. The following incident illustrates this point.

A repentant sinner was making his First Communion on his death bed; his wife and his three sons were also receiving our Lord for the first time. The whole household had arisen to a new life! With tears in their eyes they all joined in thanksgiving to the Sacred Heart who had been so merciful

---

7 1 Cor. 28, 20, 21, 23

to them. An aged servant, evidently overcome with joy, came near the sick man's bed. "Master," she said, "at this heavenly moment, allow your old cook to congratulate you."

When her master, deeply moved, had shaken hands with her, she continued, "For over twenty-five years I have served you, and during all this time I have not only done my humble duties, but I have prayed, made sacrifices, received daily Communion as an apostle of the Sacred Heart, begging for one only grace, that I might not die and enjoy heaven before I had seen our divine Lord triumphant and victorious in this house, as He now is. The Sacred Heart has granted this great miracle. Now I can die content. My mission is fulfilled." How touching is the *Nunc Dimittis* of the poor servant apostle!

Thus you see that our faith is the surest solution to all the difficulties which must needs beset us. You will meet numberless obstacles along your path. How will they be removed? Only by your faith. Believe in Him who said, "I have overcome the world."[8] You, the apostles, will overcome it through Him and with Him, in so far as you believe in Him who sent you.

Many apostles only believe when they are successful in their endeavors. This is fair weather faith. It is especially in the hour of apparent defeat that our faith must be firm and unshaken. I say *apparent* because very often a seeming failure is a real success, if not for us, then at least for Jesus. Pray to Him during these days that the scales may fall from your eyes, that you may begin to understand the omnipotence of His Heart, and feel its effects in your interior life. Fix your eyes on Him, only on Him, and then forward! May His Kingdom come!

---

8 John 16: 33

Chapter 2

SPIRIT OF FAITH

"Lord, that I may see."[1]

"IF THOU DIDST KNOW THE GIFT OF GOD and who it is who says to thee, 'Give me to drink,' thou perhaps wouldst have asked of him, and he would have given thee living water."[2] If thou didst know! Know once and for all. Jesus wishes that you should know, that you should see clearly, since you have to guide others. Open the eyes of your soul, drink in torrents of the light. See!

To live by love we must live in the full light. Life is such a coming and going, a continual ebb and flow, that it needs a center around which it may safely gravitate. Our peace should be founded on the rock. This rock and this center can be none other than *Jesus Christ*. There is no greater wisdom than that of knowing Him, there is no truer happiness than that of being on intimate terms with Him. Jesus is all we need! How grand, consoling and safe it is to live by the conviction of faith. God will realize in us and through us His designs of mercy in proportion to our faith.

"Dost thou believe?" Jesus always inquires before performing any miracle of love. "Do you believe that I can do this to you?" said Jesus to the blind men. They answered him, "Yes, Lord . . . and their eyes were opened."[3]

"Who do men say the Son of Man is? . . . But who do you say that I am?" Simon Peter answered and said, "Thou art the Christ, the Son of the living God."[4]

---

1 Luke 18: 41 2 John 4: 10
3 Matt. 9: 27-30 4 Matt. 16: 13, 15, 16

37

Every time any appeal was made to His Heart and to His omnipotence, our Lord made answer; "If thou canst believe, all things are possible to him who believes."[5] "When I laid before Him," says Margaret Mary, "my little petitions about things difficult to obtain, I always seemed to hear these words: 'Dost thou believe that I can do these things? For if thou believe, thou shalt see the power of My Heart in the magnificence of My Love.'" Once more, then, it is clearly manifested that as faith is the basis of all sanctity, so it is also that of every apostolate.

The majority of the saints certainly lived ordinary humdrum lives such as ours, but they bore within them a Sun which marvelously illumined them. Hence it is that, though subject like ourselves to unavoidable ups and downs, they appeared to be — and in truth were — established in an unalterable peace, and a confidence stronger than all their interior crises.

In spite of all, they were able to keep the even tenor of their way. Whence did they derive that interior tranquility and unshaken confidence which never forsook them?

The world, which lives in darkness and hates the light, thought them mad, but their folly was the holy outpouring of an immense, unfailing light which permeated their souls. Few, even among Catholics, fully realize and believe in the love of Jesus which is something so mysterious and divine that only a very lively faith — that of the saint — can penetrate and understand it. But in proportion as any creature whatsoever, and especially an apostle, is "enamored" of Jesus, and believes blindly in His love, in that same measure the apostle may reckon on a veritable omnipotence, and have the power to transform the world.

O Jesus! give us the omnipotence of those saints, above all of those who believed with a blind faith in the madness of Thy love, in order that like them we may bring the world captive to Thy blood-stained feet.

Ask Him during these days for the faith of the saints. You

5 Mark 9: 22

certainly have faith, but is it truly a living, fiery faith, fit to be the root and the spirit of enterprises to redeem souls? For to believe is not merely to have that common faith in a vague, far off, impersonal Being. To believe is to throw oneself into the arms of Jesus, the supreme revelation of the Father, to give all to Him, to live in Him, the Light that came down from Heaven to show us the way which leads to Him. And it is not enough to believe that He came, we must also believe that *He remained and is still living among* us, and we must live accordingly. In short, to believe in Jesus is the secret of a close and divine brotherhood between Him and ourselves. Since, as apostles, we are called to give light to the world, let us seek it in Him who calls Himself and is "the Light of the world."[6] Oh! may this light be kindled in so many unfortunate souls who are misled by error.

The blind man cried out, "Lord, that I may see." Let us with a slight alteration repeat ceaselessly to the point of tiring Jesus, if that were possible: "Lord that I may see Thee! Let me see Thee and penetrate into Thy heart; let me see Thee and live joyously by Thy doctrine of love; let me see Thee even though it leave me blind, if that be Thy will, to the flowers, the stars and all creatures of earth."

Such a life would be the prelude to heaven, for the Beatific Vision consists in seeing and knowing everything in that light which is God. Thus, if by a great spirit of faith we anticipate, so to speak, though under a veil, that ineffable Vision, we also foretaste a drop of the future bliss of Paradise.

Such was, assuredly, the corner of heaven which we call Nazareth. To all the neighbors of the King of Kings, Jesus the child, and later the growing lad, the youth, the workman, was of no particular account, just one of many. But Mary and Joseph saw behind that mortal veil the Word made flesh; they adored the son of the living God and in the secret places of their souls they experienced ineffable joys and unspeakable delight.

Let us contemplate and reproduce the life of faith and

6 John 8: 12

love in Nazareth. Like Mary and Joseph let us learn how to labor, to suffer, to struggle in the company of Him who continues to share our life. Any distance between Him and us arises from our want of faith. The autobiography of the Little Flower will help us to understand this lesson, and will open up new horizons in relation to it. It has been said, and not without reason, that since St. Joseph there has never been a saint who realized better, more intimately and more simply the life of Nazareth than the Little Flower. Consult this doctor-child, that she may lead you in a way so suited to your vocation and to hers.

But how are we to see Jesus in everything, to draw Him to us and stamp Him on our souls so that He may be the obsession of our lives? Clearly we are not alluding to that vague, hazy vision of His Divine Person, a chance remembrance of Him from time to time, like a ray of sunlight piercing the gloom of the soul. See Him where He is, not only in heaven and in the Tabernacle, but in yourselves. Find Him in the everyday occurrences of your lives, in the trials and joys which He in His Wisdom sends you. See Him in the countless graces He pours out upon you; and when you feel Him bless you, as He passes, give thanks to Him, for gratitude brings down abundant favors.

See Him in your prayers, those you offer up in church, and also those informal ones you say at home. See Him inspiring your prayers, teaching you how to pray, receiving your homage and petitions, and answering them in His divine mercy and liberality.

See Him in your daily tasks and occupations. See Him at your side in the fatigue which He Himself experienced. While your hands labor, His Heart is sanctifying you, in proportion as you cooperate with His grace.

See Him sharing your table, seated with you in your home; but, above all, understand that He hungers and thirsts for your heart and He, in return, will give Himself to you.

See Him at night time, when you are about to go to rest. Repose, like John, upon His Heart, and in your sleep let your very breath say to Him, "Jesus, I love Thee." In this way your eyes will sleep while your heart keeps watch.

See Him in the hour of sacrifice which meets you at every step. The vision of Jesus crucified will be a divine encouragement and a recompense. Do not lose a single splinter of your daily cross, never fail to unite your sufferings to those of Jesus.

See Him in those hidden sorrows which no one would understand, your hours of Gethsemane. Do not seek a Cyrenean, nor call, then, on an angel; Jesus will be enough for you. Call to Him, feel Him at your side, see Him in the disappointments caused by your fellow creatures when they fail or forsake you and do not respond to your affection as you would have them do. In that hour see Jesus soothing your sorrow and listen to Him for — by that salutary trial — He is teaching you not to put your trust in creatures, and is loudly proclaiming to you that He alone is good and true.

See Him in those hours of moral weariness and darkness, when your whole nature seems rent and shattered, when you feel more than usually oppressed by your poverty and wretchedness. See Him then close to you and exclaim with heart and voice, "I believe in Thy love, Jesus, I do believe."

When the storm and tempest of temptation is about to overwhelm you and shipwreck seems imminent, hear Jesus above the tossing waves, inviting you to enter into the barque of His Heart; and if you think at times, as Peter did, that the Master sleeps, do not greatly fear, for to go down with Jesus will be to find heaven in the depths. He will, at the fitting hour, calm the tempest and restore peace to your troubled soul. In that dark hour trust His Heart.

See Him each time you sink down and feel guilty. He Himself willed to fall on the way to Calvary to encourage you by His own weakness; all may be scandalized, but He will never be. No one understands as He does the weakness of our humanity with which He clothed Himself,[7] that He might really be our Brother. However great and numerous your falls, fear Him not; He, the Mercy of the Father, the

7 *Cf.* Phil. 2: 6, 7

divine Compassion, will go down into the depths of the abyss for you. We have cost Him so great a price that He cannot easily resign Himself to the loss of a single soul given Him by the Father.

Remember how beautifully He depicted Himself in that Samaritan[8] who raised up in his arms from the wayside, the poor wretch attacked by robbers. Who does not know by happy experience the tenderness and gentleness of this adorable Samaritan? You may be deep in guilt and covered with the stains of sin, yet He is ever ready to change your soiled garment into a royal robe of glory. How eloquent was the look[9] Jesus cast on Peter after the denial, conquering His ungrateful apostle by His love.

"Peace, be not troubled," says the Savior in our hours of darkness and loneliness. "Peace, with Me thou shalt gain the victory."

And lastly, see Him, and only Him, in the thousand and one difficulties of your apostolate. You were expecting encouragement and approbation from virtuous souls, and they oppose you like unlooked for barricades. God knows for what reason He allows this opposition and persecution *on the part of good people;* it is often a prelude to great victories. If we seek His glory, we shall believe in divine Love and Wisdom more than ever in such moments.

Let us be *beset* by the love of Jesus, seeing Him and only Him in everything. What was the earthly life of our Lord but an obsession for mankind? And it is still so today. See how He follows and pursues us, determined to draw His glory and our good from everything; from our virtues and from our very vices, from our good qualities and our defects.

Saint Therese one day heard how it is possible to hypnotize others and to take possession of their faculties. "Ah," she at once exclaimed, "how I should like Jesus to hypnotize me! With what boundless joy would I yield myself to His will!" And it was because the Little Flower sought to be, and really was, hypnotized by Jesus, that her life was so great a marvel

---

8 Luke 10: 30-37   9 Luke 22: 61, 62

of faith. Why should Jesus not attract the soul as much and even more strongly than human beings, such as a husband, a friend, a lover or a son?

Scientists and great artists are often obsessed by their work and ready to sacrifice everything to win admiration from their fellow men. Surely apostles of the King of Glory, may well be in love with Jesus Christ, the uncreated Beauty, the sight of whom entrances the angels and rejoices paradise. Let us allow Him to take full possession of our hearts and so fill them with love that we may truly cry with St. Thomas, "My God and my All!"

O Jesus, Sun of Justice, dazzle and enlighten Thy apostles! Become their divine and only obsession, that they may take pleasure in no other thing but Thee.[10]

---

10 St. Margaret Mary, speaking of a grace which our Lord accorded her on all First Fridays of the month, expressed herself thus: "This Divine Heart appeared to me as a resplendent Sun, whose fiery rays fell directly on my heart, which felt as if it were reduced to ashes by so fierce a fire."

Chapter 3

LIFE OF LOVE

"Abide in my love."[1]

"THESE WORDS ARE THE FULFILLING of the Gospel and the law.[2] I have loved you to the point of humbling Myself in the crib, on the cross, and in the Eucharist. I have loved you without the least merit on your part, nay more, in spite of your having a thousand times been unworthy of My love. I have loved you as your Redeemer, not only in spite of, but because of your iniquities!

"I have loved you with a love of preference. Did I not leave My Father and My heaven and My angels for you? I disdained the treasures of the world and was born naked in a stable for you, My erring children. I have loved you more than My own life, for I gave it freely, seeking death that life eternal might be yours. And to give one's life is to give everything. This is the supreme proof of love. You had incurred the chastisement of infinite justice, but I interposed Myself between you and the Father. I suffered death for love of you!

"I have loved you more than My own majesty: Behold Me, covered with ignominy, clothed like a fool, upbraided, mocked, trampled upon like a worm — I, God! I have loved you more than My own glory, which was shrouded with the veil of death on Calvary, and has since been hidden for twenty centuries in the Eucharist. Who would ever guess that in the

---

1 John 15: 9   2 Rom. 13: 10

44

poor tabernacle of some village church there dwells the God whom the very heavens cannot contain?

"I have loved you, and I love you with an infinite charity. And you, my little children, do you love Me in return? In any case you were not the first to love, for I have loved you from all eternity. I first offered you My Heart. 'I have loved thee with an everlasting love!'[3] Have I the first place in your hearts? In your affections do you place Me above creatures, pleasures and comforts?

" 'Behold, I stand at the door and knock.'[4] I stand waiting patiently, I call again and again, and too often the reply is: 'Lord, wait one moment; I am now too busy about my future, money matters and my business. Wait a moment!' Time passes, bringing with it reverses and successes, flowers and thorns. I return again and call with a voice of supplication: 'Let Me in, I am Love and Peace.' 'Yes, Lord, but not just yet. See how worried I am about my welfare, how close I am to the goal of my ideals. I cannot waste a moment, each second is precious. Come back another day.' I have come back, hungry for love. Like some poor beggar, I hold out my blood-stained hand. I plead in vain.

"Suddenly that soul is invaded by anxiety, worry, human ambitions and illusions, which cause uneasiness and sorrow. Then I say to Myself: 'Perhaps such a bitter chalice has served to show them that I alone am p⅄ace — happiness and love.' I redouble My knocking; no answer comes. I knock again: 'Open to Me. It is I, be not afraid, I am the Consoler. I am Jesus, the one sure friend in days of darkness, He who never forgets, who never turns away those who neglect Him. Open to me. I am Mercy.'

"The door is half opened, and I am politely given a thousand excuses ... 'Will you return again, for after many nights of insomnia and pain I am just about to fall asleep' — alas, perhaps the sleep of Death! 'On some other occasion ... at some other time ... at present it is impossible.' Ah! too often

3 Jer. 31: 3   4 Apoc. 3: 20

45

when I return and they open to Me, death has got there before me."

This is a sad and harrowing story, but a very true one. How patient and kind is Jesus, true God and true Man, who thus lovingly waits and watches for me, an atom which He has created from nothing, a poor, ungrateful, erring creature overwhelmed with mercies! Truly it has been said that Jesus is a Heart infinite in love.

But why does He not, in holy anger, force a door barred against Him? Is He not the Lord and Master? Yes, He could do so and certainly has the right to force it; but what He seeks is *love*. He wants less the open door than the affection of him who opens, and it is the more incredible that He, a God wholly love, tenderness, compassion and mercy, should be thus rebuffed!

Here let me sadly repeat what St. Francis of Assisi used to say: "Love is not loved." The Heart of Jesus is not understood, not even by those who call themselves His friends. No, He is not loved!

Did He become man, die upon the cross and make Himself a Prisoner in the Tabernacle to inspire us with awe? He might have used the lightning as His scourge, and founded His empire upon fear, as we deserved. He came not to rule over slaves, but over sons and children, joint-heirs of the Savior by divine right[5] though we hardly merit such a title.

It may be alleged that "the fear of the Lord is the beginning of wisdom."[6] Yes, but only the *beginning*, the first rung of the ladder which reaches to God. Too many remain on that first rung, when they could and should climb to the second, to the third, to the thousandth, to the very top. "Love," says St. Paul, " . . . is the fulfillment of the Law."[7]

Apostles of the Sacred Heart, never forget that at the base of conversion is the rock known as holy fear. Surmount it without seeking to remove it, and climb with humility and confidence to the topmost peak of perfection, which is Love only.

---

5 Rom. 8: 15   6 Ps. 110: 10
7 Rom. 13: 10

Love, as we have said, is the whole Gospel. It is Jesus who offers Himself in the arms of Mary, on the Cross, and by His Church; it is also the whole Christian law.

Christ's masterpiece, the Church, is a perfect figure of His love. The priesthood, too, is another abiding miracle of His love; its only purpose being to save souls and to raise them by the road of love to Christ. The priest is by right the dispenser of love in the sacraments, those wonderful channels of grace, and from the pulpit his voice is the true echo of that "Come to me all you. . . ."[9] "It is I. Do not be afraid."[10]

What is prayer but the fusion of the soul with God through love? Grace with its manifold effects is but the net of love and mercy in which the God-Redeemer seeks to ensnare our souls. The very illusions and bitterness of exile, the disappointments caused us by our dealings with fellow creatures, the passing away of all that is human, proclaim aloud that the love of Jesus is the one reality for the human heart and that apart from Him, "all is vanity, and a chase after wind"[11]

The only language our Lord ever used, at Nazareth, on the shores of Genesareth, on the mountain top and at Paray-le-Monial, was that of His Heart, that of Love! Jesus said to St. Margaret Mary these remarkable words: *My Heart is so impassioned with love for men, and for thee in particular. . . .* This love was and is the supreme reality dominating all time. It is the very substance of Him who commands, who reigns, who conquers, because He is King and because "God is Love."[12] His law is summed up in the words: *Thou shalt love!* All perfection here below, all reward in heaven is simply love.

Oh, unfathomable mystery of infinite charity! Is it possible that a God to whom no person nor thing is necessary, should have made a law which constrains me to love Him with all my heart, with all my soul, and with all my strength?[13] It

---

8 Prov. 23: 26   9 Matt. 11: 28
10 Mark 6: 50   11 Eccles. 1: 14
12 1 John 4: 16   13 Luke 10: 27

seems as though without my love something would be lacking to that absolute and infinite Being; as if without it our Lord would have felt some kind of void, and therefore He desired to fill it with such an atom as my heart.

There is no doubt that the first and the most adorable of His rights is that of *being loved*. At the same time He has a great longing for our love which He tearfully begs for, when we refuse it to Him.

Woe, then, to those who under pretext of avoiding sensible devotion pride themselves on shunning the life of the heart, declaring that love is a romantic outgrowth of sickly sentimentality. I protest angrily against this absurdity, which moreover carries with it a good dose of human respect, a large measure of pride, and no little lack of generosity in the service of the Lord.

To love, a weakness! Yes, the holy weakness and the folly of St. Francis of Assisi, St. Therese, St. Paul, and all the saints; Thine, too, O Jesus! True love, charity, was never mere sentimentality. On the contrary, it has ever been the soul of all great struggles and victories in the interior life and the hidden power to be found at the root of heroical acts. Fear may easily become feminine sensibility, but there is no virtue so strong or so virile as love.

It may also be said that the best theologians are those who — besides possessing a deep knowledge — have souls aflame with love and hearts transfigured by a divine intimacy with our Lord, the God of charity. Unfortunately there are, and always will be, men of much book-learning, who have studied St. Augustine and St. Thomas, but who are far from loving as those holy doctors did. I abjure that lifeless knowledge and I cling exclusively to the teaching of St. Augustine and St. Thomas, the true and genuine doctors of the Church. Love is the only true theology. It gives us all we need; whereas science, erudition and intellectualism without love fill the soul with self-sufficiency.

I repeat, charity is not effeminate sentimentalism! It is the greatest of all virtues.[14] To love is to live heroically, divinely.

14 1 Cor. 13: 13

48

It would be a most grievous error to attach over importance to faith apart from charity. It is one thing to believe and another to love. "If I have all faith so as to remove mountains, yet do not have charity, I am nothing,"[15] worse, I am a danger to myself and to the souls around me.

We can believe without loving. Millions accept and acknowledge speculatively the principle of the Gospel, but neither observe nor practice it *because they do not love.* We cannot love without faith, but love brings life to our faith. Let us lay much stress on the doctrinal foundation of our faith, and still more let us increase our love. Our teaching should be to believe through love and to love that which we believe. Many make shipwreck of their faith because they have not been taught to love. The faith of a dried up heart will never wing us aloft to God. It ties us down by odious bonds.

It is evident that the fulfillment of the Christian law demands that we return divine love with our fervent love and the gift of our hearts. *"My son, give me your heart."*[16] *Love is not shown by feelings.* We may be as cold as ice, and, what is more, even experience a real distaste and disgust for spiritual things and yet be aflame with true charity. When speaking of love, therefore, we always mean an interior, steadfast, virile, resolute will together with an intense desire to love which, in the eyes of God, constitutes loving. Hence the primary element of our charity is a sincere *longing* to love. A great longing is always a great love.[17] Love is nourished and lives by noble aspirations, ambitions and yearnings which are the gift of the Holy Spirit. These desires destroy in the soul the routine and mediocrity which in pious souls are always great obstacles to sanctity.

There is nothing ordinary about a soul borne aloft on the wings of great desires. Its abode is on the heights, it is ever in pursuit of the divine eagle, it ever longs to mount higher and higher.

---

15 1 Cor. 13: 2   16 Prov. 23: 26

17 "I, the Infinite God, desire to be served in an infinite manner; but thou has of infinity naught but the desire and longing of thy soul." (St. Catherine of Sienna, Dial. 4).

It is clear that we are not referring to those fickle, dreamy souls, whose apparent sanctity is as unstable as a house of cards. Our desires must be strong and generous, not mere passing whims nor fancies, which the first humiliation shatters, but a holy ambition to sacrifice ourselves and a willingness to be forgotten and despised.

St. Mary Magdalen of Pazzi, speaking to our Lord of St. Aloysius Gonzaga, asked, "How did he rise to such a height, in what time and by what works?" Jesus answered, "He rose on the wings of great desires."

This, too, was the secret of Saint Therese, so great in her ambition to love. She must be even higher than many of the seraphs in heaven "because she has loved much,"[18] because she *desired to love Jesus as no one had ever loved Him*.[19] And this must needs be so, for God reads the hearts of men. Many good works are beyond our power, whereas the *interior work*, that is to say the great desire to love, is always within the reach of everyone. The longing to love is much, and often indeed is all.[20]

What Jesus asks above all is the will to love, but it must be resolute and generous. Give Him your whole, entire heart, not the leavings as so many do. St. Peter did not give all at the outset. "We have left all,"[21] he said. But this was not entirely true, for he had kept back the best part of the gift, and had only given his fishing nets and his boat. Jesus might often say to certain souls, "I do not ask this or that. You deceive yourselves and try to deceive Me, if that were possible, with such gifts! Keep them, but give Me in exchange your heart; for this reason I have given you Mine. Love Me as I have loved you; give yourselves to Me as I give Myself to you." To love is not merely to give but *to give oneself without reserve*.

---

18 Luke 7: 47   19 Letters

20 "Thou wilt satisfy Me wholly," said our Lord to St. Margaret Mary, "by loving me without reserve or restrictions; neither apply thyself to anything, nor think of aught but perfect love of Me."

21 Luke 18: 28

Once and for all, rid yourselves of that network of petty affections and attachments which share your hearts, small as they are. Jesus is a "jealous God,"[22] He has a right to be the sole and absolute Master. If a husband claims this right, how can you refuse it to our Lord?

The cross and the Tabernacle prove that He loved us without measure.

Think how He has given Himself in the Holy Eucharist, that folly of love. There He is our own entirely, for ever, and with all His treasures. If our Lord had measured and calculated as we do, He would never have gone to such extremities of love. But when Jesus, wounded by the ingratitude He meets with, finds a soul, one only soul, who loves Him with the love of absolute surrender, He appears then to forget the betrayal and hatred He has endured for centuries. Oh, that He might always say to us in Holy Communion as to St. Gertrude: "When thou receivest Me, thou art in truth My heaven."[23]

Establish a kind of rivalry between Jesus and yourselves as to who will give most! He will easily come out the victor, for, having infinite treasures, He can give the infinite. But remember: he who gives his all, be it only a mite, heaps up the measure. You cannot give the infinite, but when you have given without reserve, when you have given your all, you can say with the Little Flower to Jesus: "Lord, we are quits! Thou gavest the infinite, and I have given myself wholly: more I can neither imagine, desire, nor offer."

During this retreat He is certainly knocking more repeatedly than at other times; He is expecting much, or at least something, from your generosity. Do not disappoint Him, you apostles. If necessary He would wait for years to conquer you completely, that in your turn you may conquer others. And if you only opened to Him at the eleventh hour, He would summon the whole of His celestial court in happy cele-

22 Deut. 4: 24

23 "My daughter," said Jesus to St. Margaret Mary. "I have chosen thy soul to be a heaven of rest to Me, and thy heart a throne of delight for My love."

bration to rejoice with Him that He had gained admittance to your soul as a Conqueror. Surely He will not call you twice. His Heart is taking you by storm, and you are persuaded that it is your duty to become saints through love.

St. Thomas, the Angelic Doctor, says, "Sanctity does not consist in great knowledge or in profound meditation, or in high thoughts, but in *knowing how to love much.*" Consequently a saint is "a chalice overflowing with charity." And if this is true of fervent Christians, who seek something higher than bare salvation, what shall we say of you whose vocation as apostles is to melt the ice of indifference and to set the world afire with love? There is a lack of apostles because there are so few who love. Many do good works, many labor with good-will; there are plenty of wheels in the machinery of catholic action. But *apostles are lacking,* that is to say hearts that are aglow with love. It is one thing to talk and be engaged in active works; but an apostle — like St. Francis Xavier, St. Margaret Mary or St. Therese — has always a soul consumed by holy zeal.

In this glorious epoch of the reign of the Heart of Jesus, you and I ought to be by vocation, chariots of fire carrying the King of Love in triumph from pole to pole.

Pray and beseech Him to sanctify you by love. The Little Flower used to say that ardent love for God purifies the soul, even here below, far better than the fires of purgatory will do. We must not dwell too much upon our faults nor be discouraged and disconcerted, however persistently they may occur. We cannot expect to become saints in a day nor even in a year. Sanctity based on love will grow and expand in you slowly but surely, permeating all your being. Grace, like nature, never proceeds by sudden leaps and bounds, but by gradual, imperceptible degrees. Make all possible use of these hours of grace and recollection. Be faithful, be generous, and the love of our Lord will flood your soul and submerge your weak nature beneath the waves of a new life, divine and strong. Plunge into the boundless sea of love, the Heart of Jesus! Close the eyes of your understanding to all else but Him and say: "Lord, Thee alone!... Thy Heart and Thy

Glory. . . . Make me be athirst with a passion for souls that will form Thy diadem! Nothing but to love Thee, and to make Thee loved! And this with no further reward here below than that I may love Thee more, and that my power to make Thee loved may be made more and more invincible! May my eternal reward be to possess Thy Heart, O Jesus, and to have my name inscribed beside those of John, Margaret Mary, and the Little Flower; to love Thee there, and from heaven to spread the fire of Thy love."

Love for Love!
Folly for Folly!
Heart for Heart!

Chapter 4

LOVING CONFIDENCE

"It is I: do not be afraid."[1]

THESE ARE MOST CONSOLING WORDS. "Have confidence, it is I, your Father, your Friend! Be not afraid!" — But how can I help being afraid, miserable as I am? — Because "it is I." If I were an angel, or a prophet, or a saint, you might fear, for even the holiest creatures can neither know, judge nor love you as I do. Fear not, for I am Jesus.

Therefore, He said, "My peace I give to you."[2] His peace, not ours which is so liable to illusions; His, not that of the world which is but a dangerous counterfeit. Through His mercy we may have peace. Not because we think ourselves holy or confirmed in grace, but because we believe, with an immense faith, in His love, the remedy and reparation of our failings.

What should we do without the supernatural and divine courage which we find in trusting Jesus? Truly, the summit of sanctity is reached by the road of confidence and there is no other. For, being what we are — an abyss of miseries and sins — we should be hurled into another abyss — that of a final and irremediable discouragement — if we were asked to fly without first being given the wings of confidence. But with them we can aspire to be saints, and rise to the heights, from the depths of our fallen state, from the abyss of our iniquities.

Do not tell me it is a pretension or an illusion. I well know it would indeed be folly and pride to think I could reach the

---

1 Luke 24: 36   2 John 14: 27

summit of sanctity by relying on my own strength, but in the "elevator" formed by the arms of Jesus, on His Heart, I am certain to succeed, precisely because I am of less account than a tiny ant. He likes to transform ants into royal eagles when they trust Him. If He, the God of pardon and grace, the God of mercy and tenderness, the Word made Flesh to redeem us, the God crucified and hidden in the Sacrament does not inspire me with a blind, immense and unbounded confidence, who will ever be able to do so?

He did not come down to earth to bring us the sword of His justice, the flames of divine wrath, the sentence of eternal death, so well deserved! No! a thousand times no! Open the Gospel at random; even in His moments of indignation and in His anathemas you will find the Heart of Jesus compassionate and irresistibly captivating. He came to pardon, to save, to give peace and heaven even to those who prepared for Him the gibbet of the cross: "Father, forgive them, for they do not know what they are doing."[3] To redeem us "He emptied Himself, taking the nature of a slave."[4] He clothed Himself with the garment of our sins, and because of this the Father sentenced Him to death. He took our sins upon Him as it is written, "He hath borne our infirmities and carried our sorrows."[5] He was "a man of sorrows and acquainted with infirmity."[6] In the Holy Scripture we read, "Deep calls unto deep."[7] These words may be applied to Him, but in a figurative sense. The deep of our iniquity and corruption may be said to call on the deep of His pity and mercy.

Bethlehem, with its poverty, is hardly even a poetical picture of that other poor, unworthy and living cradle, which is the heart of one who receives Him in Holy Communion. However, Jesus who knows this commands that we should receive Him, and when we approach the altar with contrition and humility Jesus casts a veil over this poor cradle. Here He longs to stay. To deny Him this right would be to wound His Heart.

---

3 Luke 23: 34
5 Is. 53: 4
7 Is. 41: 8

4 Phil. 2: 7
6 Is. 53: 3

Do you know which transfiguration most entrances me? It is not that of Thabor where for a moment He appeared to recover the mantle of His radiant majesty which He had laid aside for love of me. The transfiguration which touches and delights me is that of Bethlehem, where I see the Creator wrapped in the swaddling clothes of my nature; that of Nazareth, where I contemplate my Judge shrouded in obscurity; and that of Calvary where I adore, beneath the bloodstained winding sheet of death, Him who is Life Itself.[8] This triple transfiguration which makes Him my own Possession, my own Brother, where in His condescension He deigns to resemble me, teaches me more than the glories of Thabor how much I ought to love Him, and with what infinite confidence I ought to approach His Heart. It is precisely the prodigious contrast between what He shows us for a moment on Thabor and what He is and remains in Bethlehem, in Nazareth and on Calvary, that preaches to me, with overwhelming eloquence, the folly of His love and the truth of that passage of Scripture: "I desire not the death of the wicked, but that the wicked turn from his way and live."[9] And again: "For the Son of Man came to seek and to save what was lost."[10]

Note for your consolation that the love which Jesus has for you is not quite the same as the love He has for His mother, who is all pure, holy, perfect, and immaculate. This is, we may say, a unique love. Nor is it the love with which He loves His angels, those pure, perfect and ever faithful spirits. Remember that the Shepherd left those ninety and nine faithful ones for the little lamb that had gone astray, and which figures each one of you, my readers. I may even say that the love of which I speak is not the love He has for that little band of consecrated souls pure as snow and aflame with fervor. These souls, dear to Him because of their heroic and constant fidelity, have been and always will be the oasis of His Heart, the little flock which is for ever singing a can-

---

8 "O Jesus, in Thy desire to make Thyself like unto us, Thou dost not appear to be like Thyself" (Msgr. Gay).

9 Ezech. 33: 11   10 Luke 19: 10

11 Apoc. 14: 3

ticle no one could learn;[11] they have merited the caresses of the King of Love. But the love He lavishes on the majority of miserable and ungrateful sinners is a *merciful love,* or rather an infinite condescension. The Word, the God-Savior, descends into the morass in order to convert a little "mud" into stars, if only the "mud" is humble and believes in the mercy of the Lord.

We have set out these differences because it was necessary to bring into relief what the Little Flower called the *merciful love of Jesus,* and to make you appreciate it, as far as possible, at its real worth. The love which enriches and sanctifies pure souls is one thing, the love which by the precious blood purifies and uplifts sinful souls is quite another. We can never merit the condescension of this merciful love. We have sinned, we have loaded Him with our iniquities, we have crucified and put to death the Lord of Life, and are more guilty than His executioners. We have all laid hands on Him, hands stained with His blood, all of us! And He stretches out His arms to us and offers His pardon, His friendship, and His Heart. This is the highest point of God's passionate love for us. Therefore, the sin of fear, the sin of mistrust, is inexplicable. I was going to say that it is almost unpardonable. Is it possible that His Heart should eagerly seek ours — the two deeps calling to one another — and that, from the depth of our iniquity and for want of trust, we should refuse to give entrance to Him who seeks and pleads to fill up our abyss of death with His Heart, the Abyss of pardon and life?

To His entreaties, some oppose the argument of unworthiness and respect, as if He could not offer freely all the treasures of His tenderness, or as if He were the monopoly of the just, or of those who think themselves worthy of His graces. One would say that such Christians have the pretension to set right a God who appears *guilty of exaggeration* in seeking to associate His immortal life with ours. When He advances, these souls retreat; when He says, "Come to Me all ye that labor and are burdened," they seem to repeat the cry of the demoniac in the Gospel: "What have we to do with thee,

Son of God? Hast thou come here to torment us before the time?"[12] And the hapless souls flee from Him. They forget that between the Father sitting in judgment and us the rebels, the merciful Son has interposed Himself as a bridge of hope, by which we who are guilty may be pardoned and drawn near our God and Father. "My little children," He is saying, "cross by this bridge, for I am the Crucified. Fear not, cross by it, for I am the Way. Why are you trembling? Pass over it, meditating on My Cross, My Calvary and My Eucharist. Go forward in peace and with full trust. I wish to fill the abyss of your fear with the abyss of My tenderness; but, I beseech you, do not re-open the abyss of suspicion and reserve which I have suppressed by My Incarnation and My Eucharist.

"Souls of little faith, do you not see that the greatest of your faults, the source of so many others and that which most offends Me is your lack of trust?" And you, trembling souls, who are never satisfied with your confessions, ever doubting the pardon for sins already confessed, listen to the following story.

One of the many souls who regard Jesus as a tyrant was preparing to make a general confession for the hundredth time. Restlessly, she spent the days of her retreat writing down the sins of her whole life. She neither meditated nor prayed, she was entirely absorbed in an examination which stifled her. At last she went into the confessional. She read out the list of her sins, repeating and explaining over and over again, in fear and trembling. When at length she thought she had finished, a voice was heard which gently and very sadly said, "You have forgotten something very important."

"I thought I must have," she answered, terror-stricken, and hastily prepared to read it all again.

"Your sin is not in your notes," continued the voice, "and it offends me much more than all that you have said. Accuse yourself of *lack of trust!*"

That voice moved her to the depths and she sought to

---

12 Matt. 8: 29

ascertain if it was really her confessor's. The confessional was empty! Jesus had come to give her a supreme lesson.

We are not, certainly, censuring general confessions, for they are most profitable on definite occasions, but we do condemn that lack of trust, that spirit of fear and exaggerated nervousness which is an outrage to the mercy of the Savior. If the blind, the leprous, the paralytic, cured by Him, had reasoned in this way and doubted of their cure because of their unworthiness, they would have deserved to relapse into their infirmities and even into a worse state as a punishment for their ingratitude, as well as for their pride which is always the root of the sin of mistrust. The chief crime of Judas, greater even than his betrayal or his suicide, was his refusal to believe in that mercy which Jesus offered him on His knees when He washed his feet at the Last Supper!

Let us not alter the Gospels, no one has ever the right to do that. The Lord came down not for the just but for sinners, not for the whole but for the sick, and the payment He asks in exchange for such condescension is a trusting love, which is ever the most sincere and humble form of repentance. "It is not the healthy who need a physician, but they who are sick. For I have come to call the sinners, not the just."[13] He who does not understand this fails to understand what is most delicate and beautiful in the Heart of Jesus!

Nothing should ever prevent you from approaching His wounded side. *Your sins, do you say?* He has cleansed them in His blood. Your unworthiness? He knows that a thousand times better than you do. He only asks of you to believe with humility and confidence in His love.

Lastly, do not abuse the term "respect." The most repugnant and odious of heresies, Jansenism, has ever hidden itself under the cover of this word. Trust in Him who is to you father, brother, and Savior. To trust is not and never will be to fail in respect, neither is it a lack of reverence to obey His call, when He offers us His Heart. To resist that call on the pretext that you are, as yet, not sufficiently purified and

13 Mark 2: 17

worthy is the refinement of pride. If such be your case, be frank to confess that you have an abundance of *self-love* and you lack love of Jesus. If you loved you would think otherwise, for humility — the twin sister of trust — does not assume such an attitude. Not without reason St. Augustine said, "Love and do what thou wilt." Yes, whatever you wish, for when true charity is your counsellor there is no danger of your offending the object of your love.

How beautiful is the thought that before Pentecost St. Peter said, "Depart from me, for I am a sinful man, O Lord."[14] After the great light of Pentecost had shown him the depth of infinite mercy joined to that of his frailty, he must often have thought and exclaimed, "Depart not from me, O Lord! Come yet closer to me, much closer, just because I am a very sinful man."

Ask a St. Francis of Assisi, a St. John of the Cross, a St. Francis of Sales, a St. Paul, where they found the secret of life, sanctity and love; it was certainly not far from Jesus, but in the eager desire to attain to intimacy with Him, by the road of simplicity and trust. Where, except in the Gospel, did Saint Therese learn that marvelous theology with which, as serious authors assert, she is bringing about a spiritual renaissance in souls; that theology of children, of those fearless little ones, who, seated on the Master's knees[15] and greedy for His caresses, learnt long before the Little Flower that love leads to union and demands boundless trust? Is not this the pure celestial fragrance of the Gospel? Who loved most, the little ones or Jesus? If there was an excess it was in the tenderness and condescension of Jesus. Children's souls in their simplicity have always been privileged to understand the demands and sublimities of love. I side with the children who contended for the place of honor on His knee, listening to the heartbeats of their Friend, rather than with the apostles who rebuked such great familiarity which they did not understand and from which they kept aloof. In life and in death I desire their simplicity, their trust, their place!

---

14 Luke 5: 8   15 Matt. 19: 13, 15

You cannot imagine how artful is the cunning of the enemy in separating you from our Lord by the obsession of your sins. There is but a step between discouragement and your sinking even lower. Ponder for a moment, before the Tabernacle, the kindness of Jesus towards the woman of Samaria.[16] Did He refuse to talk with this great sinner? Was His tone or were His words such that she departed abashed at having been so close to Him who is Sanctity itself? What was the immediate fruit of that proximity? The confusion and flight of the Samaritan woman, or an expansion of trust, contrition and conversion? Let us take the lesson to heart for our own good and the good of souls. Every serious evil begins and ends with separation from Jesus. Every virtue, especially those of repentance and humility, brings us, as if by instinct, to the Heart of the Redeemer.

If at times when seeking this intimacy you do not see or feel any progress in the correction of your defects, do not attribute this apparent sterility to the proximity of Jesus, for spiritual progress cannot always be felt. It even happens that after spending long years in this life of love and trust, you see more clearly than before the infirmities of your nature. This does not mean that you have become worse by living close to Jesus; far from that — I should rather say the divine light from His Heart has grown more intense and is now showing you those "microbes" of your soul whose existence you had not identified in the fainter light a few years back. Still more, He allows you to feel the discomfort of your sin even after you have been cured, in order that you may expiate it and your soul be restored to perfect health through humiliation.

As I already have told you, in order to know yourself, look into the divine mirror of the eyes of Jesus;[17] the Sun of His Heart will show you what you are and at the same time He will comfort you with the vision of Its mercies.[18] If we read

16 John 4
17 "Guard against looking at thyself anywhere except in My Heart."
18 "He made me see myself as a compound of all the iniquities which He desired to change into a sum of all His infinite mercy." (St. Margaret Mary).

the Gospel carefully, we must come to believe that Jesus thirsted for the souls of sinners. Let us meditate on the pages which tell us of the Good Shepherd, the Samaritan, the Magdalen, the woman taken in adultery, the meals with the publicans, and wherever we look we find the merciful Heart of Jesus beating with compassion for them. Those publicans still exist; we are such ourselves, and Jesus seeks us out eagerly, precisely because we are publicans. Let us understand, then, once for all, that the only way in which we may repay the Divine Physician is by giving Him our hearts overflowing with trust. "Our confidence can never be too great," said Saint Therese.

How many there are who think the devotion to the Sacred Heart a novelty, a pretty little poetical devotion, which originated in Paray-le-Monial. This is anything but the truth. In the Gospel itself I find the whole doctrine of the Heart Of Jesus showing me that divine Heart as Life and Mercy, as Center of all hearts. I believe, of course, in the great revelation made to St. Margaret Mary, but what moves and convinces me most (next to the authority of the Church) is precisely that I find the Gospel and the writings of St. Margaret Mary in perfect accord with one another. Moreover, I need neither her words nor any other help to know the Heart which revealed Itself so marvelously in Bethlehem, in Nazareth, on Calvary and which continues to dwell with us in the Sacrament of the Altar. Paray-le-Monial has shed a great light and it is, in all truth, a revelation, for the petitions and promises are a divine mark which bring the doctrine into relief. But that doctrine is to be found in every line of the Gospel, this supreme and definitive revelation of the Heart of Jesus. And all He said in Paray may be condensed into these words: "Believe in My love, fear not, it is I, Jesus. . . . Love Me, give Me your whole heart, and make Me loved, for I am Jesus."

Before the apostles were taught by their divine Master they said, "Lord, wilt thou that we bid fire come down from heaven and consume them?"[19] They had not yet fully under-

19 Luke 9: 54

stood the spirit and the Heart of their Teacher. But when the Holy Ghost enlightened them and filled their hearts with divine love, they commanded the *fire of charity* to come down in order to set ablaze the souls of men and nations with the love of Jesus Christ.

There are some who say that for them God has but one single attribute, that of an ever-terrible justice. Evidently God, since He is God, must be infinitely just. But, precisely because He is just and knows the clay from which He has fashioned us, He must, while we are traveling this rugged path of ours here below be much more kind than rigorous, the Savior and Father rather than the inexorable Judge. He came to earth, and He still remains in the Eucharist and in the Church, in order to save us. It is we, unfortunately, who force Him to condemn and to show us His severity. If there were nothing but justice in the providential government of souls, or if there were more justice than mercy, or exactly as much justice as mercy, what would be the good of the confessional, the priesthood, the Eucharist and the whole of that system, marvelous beyond words, of our merciful redemption? For any one who has the slightest experience of souls, the practical and daily application of that system constitutes an ever-enduring miracle of miracles.

Again, our Lord must be much more a parent than a dreadful Judge, because He knows where our evil intentions end and where our weakness and ignorance begin. Hence that saying of Saint Therese: "I have absolute trust in the justice of God and I hope as much from it as I do from His mercy." And this is in perfect accord with theology. As for me, the more firmly I believe in the justice and equity of the King of Glory, the more do I believe in the mercy which I preach. For justice does not always — and still less exclusively — mean severity and punishment, but *equity*. Therefore, because God is just He must needs give me sometimes tenderness and compassion and, at other times, show severity and rigor. But, as a matter of fact, this Crucified God is much more inclined to pity than to anger while we are in our earthly exile.

Do you want a simple and eloquent proof of this? Let us suppose that the reader of these lines has committed a single mortal sin. If, here below, God were inexorably strict and severe why is not this soul already in hell, which it so justly deserves? Why is it still enjoying all the sweet blessings which this doctrine of redemption offers? It will be another thing when death closes our eyes and we stand on the other side of the eternal river, before the judgment seat of the Most High. There the work of mercy is consummated and strict justice will be our share, but meanwhile, *here below*, "where the offense has abounded, grace has abounded yet more,"[20] and mercy.

There is a very beatiful story of a miraculous crucifix. At its foot, a sincerely repentant sinner was making his confession. His sins were so great that the confessor hesitated for a moment to give him absolution, but, moved by the man's tears, he said "I will absolve you, but take care not to fall again!"

After some time the penitent returned. "I have struggled bravely, Father, but, in a moment of weakness, I have relapsed, and I came at once humbly to reconcile myself with God." "No," said the confessor, "this time I cannot give you absolution." "But, Father, have pity on me! Remember that my soul is still very weak after a long and serious illness. Have pity, I am truly sincere!" With great hesitation, and after severely censuring him, the priest, once more, gave him absolution.

The penitent was truly contrite, but, after a long period of perseverance, the habit of so many years of sin, plus his whole nature, corrupted and deadened by vice, combined to break down his good resolutions. He hastened to his confessor with simplicity and confidence in order to regain the grace of God. "This time, I cannot absolve you," said the confessor. "You are not sorry." In vain the poor man wept, implored, argued: "I am weak, not wicked," he said. "I want to be faithful, but to do that I need the pardon for which I

---

20 Romans 5: 20

beg." "I cannot," said the priest, and he rose to go away, trying to break loose from the penitent who was holding him with both hands.

At this moment, a sigh of immense love and compassion was heard. Both at once looked up. What did they see? The breast of the Crucified heaving with emotion, His eyes full of tears, and His right hand unnailed. Then, they heard His gentle voice saying, as He made the sign of the Cross: "I myself forgive thee, for thy soul is the gem for which I shed My Blood." Needless to enquire if this really happened or is only a legend. What enchants me is the lesson and the doctrine. The Lord is gentle and kind, compassionate and merciful to a degree past our imagining, for He shed His blood for us!

Want of trust is great ingratitude and a lack of simplicity and self-abandonment. Be more childlike with your Father who is in heaven. You may certainly acknowledge your failings, but do not let yourselves be crushed and disheartened by them. Imitate our Lord, who turns even your sins to His glory and your good. With the exception of the Immaculate Virgin, what saint has there ever been without defects? Throw them into the furnace of the Heart of Jesus and let yourself be consumed with them.

Do you know the beautiful dialogue between Jesus and St. Jerome? "Jerome," said our Lord, "dost thou want to make Me a present?" "But, Lord," replied the saint, "have not I already given Thee everything? My life, my possessions, my faculties, my griefs, my joys, my soul, all are Thine and Thine alone." "Jerome, give Me something else." "But what, Lord, what? Is there anything, any single fiber of my heart which does not belong to Thee?" "Jerome, Jerome, give Me something which is not yet Mine; something which thou keepest to thyself and which ought to be Mine." "Speak, Lord, ask what Thou wilt, what is it?" "Jerome, *give Me thy sins!*"

Yes, give them to Him, abandon all of them to Him; they are the disease He seeks to heal with the solicitude of a physician and a Redeemer. Say to Him, "Lord, take them away entirely and for ever! I believe in Thy love. I cast myself on Thy Heart. May Thy kingdom come!"

In speaking thus I do not claim to lessen your defects, whether in their hideousness or their number. Humility should be the truth. I will say more. Commit yourselves to Him, because Jesus who invites you to His intimacy sees more clearly than you. Where you notice a hundred defects He will find a thousand, and yet He loves you and calls you to Him. His love is not, and cannot be, like that of a friend or a lover, based on illusion, but is grounded on the truth. He does not love you because He *imagines* you to be what you are not, since for Him there can be no pretense. He loves you such as you are. That is why St. Teresa said boldly but rightly, "What bad taste You have, Lord, to love me, hideous as I am; but do not, on any account, change that bad taste, lest I be exposed to the danger of your putting an angel in my place."

In earthly friendship, excess of familiarity reveals defects. Hence it is that so many affections founded on illusion gradually cool off. "Jesus loves and forgives you as no one else does," says Father Faber, "precisely because no one knows you as He does." For Him alone there can never be any surprises, since even in the saint who works miracles, He still sees an abyss of frailty. It follows then that He who knows everything is satisfied with great and holy desires, because many of them, however sincere, cannot be realized. And these great desires are considered as a real *work of love* by our indulgent Savior, provided they are true and not mere passing fancies. "Peace on earth among men of good will."[21] Peace to those who have understood and tasted how good the Lord is! Peace to those who have experienced that His yoke is easy and His burden light![22] Therefore, be more concerned for His glory than for the curing of your ills, however legitimate this desire be. "Think of Me and only Me," said Jesus to St. Margaret Mary, "and I will think of thee and all that concerns thee."

---

21 Luke 2: 14   22 Matt. 11: 30

Apostles who do not understand this waste both time and energy in making many petitions. It is only when they have tired themselves out that they will add, "Thy Kingdom come." Do not follow their example; begin the work of your sanctification and apostolate with this prayer from your very heart: "Thy Kingdom come, the Reign of Thy Heart, of Thy Love." And at once He will say: "I Myself will see to all your interests!" You see, now, how ample, sure, solid and beautiful is the doctrine of the Heart of Jesus. How good it is to live, to struggle, to labor in that refuge in which all is truth, peace, strength, and joy in the Holy Spirit! Drink your fill of that Heart, the unfailing fountain of life and of merciful love. In Him I wish to have my abode, my school, my resting place, my heaven. That Heart suffices me. I am the poorest of the poor, but in that Heart I have no fear.

There are many who think it is arduous and most difficult to be saved. I believe, on the contrary, that it is not so easy to lose one's soul, for to do so we should have to break loose from the Savior's arms and escape from that citadel of redemption which is His Heart. Steep yourselves, zealous apostles, in this grand doctrine, which is assuredly not new — for there has been nothing new since the Gospel — but which, by the explicit will of heaven, is today like a spiritual atmosphere embracing the whole world under the title of "The Reign of the Heart of Jesus." Nourish yourselves on this bread of love and unbounded trust, in order to give this manna to the many souls who have but a mean and false conception of Christ our Lord. Be yourselves aglow with love that you may set other souls aflame with charity. Speak to the weak, the perverse, to sinners, as the Sacred Heart would do. Hearken to Him as He passes judgment on the sinner crouching at His feet: "Neither will I condemn thee. Go thy way, and from now on sin no more."[23] You who are His disciples, form your ideas and your language on the pattern of that Teacher!

I will end with one of Saint Therese's most admirable sayings both in doctrine and eloquence: "It is not merely because

---

23 John 8: 11

I have been preserved from mortal sin that I lift up my heart to God in trust and love. I am certain that, even if I had committed every imaginable crime, I should lose nothing of my confidence, but would throw myself broken-hearted into the arms of my Savior. I know how He loved the Prodigal Son; I recall His words to St. Mary Magdalen, to the woman taken in adultery, to the Samaritan woman, and no one could ever discourage me, for I abide by His mercy and His love. I know that the multitude of my sins would vanish in the twinkling of an eye, *like a drop of water dropped into a blazing crucible.*"

Chapter 5

HUMILITY

*"Learn from me, for I am
meek and humble of heart."*[1]

OUR NATURAL LIFE IS SUCH A SMALL THING that it seems hardly
worth while living. An apostle, above all, cannot content
himself with so small a thing; his true ideal is to live in Jesus
and by Jesus, lost in the heaven of His Heart. Such is the
one life worthy of the name and a fitting prelude to that
which will be eternal.

But in order to attain to these sublimities, it is fortunately
not necessary for us to take wings to the heights. We should
rather descend, disappear and annihilate ourselves as Jesus
did. Think how, in order to raise us, He came down to Mary's
womb, and from there to the crib of straw, lower still to
His annihilation on the cross, and even lower, when He abases
Himself and disappears, not even keeping His human form,
in the Sacred Host. Such is His grandeur, such should be ours.

It is really necessary that I should make myself small. In
the divine order this is always the first and the last step. Alas!
we are far too big to be saints. "Big" and "saint" are contradictory terms. For to be a saint one must be little, and to be
a great saint it is indispensable that we should be very little.
Divine grandeur — the only one — always means a lessening
and a disappearance. If, then, we wish to transform ourselves
in God, we must begin by making ourselves very little. And
to give Him to other souls, to be His friends and His apostles,

---

1 Matt. 11: 29

we must at once prepare ourselves to be particles of the Host which is Jesus Himself. Is it not wonderful to think that the Word, in order to give Himself to us without reserve, comes under the appearance of bread? We are not greater than the Master. We shall never be able to work miracles of conversions unless we begin by this miracle of grace: namely, we must decrease that He may increase in us and in souls.

Contemplate the great forsaken King in the thousands of tabernacles scattered over the world, with no other splendor than that of silence, the poorest of the poor, mute, still, neglected. What shame and reproach are ours when we meditate on our dreams of self-love and ambitions before the tabernacle. The Incarnate Word has humbled Himself to the dust, and we think of our right to esteem, affection, credit, consideration and honor. Let us blush for shame to have our thoughts thus occupied in the presence of Jesus in the Blessed Sacrament and promise to forget ourselves as He forgets Himself, to lay aside those foolish thoughts and to rejoice in having but one right, that of having none! *"Learn from me, for I am meek and humble of heart."*[2] This is the same lesson of profound abasement and humility which He gave in Paray-le-Monial to His servant St. Margaret Mary, and through her to His apostles.

O Jesus! conceal me in Thy wounded side: free me from the yearning to be loved and appreciated; deliver me from the evil of wanting to put myself forward and win distinction! Humble me till I am an atom of dust, a spark of fire in the flame of love of Thy Sacred Heart. Let me there forget creatures and my very self.

"IF THY EYE BE SOUND, THY WHOLE BODY WILL BE FULL OF LIGHT"[3]

The characteristic of the spirit of Jesus in the entire Gospel is love in the most perfect and sublime simplicity. Truly, simplicity is a rare, a very rare virtue, even among good people. It may be described as the splendor of humility and

---

2 Matt. 11: 29   3 Matt. 6: 22

the reflection of truth. Hence, the guileless child is instinctively truthful, because it is simple. Simplicity is a moral limpidity in which an extraordinary and celestial beauty of soul is always reflected. Faulty upbringing, a systematic breakdown of the Gospel ideals and bad example, have made us very complex and prone to duplicity; we live by many fallacious arguments and compromises! Alas! our hearts are an inextricable maze and Jesus cannot abide in such confusion. He is supreme simplicity. His words were not in vain when He said: "Unless you turn and become like little children,"[4] and "he who is the least among you, he is the greatest."[5] And again, "Let your speech be: 'Yes, yes;' 'No, no';"[6] and "If thy eye be sound, thy whole body will be full of light."[7]

Be simple, very simple, with God your Father since you you are His children. Go to Him, turn to His Heart with the lawful and sacred audacity of little children, without complications, "like a bullet to its mark," as the Curé of Ars used to say. How easily His Heart is won by such a way of acting. You then prove you know Him and understand the teaching of His Heart and of the Gospel; you are then but a step from winning a great victory.

Compare the high-sounding, obscure and pedantic language of the would-be "intellectuals" with that of the saints. The angels must sometimes be amazed when listening to a dialogue between such souls and Jesus. On the contrary, we have an exquisite, daring expression in the words of Saint Therese: "If I were Jesus and Thou wert Therese"; and that of St. Margaret Mary: "Why dost Thou not let me go the ordinary road of the Daughters of Holy Mary? Lord, Thou wilt be the cause of my being sent away." And St. Teresa of Avila on hearing that the Lord tried His friends more than others replied, "That is why Thou hast so few!" Never be afraid to talk to Jesus like little children and like the saints. Remember that He Himself taught us to pray in the simplest fashion: "Our Father who art in heaven — Thy Kingdom come

4 Matt. 18: 3   5 Luke 9: 48
6 Matt. 5: 37   7 Matt. 6: 22

71

— Give us this day our daily bread." But, above all, give us the Living Bread which is Thyself and Thy Heart. Be our life, O Jesus!

While a royal audience is altogether a difficult and puzzling problem to face — because of having to study and observe all the rules of etiquette concerning our words and attitude — a visit to the Blessed Sacrament fills our heart with peace and comfort; we are in our own house and perfectly happy at the feet of the King of Kings, at Thy feet, O Jesus!

The following story will teach you a great lesson. Let us call it a *dialogue in Nazareth*. A little girl of eight had been well prepared for her First Communion and had made it with fervor and generosity. Our Lord, who never lets Himself be outdone in generosity, willed that such great love should be repaid by a miracle and, from that day on, used to converse with her. She was not in the least surprised, for in the simplicity of her heart she thought that everybody could hear Jesus and speak as she did to Him. They talked together as naturally and familiarly as a little brother and sister.

One day Jesus said to her, "Do you really love Me very much?" She was up in arms at once, for the question seemed to imply a doubt and she replied, "You oughtn't to ask me that, dear Jesus." "Why not?" He inquired. "Because You know quite well that I have given You my heart and it belongs to You." "Yes," answered Jesus, "I know, but I wanted you to tell me so. Very few people love Me nowadays." Shortly after in a moment of fervor, the little girl said to Jesus, "Is it really true that You, who are God, can love a little thing like me?" Then Jesus paid her back in her own coin, saying, "You ought not to ask Me that." "Why not?" she asked, quite upset and fearing she had done wrong. "Because you know quite well I do. You are My very own, My little apostle, and My Heart belongs to you." "Well," said the child, "I knew You loved me, only I wanted You to tell me so Yourself, dear Jesus." And so it went on nearly every day.

However, as it was a delicate matter and imagination might easily have crept in, I resolved, in all confidence, to make a test to draw from our Lord a proof that it was really

72

He who talked to the child. One day I told her to ask for the conversion of a great sinner. The next time she came to confession she said in her usual simple way, "Father, he's coming." "What do you mean, child, who's coming?" "The sinner you asked little Jesus for, Father, don't you remember?" Without further ado, she went on, "Next day, when Jesus began to talk to me, I said, 'Please, Jesus, wait a minute. I want to speak first today.' Then I told Him what you had said to me and that He would know quite well which soul you meant, since He was God. With a lovely smile Jesus said, "Yes, I know. Ask Me always for souls, and tell Father to ask, too, and he shall have them. After your next confession the man he means and whom nobody has been able to convert will go and make his confession to him. But to get him to do this, you must be my little missionary. Pay the price for his soul by earning "three golden pennies." Do this by offering to Me your prayers, your sacrifices (especially by obedience), and your Communions."

Then she stopped short and added hurriedly, "Father, please, hadn't you better give me absolution at once? the soul's just coming here." I did so and as the child moved towards the altar to say her penance, I saw coming toward my confessional a man who was known to lead an absolutely irreligious life.

"Father," he said, "I do not know what has happened, but since this morning I am quite changed and I have come to make my first confession." Jesus had vanquished him, giving this soul as a reward for the loving prayers and sacrifices of a little child.

I really think that we are altogether too solemn to be saints. Blessed are the little children, and those who make themselves like unto them. "Whatever our age and however lofty our station, we can always be children in sincerity and simplicity," little Therese wrote. I have already said, "Pray as you love." Let there be less ceremony in your way of speaking to God and be more like a child talking to its mother. Do not seek fine words or ramble off into useless reasonings. Think how marvelously simple are the prayers of the Church.

73

The same words are repeated hundreds of times in the litanies, in the missal and in the breviary: "Amen," "Have mercy on us," "Glory be to the Father and to the Son and to the Holy Ghost." The whole system of the official prayers of the Church is of this kind. There are no complications. Everything is beautiful, divine and simple.

Simplicity has its chief practical application in the spiritual life. A teacher of the very first order in this school is St. Therese. Cardinal Bourne aptly and truly said that she had had the privilege of suppressing mathematics in sanctity. Analyze her famous little path; study her spirituality, her life of prayer; observe her method of dealing with her fellow-creatures, with her sisters; in everything she has the supreme, divine art of enchanting simplicity. It seems as though heaven had presented her to us with the credentials of miracles precisely to recommend her as the finished model of evangelical simplicity. The failure to understand the lessons which, at different times, God has given to souls, through certain saints providentially sent at opportune moments, has always been a bad symptom. Few among these lessons have been more eloquent, suggestive and rich in doctrine than that of the Little Flower: Let us try to understand it!

"Thank you, sweet and marvelous little saint," wrote a great author. "Thank you for having, with your gentle smile, made us understand that according to the Gospel, greatness does not lie in the knowledge acquired in books, nor in the minds of those who pretend to interpret them. Thank you, little Therese, for having awakened so many of the learned and conceited from the moral depression in which they lived, believing only in false lights, and intellectualism. More prudent, wise and learned than all of us, you have been able to prove by your life, which was a marvel of simplicity and heroism, that he who humbles himself is exalted, he who is simple is profound, he who knows how to love knows everything and he who can lovingly die little by little is the most fruitful of apostles."

There still exists in Lima a part of the garden in which St. Rose and the Child Jesus often walked *hand in hand.*

There still remains the old tree-trunk on which the saint used to sit while the divine Child picked flowers to place in Rose's lap. She would at once make a crown with them and put it on the brow of the Little King. He would then smile and say, "Dear Spouse, because thou hast chosen the thorns for thyself, I want thee to have the flowers." And, with this, the Child Jesus would take the crown from His head and place it on hers, saying, "My Heart is thine, dear Rose."

Note how Rose of Lima and Therese of Lisieux, in spite of the centuries between them and their apparently different paths, speak the same language and sing the same canticle. They are two roses of which the Child Jesus loved to pluck the petals of His glory. He found them worthy of Himself because of their simplicity, littleness and meekness of heart. Each of them could say, as she played in her own way with the Child Jesus, "Because I was little I was pleasing to the most High."[8]

I repeat, let us be simple in our relations with God, for simplicity implies humility and trust. Let us be simple in our relations with our neighbor, in seeking and loving nothing in them but Jesus and forgetting our personal interests to serve and help our brethren for love of Him. Finally, let us be simple with ourselves; to deny our good qualities would be ingratitude and mock humility; to attribute them to ourselves or to lay stress upon them would be pride. Let us likewise acknowledge our defects, but without pessimism or irritation. We shall then find light and strength to correct them in a real intimacy with the Heart of Jesus.

---

8 Office of the Annunciation

Chapter 6

INTO THY HANDS . . .[1]

FATHER, MY SPIRIT, MY LIFE, my desires, my hopes, my eternal future — I commend all into Thy hands. Properly speaking, abandonment is nothing but a logical consequence of the spirit of faith. The summit is easily reached through confidence and a love as strong as death. Needless to say, there is nothing in common between a "stupid quietism," an indolent folding of the arms, trusting that God will do everything without any cooperation or sacrifice on my part and this genuine self-abandonment which is the supreme expression of true love.

In this, as in everything, Jesus can say, "I have given you an example."[2] Think of His abandonment in Holy Communion, not to speak of His Incarnation in the heart of His Immaculate Mother, or of His life in Nazareth when He was subject to Mary and Joseph. I would make special mention of His abandonment in the forgetful, frivolous, often disloyal heart of a communicant. Given that he is at that moment in a state of grace, was he so yesterday? How justly Jesus could, at times, interrupt our many protestations of fidelity and say, "Stop, do not keep on affirming that you love Me, nor promise that you will love Me. I have heard the same words so often, and as many times afterwards you have pierced My Heart." Is that how Jesus speaks? No! When we receive Him, poor frail beings as we are, and assure Him that we are His, He lovingly listens to our words and never tells us He does not

---

1 Luke 23: 46　　　　　　2 John 13: 15

76

believe us. Still less does He lock the Tabernacle to those who offended Him grievously yesterday. Holding out His arms, He comes to us keeping nothing back, and giving His soul, His body, His blood, His divinity. Jesus is wholly ours, as if we were saints, as if we had always been such, as if He were sure of our eternal fidelity. He abandons Himself to us through love. What a sublime and entrancing example! Let us do as much. How reasonable it is that the slime of the earth should abandon itself to the Ark of Gold, the Heart of Jesus. But what divine folly that He, the heaven of heavens, should commit Himself to the vessel of clay, the stained earthenware chalice of our poor little hearts.

"I give thee an example; copy it, follow Me!" True love consists, for Jesus as for us, in abandonment one to the other, the son to his mother, the wife to her husband. But what mother or spouse can ever be compared to Jesus? If then, I firmly believe in His wisdom and justice, above all in His merciful love, I must, logically, give myself up to His designs, to His Heart. Jesus knows and understands as no one else does both my temporal and eternal interests; guided by His infinite love, and constantly anxious about me, He turns everything to His glory and my good. Is it not, therefore, supreme wisdom to say to Him, "Lord, do whatsoever pleaseth Thee, dispose of me, burn or rend, heal or wound me, as Thou wilt; blessed be Thou in life and in death?"

The most instinctive and at the same time rational gesture of a child is to throw himself into his mother's arms. There he will play and sleep, be tenderly fed and cared for. Why should we not do the same in the spiritual life, since for us there is not only a question of confiding ourselves to the most loving of mothers, but to Jesus. Can I truly love Him without giving myself up to Him?

Is not self-abandonment through love the most sublime and simple realization of the prayer "Thy Kingdom come, Thy Will be done?" How do I know whether sickness or health, riches or poverty is for my good or ill today? But He knows. Let Him, therefore, proceed with a free hand and a Father's Heart. Let Him dispose of me, make His decision, without consulting me, wayward, ignorant child as I am. Is not this wisdom and prudence? Is not this loving God above all things?

Thus, in a life of struggle or of ease, my place will be within Thy arms, on Thy Heart, O Jesus. As for the rest, whether I rise or sink, whether my portion is sweet or bitter, let it be according to Thy Will. I cannot say it is indifferent to my weak nature, which never hesitates in its choice between the bitter and the sweet; but with the help of Thy divine light and grace here I am, Jesus. I come to say that I wish to do Thy Will in everything and to abandon myself entirely to Thee.

The unalterable peace enjoyed by the saints had no other secret. Like us, they passed through countless vicissitudes and temptations which tried them like a fiery crucible. Nevertheless, their souls experienced perfect tranquility; nay more, a happiness so deep, so enrapturing, that in this exile they had, at times, a foretaste of paradise. Oh! if we knew how good it is to live in the Heart of Jesus, entirely submissive to His will and desires, wishing for or refusing nothing, but accepting equally and with love the thorns as well as the flowers! Let us during these days resolve to reach that height where perfect calm reigns, where everything but Jesus is indifferent to us. May His Heart find us perfectly docile even in our attempt to accomplish these our resolutions.

Then indeed He will be able to say to us as to St. Margaret Mary, "I am a very wise director and can guide souls without the slightest danger if they will only submit entirely to Me and forget themselves!" This director never fails, never leaves you. He is never transferred, nor does He die. You will find Him always within reach, faithful and vigilant. Oh! give to Him the tiller of your little barque! How holy will then be your voyage! How sweet it will be to wake on the other shore, having been borne, piloted, guided there by Jesus!

Abandon yourselves blindly into His Arms; abandon yourselves upon His Heart.

Chapter 7

BE SAINTS

"For this is the will of God,
your sanctification."[1]

THOUGH THESE WORDS ARE ADDRESSED to all Christians, they seem to refer most specially to you and to all those who by vocation are called to be the friends and apostles of the King of Love.

"Come, follow Me," for "I am the light of the world"[2] "I am the way, and the truth and the life."[3]

And whither leads this way?

Here below to the goal pointed out to you which is sanctity, and then to your supreme and final goal which is eternal life, that is to say the consummation of all sanctity.

This sanctity is God Himself, because He alone is life and the beginning of life: I am "the beginning I who speak with you!"[4] Whence it follows that sanctity is our true life as well as our moral beauty and the sole secret of happiness and peace for us.

How often in our desire for happiness and all that is beautiful we deceive ourselves through misconceptions and only meet with deceitful charms.

Christ in His vivid radiance is the sole beauty which gives tranquility and happiness to the heart. For this reason the

1 Thes. 4: 3
2 John 8: 12
3 John 14: 6
4 John 8: 25 (Clementine Vulgate)

saints were the greatest and only philosophers, because they knew how to drink their fill from that fountain of peace and life which was, is, and ever will be Jesus, His love, His Heart.

WHAT IS SANCTITY?

"What would you like to be? An angel? An Aloysius Gonzaga?" I asked a child who, after his First Communion, was wont to spend whole hours in an ecstasy of happiness before the Blessed Sacrament. Without a moment's hesitation and with a heavenly expression on his face, he replied, pointing to the tabernacle; "To be changed into Jesus!" Such is also the simplest and most exact definition of sanctity — to be changed into Jesus.

Sanctity is Jesus assimilated, ever growing and developing in us, supplanting our poor fallen nature and giving us His own. It is Jesus as principle: of our thoughts, our soul, our will, foundation of our joys and source of our strength; it is, in short, the practical realization that "to me to live is Christ."[5] In proportion as we disappear He fills our whole being. This transformation is begun in a mystery of intense faith and it is consummated in a mystery of burning charity.

Speaking in a figurative sense we might say that sanctity is the ray of light which returns to the Sun, the atom of dust which regains its center, the life which finds at last and for ever the inexhaustible fountain of immortal Life which is God and only God. Or, if you prefer, sanctity is Jesus Christ giving our earthly life an eternal duration, and we living here below on that one immutable reality which is Christ, with His Heart for our school, our refuge, and our habitation.

IS SANCTITY POSSIBLE?

Entirely possible for the simple reason that we are called and invited to it by the all-wise God. Therefore we can attain it. He gives the first impulse. He makes the first step easy and also the second. Remember, sanctity does not principally

5 Phil. 1: 21

consist in laying hold of God up in the heights of heaven, but *in letting ourselves be seized by Him* when He swoops down like an eagle hungry for its prey. He invites and welcomes, He offers graces, light and strength, He draws and guides, He gives Himself; our part is to love Him and to give ourselves with docility, trust and generosity.

Take the case of a soul in a state of great wretchedness, full of defects — such were assuredly very many of the saints — but this soul lets herself be loved and taken by Jesus without feeling alarmed; in spite of the resistance of nature she submits to divine inspirations. Thus, notwithstanding a thousand difficulties, the Creator and the creature have worked a miracle of grace, and even before death that soul has risen to the heights of sanctity. Love, then, with a divine passion, with a blind and boundless trust and you will be saints.

SO I CAN BE A SAINT?

Evidently, why doubt it? Moreover it is a duty for you who read this and on whom abundant graces have been bestowed. A duty is not impossible. Think how much Jesus has loved you and do not be ungrateful. Do not imagine that under pretext of humility you can refuse to acknowledge so many favors and through unpardonable cowardice release yourself from the obligation of being a saint. Do not say that you want to be an apostle only and not a saint; an apostle who does not rise above mediocrity, good because not bad, and nothing more! Such souls are not worthy to be admitted amongst those who fight for God's glory.

And here I wish to lay stress on an idea which is as fundamental as it is simple, one on which I have much insisted when preaching to apostles, in order to give them great courage in the work of their sanctification.

It is incredible how wide-spread, even among Christians, is the opinion that saints are more or less beings cast into a special mold, and, like another John the Baptist, they neither eat, drink nor sleep; in other words they enjoy a glorified body and are confirmed in grace.

81

This very mistaken conception has already disheartened numberless souls and continues to discourage many who are keenly conscious both of their own fallen state and of the call to sanctity.

Let us see what happened, for example, in the case of the Little Flower. In spite of her canonization there are still fervent souls, even nuns and priests who say, "But this Carmelite *was just like others*, what did she do beyond the ordinary?"

Do you catch the wrong, discordant note? "What extraordinary things did she do — she *was just like others*," consequently "she can hardly be the saint they say she is." Such people, though pretending to have great love for the Blessed Virgin, have never meditated on the sanctity of that queen, in whom all appears normal and ordinary whereas all is sublime and divine. According to their criterion, sanctity consists in ecstasies, apparitions, the power of restoring the dead to life, the gift of prophecy, therefore those who live hidden lives like Mary and Joseph in Nazareth are not and cannot be saints.

Be very sure the saints had to struggle as we have and still more against interior darkness. Remember the tremendous and long temptation little Therese had against the Faith until her last agony. "I do not see," she said, "but I believe as I never did. That is enough for me!" Such darkness begets a marvelous celestial light.

The saints had to struggle as much as and more than we have against injustice, and, what is a greater danger, against the seduction of creatures, this living barrier or, if you prefer, this abyss of enthralling beauty which draws us to its brink and causes a fatal giddiness. But, constantly faithful to divine grace, they could say with St. Paul, "I can do all things in Him who strengthens me."[6] They conquered through love.

The saints had to struggle as much as and more than we have against their own indolence and that natural instinct, which, like the force of gravitation, always tends to draw us

6 Phil. 4: 13

towards the earth. How many times did they not feel the fatigue of battle, the tediousness of virtue, the weariness of climbing the slope above them, while, down below, they could hear the caressing, lulling sounds of singing and merry-making. Many a time they had need of all their courage and had to close their eyes and ears in order to persevere on their upward path. Nature can never get used to living a dying life, but grace supported by generosity is all powerful.

The saints had to fight as much as and more than we against that discouragement which comes from within and without, against their own weakness, which cries out, "Enough! Why so many efforts!" At times, they slipped and fell; there were moments when they doubted of their duty to become saints and when victory seemed impossible to them. But soon, recovering and increasing their energy by penance and generosity, they rallied their frail natures with love and died on the summit, hymning the victory of Jesus.

"To will is to be able." This axiom is always true in the supernatural order, given the fidelity of God and the mercy of His Heart. If I truly wish to be a saint, I can be one; I can even be a great one.

ONLY THE SAINTS ARE HAPPY

We do not say this to the world, for the world is not capable of understanding this truth. Remember that Jesus did not pray for the world,[7] for it is wilfully blind. But we do say it for the group of fervent souls who often consider virtue and especially sanctity as a burden of crushing glory, as the bloody glory of martyrdom, and do not give a thought to the heavenly peace and happiness which our Lord grants here below to His heroic servants. This is why I assert that only the saints are truly happy. Union with God, the casting off of everything which interiorly or exteriorly is a cause of moral conflict, the cross itself sweetened and changed into a heavenly gift and gain — in short the living on that truth which is Christ crucified, and that love which is Christ in the Blessed

7 John 17: 9

Sacrament — all this can but produce a delightful tranquillity of spirit and a contentment of heart which the world can never know. And if the earth is a place of exile, a real Calvary for the saints — and perhaps more so for them than for others — it happens to them as to our Lord in the Garden: Jesus sweated blood in His agony, but His soul was transported by the delights of the vision of His Father. The saints are happiest on Calvary.

Divine love has the virtue of transforming what is bitter into sweetness. "I have come to the point," said the Little Flower, "of not being able to suffer, for I have converted suffering into unspeakable joy. My great sorrows bring me great delight, and my little crosses lesser delight." Far from being nonsense, this divine folly is wisdom, the sublime folly of the Crucified and His friends. Mary, the queen of martyrs and the most sorrowful of creatures, was surely the happiest in her mortal life. After her, millions of saints have gloried in the cross, taken their delight in it, and hymned it in ecstasies of happiness; thus did Francis of Assisi, Mary Magdalen de Pazzi and John of the Cross.[8] All bore in their souls the stigmata of a spiritual martyrdom, all could truthfully say with St. Paul, *I overflow with joy.*[9]

The saint, still less than simple Christian, does not suffer alone, for he has a Cyrenean at his side who helps him to carry his crosses and to reach Calvary. This Cyrenean is his intimate Friend, Jesus Himself. As the saint lovingly drinks of the chalice of the Crucified King, so, too, the Lord in His turn rewards the friend of His Heart with consolations and increased fortitude. Jesus is the soul of the saint's endurance; he suffers and Christ supports him.

You will agree with me, dear apostles, that it is a far better thing to take the chalice from His hands and to drink of it leaning on His Heart, than to laugh and sing in the desert places of the world where He is not.

We rub shoulders with saints without knowing it. Many

---

8 In that Divine Heart the most bitter pains are changed into love.
9 2 Cor. 7: 4

imagine that the saints are only to be found in the glory of the past but never met in modern times. This false and pessimistic argument does nothing to encourage the reproduction of that race of giants, which is supposed to have become extinct as a result of progress and our present mode of life. But the Church has been gifted with a perpetual fecundity and just as there have always been saints, so there always will be until the consummation of the world. They may vary and do vary in style, form and modality in accordance with divine ordinance, but sanctity remains an actual and permanent reality. Thus, it is very possible that at the present day we may not find a saint like St. Vincent Ferrer, but it would not be surprising to come across one of the school of Nazareth without suspecting it, for such a one neither blows his own trumpet, nor raises the dead to life, but lives, like St. Joseph, in the silence and obscurity of his cottage.

St. Pius X, pointing to the portrait of little Therese, exclaimed one day. "She is the greatest saint of modern times." But a few years ago who ever knew of the existence of the Little Flower? Hundreds of contemporaries of the little saint are alive, those who have seen her and conversed with her, those who could appreciate certain of her qualities and even testify to certain defects. How many of them imagined that they would see her raised to the altars and that her virtue and her miracles, *till then ignored,* would shake the entire world and make of her "a miniature of grace," as Pius XI said? And this story is one of yesterday. It was but yesterday that she traveled our road. Her footsteps are still fresh, and she is already canonized. So, too, on that same road of obscurity and simplicity, we have saints today, both in monasteries and in the world. As soon as death has broken the vessel of clay, the light and flame which they bore within them is manifested.

There is certainly much that is evil today, but there is also much that is good, and with daily or frequent Communion, with the spread of the devotion to the Heart of Jesus — I mean the health-giving doctrine of love — there are hidden gems of sanctity which tomorrow perhaps will blaze forth in the eyes of the whole world.

To illustrate this, let me tell you the story of a young girl who displayed heroic virtue. She was of high social standing, extremely well educated, of striking appearance, lively and most intelligent. Her father, a very worldly man, doted on her, indulged her every whim and loved to show off his little queen as his jewel. There was no play, no party, or ball that he did not attend with her. She was only sixteen years old, but she bore within her a longing for God and for heaven; she was fond of prayer and a true contemplative, without, however, having a religious vocation.

You can imagine how much she suffered from being shown off in worldly gatherings. She begged and entreated her father to excuse her from leading a life that was anguish to her. But he always refused. He had to go, he said, and he would not go without her. She, out of respect and submissiveness, had to resign herself to the torture.

So there she was, constantly arrayed in all her finery. No one suspected that she wore a hair shirt beneath her costly dresses and that her soul was as white as snow and her heart on fire for Jesus.

What is most remarkable is that after she had spent the time from ten o'clock till one in the morning in a box at the opera, at a social gathering or ball, she came away from them wholly absorbed in God. Moreover, if any one had asked her, she could not have told what play she had attended or who had asked her to dance, for, by a miracle of grace and in reward for the heroic fidelity of her heart, her soul had passed those long hours in an ecstasy of love even though her body was where her father obliged it to be. When she reached her house, in the early morning, she would spend an hour on her knees in adoration and reparation, and at seven o'clock she was at the altar rails, so rapt in God that they had to rouse her when it was time to return home again.

"I feel," she told me, "as if a very sweet drowsiness seizes me and entirely overcomes me as soon as I set foot in the theater or in the ballroom, and I am unaware of anything that is going on. It is as if I were there alone. I wake up completely as soon as I get back home, and therefore I am often much puzzled when people, talking about some party or opera at which I have been present, ask me what I thought of it. If it were not for the program or my father I should not know where I had been nor what had happened."

This is what the love of Jesus is always capable of working among rich and poor, in the cloister and in the world, when He has once taken possession of a heart. Today, more than ever, heroic souls may frequently be met. The Heart of Jesus is everywhere producing an outburst of sanctity which has perhaps never been so rich and varied, but in the style of Nazareth. The interior is splendid and worthy of the King of Love, but the outside is humble and simple, like Joseph's workshop.

God is wonderful in His saints.[10] He is forever adorning the firmament of His Church with these divine jewels, and, if you are tempted to give up the struggle for sanctity because of your unworthiness, your past or present sins, call to mind these words of His: *I make My masterpieces out of the refuse of the earth.*"

Apostles of the Sacred Heart, rejoice: *If you are or have been the refuse of the earth, you have all the more right to be a masterpiece of His love!*

---

10 Ps. 67: 36

Chapter 8

HOW TO BECOME A SAINT

WHEN WE CONSIDER THAT PROVIDENCE is insistently calling to a life of perfection men and women of every class on whom graces have been bestowed in abundance, we cannot help feeling sorry that there are not more saints. How sad it is to see marvelous treasures of light and love disdained, wasted and frittered away. And yet all the materials needed for the forging of heroes of virtue, *or saints* — the bronze, the crucible, the workmen — are ready at hand. Favorable circumstances have been wisely accumulated by the skill and foresight of Providence for the realization of a masterpiece, so the success, as far as heaven is concerned, is assured.

In the midst of the forge stands the Master of masters, the divine Craftsman, whose eyes are increate Beauty, whose hands are Truth and Omnipotence, whose Heart is throbbing with divine eagerness. He is anxiously waiting there for the decisive *fiat* of the human heart, and whenever this rings out resolute and generous the Master sets to work, and soon breathes into the bronze the breath of immortality which, in the garden of Eden, transformed a body of clay into the perfect Adam.

This prodigy of grace is unfortunately realized only at rare intervals and meanwhile the furnace dies out, the bronze becomes rusty and the workmen who have been called in to help are dismissed as too exacting and inopportune.

That bronze represents innumerable chosen and favored souls; the glowing forge is but a pale image of the thousand afflictions inherent in every state of life; the skilled artisans are the creatures, the daily events, all the things used by our Lord as blind instruments to mold man into the image and likeness of the new Adam, Jesus Christ. The workshop is the home, the office, the world or the convent, the palace or the cottage, in short the transitory dwelling place *whatever it may be*, where daily duty and God's Will have placed the temporary abode in which the soul believes, suffers and loves in this world, preparing for eternity.

Unfortunately many richly endowed souls neither understand nor heed the solicitations of a God of love, and few respond to His call. This is the more to be deplored as their very circumstances often give these favored souls the opportunity of being heroes and saints. They had but to take the one decisive step to reach the threshold of the forge where heroes are fashioned and there, without changing their vocation or dress, by merely *sanctifying the heroism imposed on them by their state of life* — that is to say *by super-naturalizing the martyrdom of their daily life* — many of these excellent Christians could be truly *saints!*

For instance, many wives and mothers — whether of high or low estate — tread the road of suffering just by leading their daily lives. Many of our Catholic business men drag out their lives in offices and factories, hampered by a thousand obligations and almost crushed under the weight of imperative and unavoidable responsibilities. They eat the bread of weariness and their future is dark with sorrow and anxiety. Many of them are really leading heroic lives and bear the scars of a noble though unseen martyrdom. Day by day they are learning the sublime lesson of generosity and sacrifice. But what is still lacking to them, if they are to be clothed with a glory that is truly immortal and *win the palm of a divine and saintly heroism, is a heart of love*, a heart burning with charity. God would raise up many a saint if these crucified souls would but make Him their life, their all.

Such is the lesson heaven is teaching us, at the present time, in the person of that sweet enchanting messenger of merciful love, that star of the first magnitude of the Church and Carmel, *Saint Therese of the Child Jesus*.

To be a saint it is not necessary to live in the strict enclosure of a monastery, to practice the austerity of Carmel, the abstinence and silence of Trappists. It is possible, though living in the world, to be detached from all, mortified, full of burning charity and without danger of presumption or illusion to aspire to and attain the height of perfection like little Therese. Why then are saints so rare, why do they not abound in the ranks of those who are not mere servants but soldiers and friends of the King of Glory?

Without *justifying* the ordinary easy going life, devoid of aspirations and high ideals, of so many who pride themselves on being the Master's faithful friends, we may give many reasons explaining this scarcity. In most cases, we do not find ourselves in the presence of lack of good faith, nor wilful resistance to divine inspirations, nor absence of real and — to some extent — solid virtue. No, it seems that such an evil has frequently a quite different origin, that is, *a mistaken conception of sanctity*, an erroneous doctrine either about the essential principle of true and genuine sanctity, or the methods and ways of acquiring it.

Then arise logically many prejudices, illusions and errors, and lastly, as a conclusion to such faulty premises, *fatal discouragement*. It is certainly this which in general holds us back on the way of perfection, and accounts for our finding so few saints in the very field where divine grace is poured out in torrents.

I should like, dear readers, to stimulate your Christian piety and generosity, to launch you on outspread wings in quest of the holy mountain! But first you must be thoroughly convinced that *sanctity is within the reach of all generous souls*. It could not be otherwise since it is our principal, nay, our *sole duty*, one which includes all the rest. "Only one thing is necessary." If, therefore, it is a duty, then the ascension of the soul *is certainly possible*. "I can do all things in Him who comforteth me and who calls me to follow Him."

A magnificent and conclusive proof of this is afforded by St. Therese of the Child Jesus. This young Carmelite Nun is gently encouraging and transforming many souls that, despite the manifold graces they have received, painfully drag out their existence in the very court of the King of Love. Being herself a lovely flower in the garden of our Lord, she is especially interested in the sanctification of consecrated souls and scatters all along her path the countless "roses" of signal graces.

Draw near her unhesitatingly and fearlessly. She is so little, so simple, so exquisitely sweet, and yet, by a mystery of grace, so compelling and irresistible in her way of calling and teaching us. Her apotheosis is invested with such extraordinary characteristics, and her power and glory are so astounding to the world, that after reading her life we may wonder how this spouse of Christ succeeded in taking the Heart of Jesus and of the Church by storm. She was only twenty four, far too young to rank among the geniuses of the world, yet she was mature enough to be a great saint. "Jesus," she cried, "open Thy book of life in which are written all the valiant deeds of all the saints. I should like to perform them all, only for Thee!" Jesus, who in His extreme condescension wrought the little miracle of the snow on the day of her clothing to satisfy the childlike whim of His betrothed, replied to this outburst of love by the infallible voice of Pius XI who in setting little Therese among the great saints of the Church declared that "she was a miracle of grace and a prodigy of miracles!"

Thus it is not astonishing that legions of souls are charmed by her spirit. Let her exercise her gracious influence upon you. If you fully comprehend the profound simplicity of her doctrine, if you value the peace and security she enjoyed in the path which she gracefully calls her "Little Way" I am certain that you will change your route as the Magi did when returning from Bethlehem.

Under the beneficent influence of the Star of Carmel, prepare your hearts to receive the seed of life and sanctity. Souls of good will that thirst for truth are the richest and most fertile soil where ripe fruit cannot fail to abound. Thus the crusade of love which I preach for the honor and glory

of the divine Heart will find the most devoted apostles among
the readers of these lines, since sanctity is always fertile as
love is, and true apostolate may be defined as a life which
radiates life, a love which sows and produces love. God
grant that each of us may be one day, like the Little Flower,
a mysterious Well of Jacob, full to the brim of living waters
which may quench the thirst for love of the Good Shepherd
and His flock.

SAINTS ARE NOT BORN SAINTS

Among the many pernicious misconceptions concerning
sanctity the following is pre-eminent. "The saints, if we except
true penitents like Mary Magdalen, *were born saints.*" Nothing indeed is farther from the truth. This might certainly be
said of geniuses and artists, since these spoilt children of
nature do, in fact, receive at their birth an extraordinary
wealth of natural gifts. These are developed and brought to
perfection in due time by favorable circumstances and personal labor. Human genius and art always presuppose a
privileged cradle. Thus Dante, Michelangelo and Raphael,
Columbus and Teresa of Avila received at birth an extraordinary rich nature. We all agree on this point.

But a saint is not born a saint, and sanctity which is a
sublime form of genius, *must be and can be acquired.* It is
an undoubted fact that the supernatural beauty of a saintly
soul is the work of grace together with the free, faithful and
heroic co-operation of the will. If we except Mary Immaculate, all the saints have had to struggle in order to bring to
fruition the talents entrusted to them. Moreover, many saints
— perhaps most of them — received at baptism only the
ordinary amount of grace bestowed on the majority of Christians in that Sacrament. But by their *extraordinary* fidelity,
their lawful ambition, and perseverance, they merited and
irresistibly drew down upon themselves that *extraordinary*
flood of celestial favors and graces which our Lord never
refuses to souls of unlimited generosity. We can therefore
safely say, without any exaggeration, that they won the divine
palm and halo by a heroic struggle.

Let us never weary of repeating that many saints only received the usual amount of grace necessary to work out their salvation. Thus if they died rich in merits we may conclude that all these treasures of virtues and rights to glory *were acquired.*

They did not spare themselves, and thus won the exceptional place which they hold on the thrones of heaven and the altars of the Church.

SAINTS ARE TEMPTED AS WE ARE

There is a still more consoling thought. All the saints *had to sustain a relentless struggle,* more violent perhaps than ordinary Christians have to face. Like their Model and Master Jesus Christ they had to pass through the crucible of temptation which humbles, fortifies and exalts. Many beautiful souls waste time and energy and are hampered in their progress by discouragement because they feel the prick of their frail and fallen nature! Lift up your hearts! Temptation is nothing but a dangerous crossroad on your journey. Confidence and humility, peace and vigilance, will get you over the crisis, not only without any loss of virtue, but with an enormous gain of merit.

There are some biographies of saints which I should like to burn, not because I condemn the saints but because, in part at least, I do blame the authors. Such writers present their heroes and heroines as being confirmed in grace from their birth, ever sailing on a peaceful sea, supreme masters of a nature totally subdued and transfigured not by hard earned praiseworthy victories, but *by a privilege* God has only granted to His Mother. You who feel discouraged in spite of your good will, read again and again the Gospels and meditate on the writings of St. Paul where such an affirmation is thoroughly overthrown.

Were not Francis of Assisi, Benedict the founder and abbot, Bernard of Clairvaux great saints who, in order to subdue low instincts and a rebellious nature, had to roll themselves on brambles and thornbushes, or stand in a pond of icy water throughout a bitter winter's night? You see, then, that temptation is no evidence of a lack of virtue; on the contrary, by fighting it unceasingly the saints covered themselves with glory.

Our temptations prove nothing against us. God in His infinite wisdom and *mercy* allows them to try our fidelity and give us an opportunity of meriting the immense glory He has in store for us. Remember what the Archangel Raphael said to Tobias: "Because thou wert acceptable to God, it was necessary that temptations should prove thee."[1]

SANCTITY IS ACQUIRED BY DEGREES

When we read these faulty biographies, we might conclude that the saints, from the mere fact of their having been enrolled in God's service, found themselves suddenly and without further trouble *immune* from all failings and weakness. They are depicted as *having been perfect and consummate in virtue from the beginning,* as if they had had to make but one bound to reach the goal. They seem to have put into practice in the supernatural life Caesar's famous saying, *"Veni, vidi, vici."* "I came, I saw, I conquered!" One is led to suppose that from the cradle to the grave they never touched the ground or experienced that weariness of soul and those waverings of heart by which all mortals are afflicted. They appear to have become perfect without effort or merit of their own, without stumbling on their road, or giving any signs of those involuntary shortcomings and imperfections which are inherent to our nature. Judging by such a criterion they may be considered as *celestial* beings and not creatures of flesh and blood.

This is not true, thank God, and the Church does not support any such theory. We may be certain that, specially at the beginning of the sublime ascent and even for long years, the saints tasted more than once of the bitter chalice of salutary remorse. More than once, too, above all at the

---

1 Tob. 12: 13

outset of their glorious career, they had to correct and wash away with repentant tears, defects and negligences. *It was only little by little, step by step* that they acquired at last what we might call an angelic nature. Even then, acutely conscious of their own frailty they had to live a life of perpetual vigilance, always like a soldier on the alert. They feared to scorch their wings as did the disloyal angels, or of falling from a great height like the cedars of Lebanon.[2] Grace, like nature, proceeds slowly, by steps wisely spaced. Sanctity increases in an ascending progression just like a mysterious ladder whose upper part will one day touch heaven, but whose point of support meanwhile is this miserable earth, as the fervent soul knows by experience.

SANCTITY THROUGH THE NORMAL TRACK OF DAILY LIFE

We have now reached the most interesting and practical point of this important subject. According to some of these disconcerting books, all the saints were quite extraordinary beings; *all of them* lived apart from the *simple, normal, trodden track,* so that between them and ourselves there scarcely exists even a distant relationship. They all belonged to a superior and select caste to which there is no admission for ordinary Christians. The reading of such lives would necessarily lead to the conclusion that to become saints we must either abandon the simple path on which we tread and thus expose ourselves to the danger of illusion, or else definitely renounce all idea of sanctity and risk the danger of never growing in virtue.

Faced with such an alternative, many would choose the second course; they would break their wings, and resign themselves to a life of mediocrity and routine.

God forbid that we should accept such an extremely dangerous theory. We can and must sanctify ourselves in the *normal, simple, beaten track* of our daily life, in the midst of the apparently commonplace cares of Nazareth.

"All her glory is from within," the Church proclaims when

2 Ezech. 31

singing the praise of our Immaculate Queen, and indeed her celestial beauty, her splendor — only surpassed by the greatness of her Son — were hidden in her heart. No exterior glory, no miracle ever revealed in Bethlehem or Nazareth the sweet majesty, the marvelous perfection and sanctity of the purest of creatures, our sweet mother. Thus sanctity does not lie in the brilliant halo of stupendous miracles; the *saint* must be, and always is, like Mary, a miracle of grace *"from within."* Moreover, the thirty years of hidden life led by the Word Incarnate in Nazareth is an argument more than sufficient to dissipate in one breath the theory in favor of these "miraculous lives," a theory whose primary danger is to exalt the imagination and to weaken the will.

Such biographies, inspired by popular piety combined with poetry and presented in the suggestive form of a pious legend, are edifying, I agree; but they must not be considered as the authentic lives of the saints. Indeed, we are not called to be the saints of a poem. We ought to be and can be real and true saints without any poetry, but *in the prose of our daily life,* ennobled and sanctified by an immense faith and love.

This certainly does not mean that there is not something "extraordinary" in many saints. Marvelous gifts have been freely bestowed upon many of them by heaven in view of some very special mission entrusted to them. But let us not confuse, as is so often done, "exceptional favors and extraordinary paths" with essential sanctity. If in Francis of Assisi or Margaret Mary or the Curé of Ars, we were to suppress the marvelous and authentic halo; if we were to leave aside the ecstasies, visions, and miracles to penetrate into their interior lives and only consider their souls, they would still keep the whole beauty and majesty of a saint.

The *pedestal,* or exterior glory, and the *real saint* are two distinct and separate elements. Moreover, how many souls there are who never had any pedestal at all! This was the case with Mary, the mother of "fair" love. Yet she is the Queen of all the Saints. Jesus Himself is as much the God of Majesty in the cradle of Bethlehem, in the workshop of

Nazareth, as on Thabor; as much Lord and King in the obscurity and annihilation of the altar as in the glories of paradise.

If then the "mansions" and the "ways" are many and varied, sanctity is one and invariable. God in His wisdom — and without consulting us — has assigned to all a certain path. He has marked out our mansion, our vocation and our way. This way is always the best for each one of us or, to put it more directly, it is the *only* way. There, and not on the lofty heights of Thabor, *we can and must sanctify ourselves*. Let us have faith in the love of Him who ordains everything for His glory and our supreme good. Taken in this light, the lives of the saints will excite in us, not merely a fleeting enthusiasm and desire for holiness, but heroic deeds which will yield fruits of glory and merit eternal life.

These principles once established, fix your eyes with divine delight on the new star of Carmel, Saint Therese of the Child Jesus. With simplicity and eloquence, sureness of doctrine and fascinating smile, she traces for us her "Little Way" leading to the highest sanctity through the entire possession of a loving and greatly loved Jesus. Heaven is daily proving by a torrent of miracles not only that she had found the true road to sanctity, but that she became a great saint by following it. This "shower of roses," to use her own expression, bears undoubted testimony that God has confided to her a truly providential mission, that of watching over His intimate friends, His priests and over all consecrated souls. It is not at all strange, therefore, that the brightest jewel of her crown is the vast throng of priests and missionaries who look upon her as the golden paten of their sacrifices, the loving guide and confidant of their interior life, the one who will provide souls for their ministry. "Come and walk in my path," she seems to say; "love greatly, for God is love; follow me!" She repeats the same words to the multitudes that approach and acclaim her. Let us now learn the gospel lesson which Jesus teaches us by means of His little spouse, the victim and apostle of His merciful love.

The most noteworthy teaching which we find in her life is that *sanctity is certainly not the exclusive privilege of a particular class of souls.* It is the right of all Christians and especially of the true friends of Jesus, whose vocation implies *the right and the duty* of aspiring to sanctity.

To see how marvelously the Little Flower embodied this doctrine, let us make a brief reference to her early childhood. Our heroine received from heaven a very noble heart. Her home — a true Bethany — was a real sanctuary in which her father and elder sisters earnestly cultivated the mind and soul of the future Carmelite.

In one sense, it is true, she was a spoilt child. But let us not judge superficially, lest we mistake what constitutes her true value. It is not so much the fine, rich casket we wish to study but the precious pearl within. If we break the rich alabaster box we shall be able to enjoy the hidden perfume of this soul so humble, yet so great.

If, then, Therese received at birth an unusually large spiritual dowry and was born rich, let us not forget that many souls — now perhaps in hell — may have received as many and even *more graces* than were bestowed on her. Sanctity must not be estimated by the measure of love which is received, so much as by the love that is given in return.

We may assert, therefore, without any hesitation, that Therese *was not born a saint,* but she *became such* by her extraordinary fidelity to grace and to the calls of Jesus. *She willed to be a saint,* she made it her purpose to be one, and in this will to follow step by step her crucified King she was strong and heroic!

There is no doubt that from her cradle she was destined for great things, and that God had great designs on her, but this did not necessarily make her a saint, for many souls frustrate and bring to naught the plans of Providence. If, therefore, the Little Flower is in deed and in truth "a saint" it is because she *willed to be most faithful* and was so. From her earliest years, docile to the solicitations of divine grace, she slowly and earnestly transformed her life through a great spirit of faith. Guided by this infallible light, she understood that, to be a saint, she ought to *give her whole being to Jesus,* and she did so without reserve. She herself declares, "I do not remember ever having refused Jesus anything." To sum up: the characteristic of the Little Flower's sanctity is a lively faith producing and developing immense generosity, this generosity keeping up the flame of divine love and the latter bringing about — day by day — a marvelous transformation.

It is frequently alleged as a palliative to remorse that the cause of our mediocrity and poverty is God's parsimony on our behalf. But this excuse turns against us and bespeaks our lack of courage to do violence to ourselves, as the saints have done. Instead of complaining of having received God's gifts in a smaller measure than the saints, we should recognize with humility the meagerness of the love we give Him in return. In all truth *God willed* we should be saints, but we did not venture on the ascent of Calvary to which the Bridegroom invited us. "Come ye to the marriage. Come, for all things are ready."

ST. THERESE THE WARRIOR SAINT

Who would guess that behind the baby features and sweet smile of St. Therese there was the soul of a great warrior? Yet she wrote, "Our Lord has given me the grace to have no fear of conflict." She was certainly too enlightened to hold the foolish opinion that saints are exempt from all struggles against temptations. Her own experience taught her that true love implies a ceaseless combat. She had no illusion of any kind when she embraced with decision and enthusiasm the career of a saint. Had it been otherwise she would never have had the courage, at the age of fifteen, to submit to the severe Carmelite rule. She had an exquisite, childlike sensibility, an exuberant, ardent nature and a loving heart! It is therefore evident that in order to undertake this ascent by such a path and to obtain the glorious triumph which today is officially recognized by the Church, she must have sustained with wonderful energy a deadly struggle against her delicate and impetuous nature.

She won the coveted palm of a moral martyrdom in a fair hand-to-hand combat, fighting with the weapons of mortification in the service of heroic love. The Church acclaims and extols a victory which was indeed bought at the high price of twenty years of conflict. To doubt this for a single moment would be wrong, for little Therese was not exempt from defects, especially in the beginning, nor did she herself ever try to conceal or disguise them. How spontaneously and humbly, for example, she speaks of what she prettily calls the "desertions" of her novitiate! But all this does not throw even the slightest shadow on the bright splendor of her soul. On the contrary, we feel her to be all the nearer, all the more accessible, more fully our own. When we are almost overcome by temptation she is at our side, bending over us like a true, affectionate sister and whispering her enrapturing and magic word: *Confidence!*

It was *confidence* that gave the Little Flower the mysterious strength which brought her peace and joy in daily struggle. Her unbounded confidence, which we may almost term holy audacity, was the secret of all her victories. Only thus can we explain the fact that in but nine years of religious life she was able to complete the masterpiece which the Church today puts before us for our admiration and imitation. It is also the explanation of the "shower of roses," and "rain of fire" announced by this marvelous Carmelite during her lifetime and now fulfilled as a proof that the secret treasures and mercies of the Sacred Heart of Jesus have been entrusted to her.

Let us, then, increase our courage and strengthen our will, so that we may abandon ourselves more fully and completely to the merciful love of Jesus. And this not so much *in spite of* our unworthiness and wretchedness, but rather *because of* our frailty and insignificance. Such is the true spirit and doctrine of this irresistible sower of confidence and love.

THE SAINT OF LITTLE SOULS

God is always admirable in His saints; but He seems to be even more so when He draws marvels out of nothingness, when He sets stars alight with a wisp of straw from the manger of Bethlehem, or when with a grain of sand He awakens and moves to its depths the moral world of souls. And this is precisely the case with St. Therese.

Even since her canonization, she still is and always will be to her countless admirers "little Therese," as the Holy Father, Pius XI himself, called her in his official discourse. On the altars, therefore, as formerly in the home and in the cloister, she will continue to be *little*, like the child-model of the Gospel. It seems evident that heaven has molded her in this enchanting form to present her as the imitable and inspiring ideal, not only of numerous "little souls" but also of all, whether priests, religious, or fervent Christians in the world. She is persistently inviting us to follow her on that path of evangelical simplicity which is, together with her burning love, her outstanding characteristic. In order to understand the importance of this great and rare virtue of simplicity, read and ponder over her life and the magnificent summary made by Pope Benedict XV in his apostolic brief on the spiritual infancy of our saint.

There is so little simplicity in the world. No wonder then if, at first, it was a matter of astonishment to hear the praises of this little soul who was so unaffected and simple, so child-like in appearance. But gradually, first a group and then a multitude of souls of every age, nationality and condition began to feel attracted by the perfume of this "rose," stripped of its petals for the glory of our Lord. In drawing near to her many met with the divine Lover and consecrated themselves to love!

This was the one sole object and desire of her life: to make Love loved, and in very truth she is realizing this in a stupendous manner. Shortly before her death she wrote, "My mission is to make God loved as I love Him." But how did little Therese love Him? She herself gives the answer: "Madly!"

Yes, that love set her heart on fire, consumed and reduced it so to speak to ashes, but simply and mysteriously. There were no raptures, no visions, no ecstasies, for it was her great anxiety that in her "little path" there should be naught but ordinary acts, "so that," as she said, "all I do, little souls can also do."

There is great wisdom in these humble words, since the moments we spend on Thabor — if we ever reach that summit — are few, and sanctity does not consist in robing ourselves in a garment of life that shines before the eyes of men, but in keeping alight in our soul that love which will sanctify our daily task and common round.

From the supernatural point of view *nothing is little, nothing is insignificant.* Our everyday life, simple and hidden like that of Jesus and Mary at Nazareth, can be, if lived in union with them, holy and in the highest degree divine. We are, therefore, greatly mistaken if we think the value of an act depends on the act itself. *It is worth only the love we put into it.* Take the case of a highly praised and successful apostolate, but one not inspired by great and noble love. The merit of such an apostolate cannot be compared with one day's immolation offered to our Lord in the chalice of the burning heart of the Little Flower. Her teaching on this most important point is summed up in this axiom of sound theology: *"All is great where love is great!"* If we live up to this, what is apparently monotonous and often wearisome in our existence disappears completely, and even in this exile we enjoy a foretaste of heaven and of eternity.

The Little Flower has been universally acclaimed as the saint of love. She possessed all the ardor and impetuosity, the tenacity and confidence of that woman of the Gospel, whose love drew from the Heart of Jesus the words that have resounded through the centuries: "She has loved much."[3] Like Francis and Clare of Assisi she lived rapt in the contemplation of a God crucified for love! And just as those saints brought about a strong reaction in the frivolous society of their times, so, too, in our days, the seraphic soul of this little queen of heaven is attracting and transforming innumerable

3 Luke 7: 47

souls. Thousands of pilgrims meet daily at Lisieux to visit the tomb of the little saint. There they pour out their souls in hymns and supplications, which she rewards with countless favors and mystic lessons on love.[4]

What is more striking still is that the glorification of this saint coincides with the epoch rightly called the "Reign of the Sacred Heart of Jesus," when many souls thirsting for love are seeking to drink of the living water which pours from the pierced side of Jesus. The Reign of the Sacred Heart is but the reign of His love in souls and in families. Like St. Margaret Mary — though following a different path — Therese had but one eager desire, one glorious vocation: to make Jesus better known and loved. And what a true Carmelite she was! Everything about her recalls to mind the noble simplicity, the virile courage, and the transverberated heart of St. Teresa of Avila. There is nothing more in conformity with the Gospel than the Carmelite life as St. Therese conceived it, and the same notes predominate in Nazareth and in Avila: child-like simplicity and burning charity.

A MISSIONARY THROUGH LOVE

Those who read the life of St. Therese of the Child Jesus without discernment — and there are many such — imagine that it is nothing but a poem. They think and say that she lived her Carmelite life like a nightingale in a grove, singing of our Lord's tenderness to her and of her own gratitude and love for Him. However, she herself writes referring to her first steps in the religious life: "I met with more thorns than roses . . . . Jesus was asleep in my little boat . . . . I received no consolation either from heaven or from earth . . . . My soul has

---

4 Here are some figures which attest the mysterious, irresistible attraction exercised by St. Therese of the Child Jesus. At the translation of her venerable remains from the cemetery of Lisieux to the Chapel of the Carmel, a month before her glorification, 50,000 people were present. The Basilica of St. Peter in Rome on the day of her beatification contained 60,000. And at the triduum celebrated in her honor at Lisieux in the August of that year, 100,000 persons attended, among them 3 cardinals, 18 archbishops and bishops, and 900 priests. The population of Lisieux is only 9,000.

experienced every kind of torture.... I have suffered much on earth."

Let us remember, too, that, on the day of her profession, little Therese carried next to her heart this prayer of heroic love which she had composed: "My Jesus, I ask that for Thy sake I may die a martyr. Oh! Give me martyrdom of soul or body. Or rather, my Jesus, give me both." Her petition was granted. Distressing aridity and spiritual darkness tortured her for many years, while a cruel illness undermined her delicate constitution. She was evidently accepted as a victim of merciful love and for nine years she was ground and crushed like purest wheat that she might be made into a "host" of prayer, silence and martyrdom in union with the Victim of the altar. She lived a dying life to the glory of God and for the redemption and sanctification of souls.

Many souls have been brought back to God by this little Carmelite of whom the sainted Pius X once said, "Little Therese is the great saint and the *great missionary* of modern times." Yes, a missionary and a marvelous one; this she was and continues to be. Countless fervent souls as well as sinners are the fruit of her intense and constant *immolation*. Little Therese is indeed renewing the apostolic feats of Teresa of Avila who is said to have saved as many souls by her prayers and sacrifices as St. Francis Xavier did by his labors and preaching.[5]

By her double martyrdom of soul and body, the chalice of her heart was filled to the brim with that unfathomable ocean of graces which she is today pouring out on souls and on the Church. It is indeed true that the Little Flower is continuing and consummating in heaven the mission begun as the "victim of love" here, on earth.

However, it is easy to explain why so many imagine that

---

5 Some time ago a group of ecclesiastical dignitaries put forward the idea of erecting a church and seminary in Rome, under the patronage of Saint Therese of the Child Jesus, for the training of missionaries. When consulted on the matter, His Holiness Pope Pius XI sent the following autographed answer: "We bless with all Our heart a project which is as holy as it is providential and well suited to a purpose which We cherish, one which is occupying Our mind greatly these days."

her life was more beautiful than profound, more poetical than heroic. Just as with immense love and exquisite grace she knew how to cover with roses the wounds of her crucified Lord, so, too, she had the divine art of hiding with the roses and carnations of her smiles the sorrows and agonies of her heart. She was indeed a nightingale of Calvary but her heroic love changed Golgotha into Thabor.

Lift up your hearts! And while contemplating this radiant star renew your confidence. St. Therese retraces both the enchanting infancy of our Lord and the blood-stained sacrifice of Calvary, emphasizing the lessons of the Infant Jesus and of Jesus Crucified: simplicity and mercy. Our modern world, with its exaggerated spirit of criticism and feverish attempts to exalt the rights of human wisdom and human science, greatly needs such Gospel teaching. Even pious souls are often bewildered and hesitate before a medley of theories good in themselves, but which they cannot always apply to practical everyday life. Thus, for instance, there are many complicated systems of spirituality but not enough simplicity and love; there are many methods for prayer and spiritual life, many schools of perfection and sanctity, but not enough spirit of faith to support and ennoble a daily hidden life. Much has been written on supernatural miracles and prodigies, but too little on self-denial in the home. As a natural consequence of these shortcomings, we find an artificial and momentary enthusiasm for corporal· penances — which are looked upon as an end in themselves, rather than as a means to an end — but not sufficient generosity in the sacrifices inherent to our daily life. Lastly, there are many *devotions,* but not always the great and true *devotion* of a humble heart consumed by charity, a love stronger than death and simple as the Gospel of Jesus and as the Jesus of the Gospel.

By following these crooked paths, many treasures are squandered and much energy is lost, because no account is taken of our Savior's reply as to who should be greater in the kingdom of heaven. Taking a little child in His divine arms and caressing him tenderly Jesus said, "He who is the

105

least among you, he is the greatest."[6] And another time when a doctor of the law asked Him, "Which is the greatest commandment?" Jesus answered, "Thou shalt love the Lord thy God with thy whole heart, and with thy whole soul, and with thy whole mind. This is the greatest and the first commandment."[7]

How consoling it is to meditate on these sublime words of the Savior which the Church seems to repeat as a divine lesson to the multitude who throng round the venerable relics of St. Therese: "I praise Thee, Father ... that Thou didst hide these things from the wise and prudent and didst reveal them to little ones"[8] — to this little one! Therese of the Child Jesus understood and lived up to this divine teaching. Hence her one ambition is to guide us along her "little way" which is so practical and leads *straight* to God who is always so near and within reach of all, whether in the crib at Bethlehem, at Nazareth, or on the altar. When we have found Him, as little Therese did, then like her we must needs love Him even unto death.

Let us follow with docility and trust this bright star of Lisieux, so that even here below we may enjoy the company of a God who is our Brother and our Friend, whose Heart is both the "*Way*" to true sanctity and the inexhaustible "*Fountain*" of everlasting life.

---

6 Luke 9 : 46-48
7 Matthew 22 : 36-37 ; *cf.* Luke 10 : 27
8 Matthew 11 : 25 ; *cf.* Luke 10 : 21

Chapter 9

GENEROUS GIVING

*"If anyone wishes to come after me, let him ...
take up his cross, and follow me."*[1]

WE, APOSTLES OF THE SACRED HEART, must not be of that
class of poets and romanticists who hymn the praises of divine
love but do not live up to what they say. If this love of ours
is to be sincere, it must not be a mere sentimental feeling but
a principle of good works and true immolation.

This immolation consists, above all, in the strict and faithful observance of the law; "He who has my commandments
and keeps them, he it is who loves me."[2] This scrupulous
fulfilment of the law, this fidelity to all its points, great and
small, constitutes the very first degree of self-immolation.
Those thousand details of life and insignificant trifles, as we
improperly call them, weave for us the roughest and most
practical hair shirt. If we are not saints in our ordinary daily
lives it is not because opportunity for doing penance is wanting, but because *the love,* which gives merit and worth to the
inevitable daily sacrifices, does not animate our souls. If your
health does not permit of your using instruments of penance,
just live your life as God planned it for you. Such a course
of action will be a more painful mortification than any bodily
penance, but accept all *with great love.*

There are three loves which really constitute but one,
namely: Love of the Eucharist, Love of the cross, and Love
of souls. You cannot separate them, nor can you have one

---

1 Mark 8: 34　　　　　　　　2 John 14: 21

to the exclusion of the others. And precisely because I preach the love of the Heart of Jesus to those who are to be its apostles, I must necessarily preach sacrifice since the two ideas are as closely linked together as the sun and light. Hence we cannot love without suffering, nor suffer gloriously and beneficently without loving. I cherish the cross for the sake of the Crucified whom I worship, but I love the crucified Jesus on the throne of His cross! He sealed, with His sacred blood, a pact of eternal love for us; we must seal with blood the pact of friendship and the pledge of apostleship which are our titles to glory. "I am Christ's wheat," said St. Ignatius of Antioch, "and that I may be made into bread worthy of God, I must needs be ground by the teeth of lions." Our vocation in relation to the glory and the reign of the Sacred Heart of Jesus requires that we should be, with Him and like Him, victims of love. By just living the life our Lord ordained for us, no more nor less, we shall be ground into the holy flour of which the "hosts" are made.

If you hunger for greater sacrifices; if, *ever faithful to your daily cross,* you feel that, a true spirit of immolation is growing in your soul, you will learn how divine love will prove your love in a thousand ways. Never doubt that the best of crosses, the safest, the most divine *is always that one which Jesus Himself ordains without consulting us.* Increase your faith in this doctrine so dear to saints cast in the mold of Nazareth. Adore, bless and praise God in all the contradictions and trials which come directly from His hand. Conquering the repugnance of your nature, say with all your heart, "Thy Will be done," or still better, *"Magnificat!"*

"I wish to give thee My Heart," said Jesus to St. Margaret Mary, "but first thou must make thyself a victim of immolation." Thus, before giving you His Heart that you, in your turn, may give it to others, Jesus requires that you should make yourselves voluntary victims of His love. But how, when and where? In all the wise and merciful rulings of His Providence, leaving Him full liberty to cut off, burn or destroy what He will, as absolute and beloved Sovereign. Why fear? He is no tyrant. He knows the exact point we can reach on the hill of Calvary and the weight of the crosses He lays on us. He knows what is lacking and what is plentiful in our home, and all that happens there. He is all-just, all-gentle, all-wise, since He is Jesus. A cross which is not of our own choosing is undoubtedly the heaviest to bear, not because of the cross itself, for that which our Lord sends us is always more bearable and sanctifying than one of our own making, but because we are so fickle and capricious, even in our efforts to attain sanctity. Our own character is one of the heaviest crosses, one which cannot be changed from day to day or left at home when we are on a journey or in public. Wherever we are, it weighs us down and covers us with confusion. In the same way, the cross of our defects and shortcomings purifies and raises our soul. "My daughter," said our Lord to a religious, "I greatly rejoice to see how generously thou art striving to correct thyself, but I leave thee the discipline of thy defects that thou mayest be sanctified thereby. On earth thou wilt never know how far thou has corrected thyself, nor what stage of perfection thou hast attained by thy constant struggle." And again He said to another: "I am building the solid shrine of My love on thy apparent failures which humiliate thee so much, and on the ruins of thy self love." How can we be surprised at it since our very impotence is, according to St. Paul, a potency of grace and a marvelous aid in our sanctification.[3] "I will make a saint of thee," said Jesus to one soul, "by making use of thy weakness, provided that thou love Me much."

He disperses our own plans, our golden dreams like puffs of smoke. We often cherish some scheme which we think will serve His glory while He has quite different projects for our own glory. It is very trying to contemplate the ruins of what we thought to be, and which perhaps indeed was, a holy project! But these ruins are holier, more glorious and richer still in merit, when we conform with generous love to the blessed will of God. "Leave Me to do as I will," Jesus says. "Tie not My hands with thy whims, trace not out the path for Me, for I am the Way. Dost thou say from thy heart:

3 *Cf.* Rom. 5: 20

'Thy kingdom come?' If so, let Me direct and order all, for I am Love. Wouldst thou be useful and happy? Put the rudder in My hands, entrust it entirely to Me, but complain not if I plan out thy life for thee." What should be your reply, apostles of the Sacred Heart? — *"Fiat, Magnificat!"* Henceforth, O Jesus, never consult us; speak, command, rule over us as absolute king of our hearts.

Even in our spiritual life we are inclined to mix with the good wine the muddy water of our own desires, and we do not allow our Lord, except under protest, to disarrange our little plans for sanctity! St. Teresa once got ready a number of penitential instruments, proposing to commence on the next day a novena of austerities for an important intention. But the following morning she was laid up with a high temperature. With her habitual trust and familiarity she said to our Lord, "Didst Thou not know that I intended to begin my novena of penance today? Couldst Thou not delay sending me this illness till my penance was accomplished?" And Jesus replied, "Thou shalt make a novena and be holy in My way, not in thine!" Happy the souls that live on truth and fear illusions in holy things, seeing and accepting in their every day lives "the discipline of Jesus and His Holy Will."

If it is true that corporal penance is absolutely indispensable to salvation — and above all to sanctification — why are many who aspire to a holy life rendered incapable of fasting, watching, taking the discipline, sleeping on the bare ground, mixing bitter herbs with their food, etc.? The Divine Master cannot be acting in a contradictory way by asking them to fly and then clipping their wings. There are thousands of other austerities that may be practiced. The severest penance, even in the cloister, is the physical pain and moral anguish which God, in His wisdom and mercy, ordains for our sanctification. This includes illness, sorrows, inclemency of weather, work, contradiction and lack of resources. We can make use of these penitential garments a hundred times a day, even a hundred times an hour!

Many fervent people, owing to the delicacy of their health, their obligations or obedience, cannot and must not fast. They

110

are ordered to sleep longer and to take care of themselves. Justice, charity and obedience require that they should submit. Yet such people are not exempt from the duty of penance; they need not renounce the ideal of sanctity. They should accept with submission, faith, peace and love, their poor health, their sufferings and all the weariness and humiliation attached thereto. They will thus become *great penitents and great saints.*

This assurance will give relief to many a troubled heart that has hitherto looked upon corporal penance as essential to sanctification. A chronic invalid may lead as penitent a life as a Carthusian. A mother whose heart, like that of Mary, is pierced with sorrows — yet who blesses God and rejoices in her martyrdom — is a penitent and a martyr of the highest order, a real marvel of grace. This luminous and inspiring doctrine is not of my invention — God preserve me from such an audacity — but is essentially the teaching of the Heart of Jesus.

Our fellow creatures, too, often cause us the most acute sufferings, and God permits this because we have often been gall and vinegar to the lips of our divine Lord. Let us do penance and suffer lovingly! We have all experienced at one time or another a feeling of utter loneliness, the suffering of being misunderstood, the impossibility of opening our hearts to anyone that we can fully trust. Here, again, let us do penance and suffer lovingly!

Another torture is temptation, the revolt of passions, the scourge of finding an incentive to evil in all around us— not because of others but on account of our own evil nature. In such trying moments let us remember our Lord's words to St. Paul, "My grace is sufficient for thee." Let us do penance and suffer lovingly!

Calvary is to be met with even in our own homes, where we encounter the cruel sufferings of disappointments, loss of fortune, sorrow, death itself. It would be a great mistake to look on home crosses as a scourge. They are but a trial of our love. Jesus spared not even His own mother. He willed that she should weep and so increase the beauty and tender

111

mercy of her soul. Why then should we be spared? Our Blessed Mother was the most sorrowful, the most afflicted of God's creatures because of her glorious vocation as Queen of martyrs and apostles. Let us do penance and suffer lovingly!

A Catholic home should nurture strong and valiant souls capable of grasping, in all its integrity, the doctrine of the Heart of Jesus, *the doctrine of suffering* and its sanctifying and redeeming power. We should set our faces firmly against the opinion that suffering is to be looked upon with horror and disgust. Indeed, though considering themselves pious and claiming to love our Lord sincerely, many flee in consternation at the slightest pin-prick and refuse to taste even a drop of His bitter chalice. Their only prayer, according to St. Teresa, is the ejaculation; "From Thy cross and my crosses deliver me, O Lord!"

On the other hand, thank God, many love to repeat with all their hearts the words of St. Therese, "Grant me either to suffer or to die," and those of St. Mary Magdalen of Pazzi, "To suffer, not to die!" Many souls of this kind are now being formed in the school of the Sacred Heart. Huby says that whereas the lovers of the cross were wont to press their lips in passionate love to the wounds of Christ, loving these wounds and seeking them with love, the lovers of the Heart of Jesus go much further. They penetrate, through the wound into His side, right into the interior suffering of His Heart, learning in that bleeding sanctuary the glory of interior immolation and the joy to be found even in the bitterest anguish of the soul. The most heroic hearts are those which have been wrought on the anvil of the wound in Christ's side and in the furnace of His Heart.

To confine austerity to fasting and other corporal mortifications is to restrict the idea of penance. The Church, no doubt, encourages these practices — as we see by the ecclesiastical fasts ordained — and she gives full approbation to certain religious orders, such as the Trappists, which go far beyond what is prescribed for the ordinary Catholic in this respect. But eighty per cent of her children unfortunately — no, providentially — are unable to live such penitential lives. Yet we are bound to preach in *season and out of season* the obligation of penance. How are they to fulfill it? By just accepting the crosses of their daily lives and so accomplishing all that is required of them.

A good Catholic once said to me, "Father, I have long given up all thought of being a saint, for I know it is impossible. My health does not allow the penance necessary for those who seek sanctity." How absurd! Just as though it were right to say, "I have no health, so I cannot be a saint." It came as a revelation to her to learn that her delicate health, if born in a great spirit of faith and love, afforded more opportunity for merit than any penance she could inflict upon herself. All this seems obvious and logical when thus argued and stated; but it is not universally understood because sufficient insistence has not been laid on the spirit of penance, *of this kind of penance,* and above all the fact that it is love which gives merit to austerities whatever these may be.

Jesus said to Margaret Mary, "Take, My daughter, the cross *which I Myself give thee and plant it in thy heart,* that thou mayest always have it before thine eyes and carry it in the arms of thy fondest desires. To carry it in thy arms means to embrace it courageously, every time it presents itself, as the most precious token of My love." Yet many of our Lord's friends do not embrace it but drag it along unlovingly and grumblingly. This is the more pitiful since we cannot get rid of it or lighten it by complaints. On the contrary, the cross we drag instead of bearing it bravely crushes us to earth, while one embraced with love lends wings which carry us aloft.

St. Mary Magdalen of Pazzi kissed the walls of her cell in a rapture of happiness and said, "Thou hast deceived me, Jesus; yes, Thou hast really deceived me!" Our Lord appeared to her and said smilingly, "Daughter, what sayest thou? How have I deceived thee?" She then threw herself at His feet and said eagerly, "Yes, Jesus, I accuse Thee of deceiving me. I was told, before leaving the world, that I should find nothing but crosses, Calvary, Gethsemane and death in immolation, and nothing of the kind has happened." "What," said Jesus, "hast thou found neither cross nor chalice in My service?" "Certainly, I have! But at the same time I found Thee, the Bridegroom, and *with Thee* pain is delight and death is life."

Dear apostles, never give our enemies an opportunity of saying that the love of the Sacred Heart is a mere sentimental devotion. On the contrary, show them that friends and apostles of the King of Love know, like St. Lawrence, how to smile on the gridiron of immolation. Do not envy the stigmata of the Seraph of Assisi, bear them within your souls like a fountain of life. As we shall see later, Jesus — our King — wills to reign from His cross,[4] He crucified with you and you with Him. Thus will you bring all men to His Heart.

Do not swell the ranks of those who follow the Master only in the breaking of bread and not in the drinking of His chalice. There are three loves which should be inseparably linked together:

> *Love of the Eucharist,*
> *Love of Souls,*
> *Love of Immolation.*

---

4 John 12: 32

Chapter 10

JESUS IN THE GOSPEL

"Jesus Christ . . . . yesterday and today"[1]

Do YOU REALLY KNOW JESUS CHRIST as He appears and reveals Himself in the Gospel? A great many Christians are only partially acquainted with our divine Lord and the great sin of our days is that Christ is not known, or known only superficially. We are not referring particularly to unbelievers who deny His divinty and account for His life by calling Him a "superman." Let us pray for these unhappy souls!

The majority of faithful Christians certainly accept His divinity, but they have not sufficient knowledge of the Word Incarnate, the God-Man, Jesus, Son of God and Son of Man, our Brother in all things except sin. Most believers look on Him as far away and unconcerned with our life, so far above us and all that is ours that they seem to ignore the Incarnation which gave Him and continues to give Him to us. For the Incarnation is not merely an historical fact narrated in the Gospel, it is and ever will be a permanent and living reality: Jesus Christ, Son of Mary, the same "yesterday and today and for ever."

"And the Word was made flesh and dwelt among us,"[2] and has remained with us: "I will not leave you orphans."[3] "And behold, I am with you all days, even unto the consummation of the world."[4] This promise is chiefly fulfilled by the Holy Eucharist and in a thousand other mysterious and marvelous ways by which He shares our life on earth. Yes,

---

1 Hebr. 13: 8   2 John 1: 14
3 John 14: 18   4 Matt. 28: 20

He was made flesh, "tried as we are in all things except sin."[5] "But when the goodness and kindness of God our Savior appeared,"[6] He made Himself as one of us in order to draw all men to His Heart. We have, therefore, the right to approach Him, to embrace Him as the shepherds did and to call Him *Brother!* "*O felix culpa*," sings the Church on Holy Saturday.[7] O happy fault which merited for us so great an honor and the consolation of being admitted to the very family of the Word. Of myself I should never have dreamed of ascending to His throne, of seating myself at His side and then in adoration on my knees calling Him lovingly and truly my Brother! But He brought this about by coming down to me, by descending to the very lowest rung of the social ladder, so as to bestow the same right of brotherhood on all, from the king to the slave. Here we have Him poor, tiny, weak, helpless, in His crib of straw, clothed in the garment of our fallen nature. If we except sin itself, we might almost dare to call Him our twin Brother, so like is He to us in all things, absolutely in everything! Let us contemplate Him thus.

GOD-BROTHER IN WEAKNESS AND HELPLESSNESS

But for the Incarnation it would have been blasphemy to address Jesus in terms like the following: "Lord, how alike we are; I have great weaknesses, so hast Thou; I bear in my human nature an abyss of helplessness and, since the annunciation, so dost Thou." Think of His weakness and helplessness in Mary's womb, where physically, in His condition as creature, He depended on His mother, He, Mary's Creator! How beautiful it is to contemplate Him on that first Christmas, born on the straw among the animals, a speechless Babe, His little limbs as frail and clumsy as our own. It is marvelously touching that He should of His own will have condemned Himself to those swaddling clothes in which His mother wrapped Him. How sweet is that God as He lies in

<hr>

5 Hebr. 4: 15   6 *Cf*. Tit. 3: 4
7 Blessing of the Candle: Preface

the arms of His Immaculate Mother, who provides for all His needs.

He is the giant of the Heavens[8] by whom all things live. See Him trying to make His first faltering steps, tottering from Mary's hands to those of St. Joseph. Listen to our adorable little Brother when He utters His first words: "Mother ... Mary," which the Virgin-Mother will lovingly remember for all eternity. When Herod schemed against the Child, desiring to slay Him, that Child, the God of battles, had to flee in His mother's arms, protected by Joseph the carpenter. Was not this the depth of helplessness? On His return to Nazareth He had to learn a trade. I say *"had to"* because, unless He displayed miraculous powers and knowledge, He would be obliged to ask questions and accept corrections regarding His task of cutting, sawing, joining pieces of wood. He earned His daily wage by the sweat of His brow, and I imagine — since He wished to be like all of us — that more than once some customer was not quite satisfied and haggled over a few pence with the "Carpenter" Jesus!

"And what hardship or penury can we mention, O Jesus, which Thou Thyself hast not experienced in Thy divine poverty. Thou didst hunger and thirst and suffer many privations. Being a humble artisan, Thou hadst to put up with the slights of those who passed and repassed Thy workshop, who regarded Thee, the King of Kings, as one of no account. To Thy fellow countrymen Thou wast neither cultured nor lettered, nor hadst Thou any greater rights than those of Thy neighbors in the village. How beautiful, how sublime it is to contemplate Thee working quickly to gain the daily bread for Joseph and for Mary, the mother of Thy Heart! Thou hast been working since early morning, *Thou art weary,* yet Thou must finish the work before eventide. The angels could lend Thee a loving hand, but no, that would be unlike our normal life and Thou hast condemned Thyself to live exactly as we do."

Therefore, being Man, Jesus retained that relative frailty which is characteristic of the clay of which we are made.

---

8 Ps. 18: 6

117

See Him overcome by fatigue sleeping in Peter's boat, so soundly that they had to shake Him to arouse Him. See Him, worn out by the heat of His journey, sitting on the curbstone of Jacob's well and begging water of the woman of Samaria. He was thirsty for water — and for that soul. Consider the dust covering His clothes and sandals as He went in search of those lambs which He could have called to Him and cured by a miracle. But no, He preferred to tread those long miles on foot by steep and rugged paths — sleeping like the foxes in caves and lairs of beasts.

But what are all these natural weaknesses and sufferings compared with what he suffered in His Passion. The infamous traitor kissed Him. He was seized and bound fast as though He were a thief. They dragged Him manacled before His judges, and then followed that dreadful but sublime night in the cell when He was mocked and spat upon, barbarously treated and crowned with thorns! He, the Judge of the living and the dead, held His peace while blood dripped from Him. He was buffeted by a soldier, insulted by Herod while the rabble, drunk with anger and with wine, clamored for His Blood and rejoiced to see fresh wounds inflicted on Him.

In climbing the hill of Golgotha He fell because He could not bear so great a weight. They had to call the Cyrenean to help Him, but He fell again. At last He was nailed to His cross and raised on high. He was parched with thirst, weak from loss of blood. He felt in His veins a fever more devouring than fire. He asked for water — for love. They gave Him gall and vinegar and mockery. And He died, suspended there, inert, *a corpse*, He who is Immortality. With fervent love and prostrate in the dust I adore Thee, my God, my Brother.

GOD-BROTHER IN FEELINGS

How beautiful it is to think His Heart beats in unison with ours. He loved as we love, all things good and lawful.

The first object of His love, was, of course, Mary His mother, and how dear she was to Him who had created her purer and more beautiful than heaven itself for His glory and happiness. He loved her, too, out of *gratitude*, seeing that He owed to her *fiat* the human capacity to weep, to suffer, to shed His blood and die, things which were beyond the reach of God, but which Mary made possible by the Incarnation. How He loved that carpenter whom He called "Father," whose horny hands labored for His daily bread and in whose arms as a little Child He tenderly reposed a thousand times. Think how Jesus our Brother must have wept when Joseph kissed Him for the last time, what grief that adorable, sensitive Heart must have felt when Mary was left a widow and He, a God, was orphaned!

To have preferences in our affections is very characteristic of our hearts; the Heart of Jesus also had its preferences and delightful ones. Apart from the little house in Nazareth, the scene of His greatest and most intimate love, He showed a marked preference for little children whom He sought out and caressed. What must the angels have thought when they saw their King among those flowers of His garden, breathing in their perfume, shedding down upon them the light of His Eyes and beautifying them for Heaven! "Behold our Friend!" they would cry when they caught sight of Him and they would run to meet Him crying, "Behold our Jesus!"

Think, too, of the poor, the ragged, the outcasts, who could not invite Him to their houses, for they had none. But He sought them out on the high roads, going to meet this horde which the world despised. Happy sufferers! Jesus had a special preference for them as well as for the sick, the crippled and those who were ill-treated. How many confidences must the most sweet Master have received upon the road, what balm did He not pour into a thousand wounded souls, without anyone suspecting it. At every step He was besieged by people, in the street, in the Temple porch. Wherever He went they were unconsciously drawn by the attraction of His heart. They had not as yet any wish to be converted, but they felt they were loved and, what is more, *preferred* above others! Later, when their sins had been forgiven them, when, after the Resurrection and especially after Pentecost every veil had been torn away, what envy must they have excited when they told how they had been the objects of His preference and how the Fisherman's cunning had caught them, in spite of themselves, in the nets of His mercy.

Then there were the twelve apostles, always in His gracious company, sharing the same bread, engaged in close, familiar, intimate conversation with the God-Man. They were rough men and the Lord had more than once to make excuses for them and defend them. Next to Mary they were the most intimate witnesses of the private life of the Redeemer. And what about the elect of the band, Peter, James and John — especially the latter — who bore the title of "the disciple whom Jesus loved?"[9] So great was his intimacy with our Lord, so evident the preference given to him, that "this saying therefore went abroad among the brethren, that that disciple was not to die."[10] His place has never been lost; we occupy it today, we the humble apostles of the divine Heart and no one can ever dispute it with us, not indeed because of any merit of ours, but by the mercy of the King of Love.

We come now to Bethany, to the house which witnessed the most intimate friendship of the Heart of Jesus. "Jesus loved Martha and her sister Mary, and Lazarus"[11] with an affection passing that which He gave to any others outside Nazareth. Bethany was His second home. Here many and many a time He must have uttered the words, "You are indeed my friends." Here He unburdened His Heart, here He received confidences which no others ever heard except *His three friends.* Here He gave tenderness, here as nowhere else He sought rest and consolation, for Bethany was His refuge in the storms which were brewing in Jerusalem; here, in this country place He passed days and nights in prayer, secure from enemies, and — in His hours of fatigue and exhaustion — from the meddling intrusion of good but importunate and thoughtless people. In Bethany, too, He was looked after and cared for in a way which would have been

---

9 John 13: 25; 21: 20   10 John 21: 23
11 John 11: 5

materially impossible in Nazareth, for neither Mary nor Joseph had the necessary means. What days and hours of paradise those three privileged souls spent there. For them only one trouble was unbearable, the absence of their Friend. Remember here all that I have said about the Bethany home, and the fidelity of the Heart of Jesus to a family which knows how to share life's sorrows and joys with Him.

O Master, multiply Thy Bethanies!

THE COMPASSION OF JESUS

No one has ever been more human than Jesus. Think of His *compassion*. "It is not the healthy who need a physician, but they who are sick."[12] Jesus had an evident tenderness for anyone in suffering, for the sad, the poor, and feeble. This predilection, which for twenty centuries has stirred the heart of man, we call His mercy. He seemed unable to resist a sorrow; a hungry crowd, a desolate mother vanquished Him at once. Let us take the case of the woman of Canaan.[13] Jesus proved her, feigned severity. Then His Heart was captivated and overcome, and the miracle was wrought. On the road to Naim,[14] when He saw the poor widow weeping, His thoughts surely must have turned to Mary in a vision of the Via Dolorosa, and, once more overcome, He drew near, took the young man by the hand and gave him back to his mother restored to life and health.

Everything that is noble and honest touched Him. The multitude which had followed Him into the desert was hungry and had nothing to eat: "I have compassion on the crowd,"[15] He said, and He multiplied the loaves. His Heart was wounded by the ingratitude of the nine lepers at Samaria. So, too, all physical and moral misery found Him ever tender and compassionate. And when sufferers could not drag themselves to Him, He went to meet them. Remember the paralytic at the pond of Probatica: — "Sir, I have no one;"[16] no friendly heart, no compassionate hand to put me into the pond, and

---

12 Mark 2: 17   13 Matt. 15: 22-28
14 Luke 7: 11-16   15 Mark 8: 2
16 John 5: 2-9

therefore I have been here for eight and thirty years. The Heart of Jesus must have leapt in His adorable breast on hearing this. He held out His divine hands to help the paralytic, and the miracle was performed. The whole Gospel is indeed a stupendous monument to the immense, the infinite *compassion of* the God-Man, who worked miracles, not to free Himself from His executioners, but to ease the wounds of the soul, to wipe away bitter tears and to lighten the crosses which all must bear.

GOD-BROTHER IN SPEECH AND IN TEARS

When the Word of God became incarnate He was called Jesus. And this Jesus who feels, loves and suffers as we do, who talks and weeps like us, is our Brother in earthly speech and earthly tears. With what ecstasy of joy and love Mary must have held on her lap the little Child, her Creator, when *she was teaching Him to speak.* Later He conversed in Aramaic, the idiom of the people. He had the Galilean lilt and in all His habits He was truly Man, truly our Brother. Thus, although He knew all things, He asked questions just as we do: "Who do men say the Son of Man is?" "How many loaves have you?" "Who touched my cloak?"[17] It is very beautiful to see Jesus adapt Himself to our ways, expressing His thoughts and needs in our words and conventional idioms. And He does this not only that He may speak to men, but because He is our Brother, *because He is Man*, and, as such, wills to employ our human language.

Nothing appeals to us more in this marvelous brotherhood than the tears of Jesus. "And Jesus wept."[18] Yes, Jesus wept, just as we human beings do in the cradle and on our bed of agony. Can we doubt that the cold and hunger in the cave in Bethlehem drew forth the first divine tears, which Mary kissed away. Again, though the Gospel does not tell us so, it is beyond doubt that on the death of His foster father, when He was consoling Mary, He relieved His own Heart

----

17 Matt. 16: 13; Mark 8: 5; John 20; 15; Mark 5: 30
18 John 11: 35

with filial tears. When He came across grievous suffering on His road, the tears of the afflicted moved Him to compassion and He wept. The Gospel tells us of His emotion when He looked down upon Jerusalem which was to slay Him, her God. Foreseeing the woes she was to suffer because of her perfidy, He could not contain the sadness which overwhelmed Him, and He found relief in tears: "He wept over it!"[19]

Recall that intensely touching scene when Jesus wept over the tomb of Lazarus. He arrived late; His friend was already buried, and Martha reproached Him with the words, "Lord, if thou hadst been here my brother would not have died,"[20] as if to say, "Thou knewest, Thou art our friend and yet Thou camest not, so it is Thy fault that he died!" Our Lord was deeply moved. He asked to be taken to the sepulcher, and when He saw it, "he groaned in spirit" and could not contain his tears. "And Jesus wept."[21] Yes, He wept, He who was about to raise him from the dead! He wept, and with those tears began the miracle of the resurrection of His friend. The onlookers, who saw in Him the most marvelous of prophets, who perhaps for this reason had held Him to be above the ordinary feelings and weaknesses of common men, were profoundly astonished to see Him thus moved to tears. They exclaimed, "See how he loved him."[22] Those tears were a token of the burning love and tenderness of the Heart of the God-Man.

The sober Gospel narrative omits a thousand precious incidents in the Master's life. Nevertheless we may make certain well-founded conjectures. For example: Let us imagine Him taking leave of His mother and His friends at Bethany on Holy Thursday. Would it not be natural for Him to have shed tears as He realized the next sad meeting would be on the way to Calvary?

Nor could it be otherwise, seeing that He is our Brother. If He gave free rein to His emotions at the tomb of Lazarus, would He not weep when giving His Mother His last kiss.

19 Luke 19: 41
21 John 11: 33, 35
20 John 11: 21
22 John 11: 36

Undoubtedly the Gospel does not tell us this, as being super-fluous and self-evident.

O divine tears, how you reveal to me the Heart of my King and Master, how you make me love Him and how firmly you bind me to Him with the bonds of the brother-hood of suffering! On seeing Thee weep, Jesus, King of Glory, I fall on my knees and, weeping with Thee, I adore Thee, my God-Brother. The fountain whence flowed those tears was opened to us by the soldier Longinus who pierced His side. From that Heart have streamed those precious tears of water and blood, of tenderness and love, which will be praised in Heaven by those of us who, like Jesus our Brother, have known on earth how to weep and lovingly adore.

Chapter 11

THE HOLY SACRIFICE OF THE MASS

The only hymn worthy
of the Blessed Tirnity

THE GREAT CARDINAL MERCIER, a saintly and learned theologian, used to say: "Give me a priest fully appreciating the
gift of his daily Mass, preparing it well, offering it devoutly,
living the grace of his Mass; I tell you, this priest will be
ready for canonization when he dies." I apply this statement
to the faithful: Give me a Catholic fully realizing the doctrine of the Mass, really and truly living the grace of daily
Mass, and I, too, will show you someone who will be a saint
at the hour of death.

I am preaching the reign of the Sacred Heart. But the
reign of the Sacred Heart presupposes an enlightened mind,
a full appreciation of the meaning of the Holy Sacrifice of
the Mass, as much as that is possible. The Mass is the only
wonderful thing on earth — the rest is mere shadow. This
is the obsession of my life; this is the foundation of the crusade I am preaching. In the measure we give to priests, to
religious, to the faithful, the true meaning, the true sense,
of this message of faith and love, the Holy Sacrifice of the
Mass, we are preaching eloquently, victoriously, through
His Blood and Chalice, the reign of the great King Who was
crucified for us, the reign of the Eucharistic Heart of Jesus,
Who wrought this miracle.

One day Our Lord appeared to a privileged soul who
asked Him this question: "Lord, what can I offer Thee for

the glory of Thy Father, for Thine own glory and for my sanctification?" The answer came back: "One more Mass!"

Let us then speak strongly and clearly about Holy Mass. May Our Lady of the Blessed Sacrament be close to us to help us properly understand the doctrine and the theology of the Mass.

LOVE, TO UNDERSTAND

The Holy Sacrifice of the Mass is the greatest and most sublime act of adoration, of worship and of reparation in the Church. Mass is the summary of all supereminent action, the *only* supereminent, supreme action. Everything is poor and insignificant if it is at a distance from the altar. Whereas, on the contrary, everything becomes bright and brilliant and heavenly when mixed with the Precious Blood in the chalice.

"Come Holy Spirit . . . ," come and shed light and fire, so that we may really grasp and live the Mystery of mysteries, this Gift of God par excellence. "If you only knew," Our Lord said to the Samaritan woman, "If you knew the Gift of God!" If *we* only knew what we call in simple language, "Holy Mass!"

Very often a strong faith is lacking in our spiritual life to grasp and realize these astounding beauties. But more than faith, LOVE — burning love — is lacking to appreciate and live these truths. I say "love" because the mystery of the altar, the Eucharistic immolation, is disclosed only to loving souls. Sometimes we find a poor woman, a poor ignorant man, a boy or girl, who grasps many things we do not grasp, BECAUSE THEY LOVE.

Only those who love penetrate the mystery of the chalice. That is why I insist so much on the virtue of charity. "Come Holy Spirit!" If you read ten books about the Mass, you would understand nothing without light from above, without love. What a pity to find good souls with a real child-like devotion, but with a mania for relics and devotions, and who do not appreciate the Mass. Do you know why? Because it is DAILY. If Our Lord had said, "I will allow a priest to say Mass and to give Holy Communion once a year, after a ten-day retreat in preparation," then we would appreciate it better.

But, O Lord Jesus, what have You done in Your divine foolishness of love? You have permitted all priests to celebrate Holy Mass every day and Christians to receive You in Communion every day. We do not say, "What a miracle is the sun," because we see it every day. Yet what are all the miracles put together when compared with the miracle He wrought at the Last Supper, on Calvary, and which He works every morning at the altar? They are as flowers compared to paradise.

A SCALE OF VALUES

Notice, please, that I start speaking of the Holy Sacrifice of the Mass and not of Holy Communion. Why? Because Holy Mass is the fountain; Communion, wonderful as it is, is the torrent. In the first place, the chalice; in the second place, the Communion rail. Never change this order. It is indeed sad to know that too often we separate the Sacrifice of the Mass from the Sacrament of Communion. We even give the first place to Communion. This evidences a lack of doctrine, and ignorance of the catechism. For many, Holy Mass is the liturgical ceremony, the "golden key," as it were, that unlocks the tabernacle door so that Jesus may be received in Holy Communion. This is not doctrinal. We should maintain the doctrinal scale of values: first, the chalice on the altar; then the Communion rail and the tabernacle. Note well, there is no Mass without Communion — at least that of the priest. But neither is there Holy Communion for the priest nor for you without the fountain, the chalice, Holy Mass.

JUST WHAT IS HOLY MASS?

But, exactly, what is the Holy Sacrifice of the Mass? It is Christ, the God-Man, the Son of God and the Son of Mary, adoring and praising God the Father and the Blessed Trinity at the altar, with you and in your name. A God praising God; a God adoring God.

What is Holy Mass? It is Christ, the God-Man, the Son of God and the Son of Mary, offering on the calvary of the altar the thanksgiving due to God His Father; making atonement for sin; the only perfect divine atonement and thanksgiving, with you and for you.

What is Holy Mass? It is Christ, the Judge of the living and the dead, the God-Man, Son of God and Son of Mary, imploring, with you and for you, a deluge of graces and blessings, through the power of His wounds, through the power of His cross, through the power of His Blood, and through the power of His sacrifice.

If all this is true, then doctrinally we can say that Holy Mass is a *daily Christmas*. The crib is the altar; the hands of our Lady, the hands of the priest. Yes, in every Mass we can say, *"Puer natus est nobis,"* a Child is born, a little Boy is born, the Son of God and of our Lady, far more little than in the crib but still the same Christ. At the altar as in Bethlehem is sung the same *Gloria in excelsis,* for the Savior is born, He is there on the altar; there is but one Jesus .... Christmas, Incarnation, every day.

There is something else — the *Last Supper*. Who was the Pontiff at the Last Supper? Jesus. Who is the Pontiff at the altar? He took the bread; he took the wine; He takes the bread, He takes the wine: "Do this in My name and for My glory, to commemorate My death; say with me (I will be your power): 'This is My Body, this is My Blood. Take, eat, and drink.'" Divine banquet, heavenly banquet, the greatest of wonders! Oh, that marvellous Gospel brought from Heaven by Christ Our Lord, the Last Supper.

And Calvary? *Calvary,* too, is there, though He can no longer suffer. There is but one Victim, Jesus, which means Savior. He is wounded unto death. Blood flows from all His wounds. In fact, He is but one great wound from His head to His feet. Is the victim of the Mass the same Jesus? He is. There is but one Jesus, crucified, but at the altar there is a difference. It is true that at the altar we have the adorable Victim of Calvary, but with one great difference: now His wounds are glorious. He keeps His wounds, the pierced

128

hands, the pierced feet, the open side, but they are the sunshine of paradise. Yes, on the altar during Mass is the same Victim of Calvary, but now a risen, a glorious Victim.

We can also say that the Sacrifice of the Mass is the Feast of the *Ascension*. Not only Christmas, the Last Supper, not only Calvary, but also the Ascension. He seems to say to us, "Come, my little ones, come. Take these wings, My arms, and together let us go to see, to embrace My Father and your Father." This is the Ascension, renewed during Mass at the altar.

Is there more? Yes. He says to His Father, "Father look at My little ones. They love You through My Sacred Heart; they bless You with My lips; they adore You through My wounds. May I command? Send down the Paraclete." And so we have *Pentecost* renewed. In fact we might say all the feasts of the Church are renewed at the altar; in that one half hour of grace and mystery are celebrated the feasts of Christmas, Holy Thursday, Good Friday, Ascension, Pentecost. That is why Holy Mother Church says that Holy Mass is the official, divine omnipotent prayer, always reaching the throne of the Blessed Trinity. Jesus alone can say, "When I speak, I command. My Father must always listen to Me." Why? Because it is a God praising God, a God adoring God, a God thanking God; it is a God offering atonement, petitioning, blessing. The Father cannot say, "Wait." No. In that case, Jesus would not be God. But He is God as well as the Father; His is the only powerful prayer reaching the throne of the Blessed Trinity. Through Him, with Him and in Him everything becomes divine. Praying with Him you are divinised; through His lips you are singing a divine hymn; you are loving through His Heart. Then you are close to the Trinity; you are knocking at the door of the Father with His hand; the door of the Heart of the Father, and then the door is opened, because it is the Son knocking with you and you with Him. Isn't this a marvellous thing? .

Have you savored the words of the preface? In all the prefaces even when they change, you will find the same thought: *per quem laudant angeli — through* Him the angels and archangels, the principalities and powers, the thrones and dominations, *through Him* they praise God. Even though they be angels, their prayers would not reach the Trinity. First they must pass, as it were, through the wounds and the lips of the God-Man, the Mediator between Heaven and earth.

<h2 style="text-align:center">HOLY COMMUNION</h2>

But you might ask, "What part does Holy Communion play in this hymn of praise?" Holy Communion is the *sharing* of the Christian, of all the faithful who communicate, in the sacrifice of the Lamb. Do you remember what Jesus said while dying in agony? *"Consummatum est"* it is finished. Holy Communion is the *Consummatum est* of the sacrifice — the sacrifice already offered. By whom? By the Victim, Jesus. To whom? To His Father. And then you come and you share in that praise, in that atonement, in that thanksgiving, in that sacrifice, by your Communion, drinking from His Wounds, drinking His Blood, eating that Flesh that was torn to death for you and for me.

Holy Communion then is the *sharing*. You come, you eat, you drink. The sacrifice is now complete, crowned, as it were, with your Communion. This is the *full* sharing of the faithful in the Mass. But never forget, first by far, comes *Jesus'* prayer, *Jesus'* immolation. Then, "Approach!" He calls to you as when He called to His Mother, when our Lady received Holy Communion from the hands of St. John.

<h2 style="text-align:center">THABOR AND CALVARY</h2>

What then, according to this doctrine, is the Catholic altar? Let me answer by two comparisons. First, the altar is Mount Calvary. But there is a difference: the calvary of our altars is enveloped in the sunshine of paradise, of glory. Why? Because the Victim Jesus is the risen Jesus of Easter Day. He keeps His wounds, but they are now glorious. For all eternity He will keep those wounds, and in the Beatific Vision you will see Him wounded unto death through love for us.

130

Another comparison: The altar is Mount Thabor, where Our Lord was transfigured. Again with a difference: the altar is indeed Thabor, but Thabor covered with the red cloud of the divine, adorable Blood shed on Calvary. Behind a white, thin veil is the astounding reality of the Last Supper, the marvelous reality of Mount Calvary, the wonderful reality of Mount Thabor. This is your daily Mass. There is but *one* Jesus, celebrating the Holy Sacrifice of the Mass.

Sometimes it is stated that the Mass is the "renewal" of the sacrifice of the Cross. Is that exact? No. It is true that because we are dealing with a great mystery it is not easy to find the proper terminology to express the reality. But it seems to me a better expression can be found than renewal, for this seems to imply "another one." For instance, yesterday I gave a lecture; today, using the same notes, I repeat it. This is a renewal. Is that the Mass? One Mass, two Masses, ten, one hundred Masses? No, there are not one hundred, one million Masses; there is only ONE Mass, the one celebrated by the Pontiff Jesus on that first Good Friday. That same Mass is *prolonged* at the altar through the centuries. Is the sun you see today a renewal of the sun created by God millions of years ago? Not at all. It is rather the prolonging of the same sun down through the centuries. It is the same with the Mass. Christ, the Son of God, the Victim, the Pontiff, celebrated one Mass and that one Mass is exactly the same Mass I celebrated this morning and will celebrate tomorrow; and the last priest who will offer the last Mass before the final judgment will be celebrating the one, first and last, Mass celebrated by Our Lord at three o'clock on Good Friday.

I have heard people say, "Oh, what a wonderful experience it would have been if I had been on Calvary, if I could have had the grace, the honor and the joy of seeing with my eyes My King, my Master and my God wounded to death and dying for me. Ah, if I had been there!" And I have replied, "Then you missed Mass this morning?" "Oh, no, Father." "Then why do you say. 'if I *had been* on Calvary?' This proves you don't know your catechism. This morning you *were* on Calvary, just as truly as was our Lady, as Mary Magdalen and St. John, at three o'clock on Good Friday. Don't say, 'If I had been there.' This is a lack of doctrine, a lack of faith."

MIRACLE OF MIRACLES

And now, to stir up your faith, permit me to relate to you some remarkable experiences I have been privileged to have. Many years ago I was in Naples on the feast of St. Januarius. Through the kindness of a prelate I was allowed to hold in my hands the glass vial containing the congealed blood of the martyr who died so many centuries ago. It did not look like blood, this thick, solid, black mass, yet I was assured it was the blood of the saint. The prelate said to me, "Now that you have seen this, you are going to see something quite different. Stay close to me."

Then we went to the basilica with the vial in a sort of monstrance. The church was packed with men, many of them scientists. While the Litany of the Saints was being chanted the prelate passed back and forth in the sanctuary at the Communion rail showing the monstrance for all to see. Suddenly he whispered to me, "Father, look, look." The black substance had disappeared. The crystal vessel was red, the blood seething — you could hear it. The miracle was evident. At once the crowd cried out, "*Vivat Sancte Januarius!*" Then they began to sing the *Te Deum*. As I looked at the seething blood of the Saint who had died a thousand years before, I felt the shock of the supernatural, for it made a deep impression. But that emotion lasted but a minute or two. Why? Because after a short while I was saying to myself, "Well, this is certainly supernatural, this is a miracle, this is wonderful, but . . . what is this compared to my chalice? Nothing, a plaything!" And my emotion vanished.

There is a scale of values in spiritual matters. There is a number one miracle, there is a number two miracle, and there is a miracle number three. Number one, by far, the chalice. Number two, the conversion of St. Paul or of St. Augustine. Number three, that little miracle of the blood of St. Januarius. I wouldn't return to see that miracle when I have my daily

Mass. Faith is lacking for many of us. Some of us would even miss Mass to witness a miracle like that. For that little lamp, you miss the sun! For that little flower, you miss the stars! I am sure you understand what I mean.

Another example. One day while in France I was in my room preparing a retreat when someone knocked on my door. It was a great friend of mine, a saintly priest. In a low voice he said to me, "Father Mateo, follow me to the sacristy. I have been sent here by the Bishop to show you a great treasure." Beneath his coat I thought I saw a surplice and a stole. We arrived in the sacristy. He unfolded a corporal and lit two candles. Then he placed a deep pyx on the corporal and knelt down. I did the same.

"The Bishop asked me to bring this treasure to you. He will call for it tomorrow. Open it, Father." I opened the pyx. It was full of blood, red and fresh, and in the blood a white, consecrated host, intact. (For more than a month, I was told.) It seems the Bishop had sent some drops of the blood to be analyzed, asking for a report. The report came back, "Perfect human blood." If the chemist had known where it came from, he could have added "*divine* blood." "What a wonderful miracle!" you say. Yes, it was, but once more, this is not a first class miracle. This is not the Mass. You see blood here, yes, but blood is *shed* there, at Mass; and the prayer of Christ is there. But that bleeding host is not the official immolation of Our Lord, it is not His official atonement, it is not His official thanksgiving. If then you had to choose between keeping that bleeding host and seeing it for a whole week and going to Mass, if you are doctrinal, if you are theological, you will say, "I prefer to leave aside the bleeding host and not miss my Mass." If you speak and act like that, then without having a doctorate you are a doctor in theology like the Little Flower.

To stir up your faith and to enkindle your love still more, listen to this remarkable case. I was celebrating Holy Mass in a private chapel in Europe. I don't know why, but a man who was scandalizing the people by his scornful attitude was present. It was really shocking the way he acted; they could feel the fury in his eyes, in his lips that were saying, "Stupid, ridiculous people, kneeling. I am the only intelligent person here." It was truly satanic. But the people were struck, you may be sure, when at the consecration this man fell on his knees, trembling and staring at the altar, wide-eyed, apparently seeing something astounding. What happened? An attack of madness? His body shook with sobs. He continued to stare at the altar as though he were dazzled by the sun. What a change!

When the Mass was over, this person rushed into the sacristy as I was taking off my vestments. "Please, tell me, what have you been doing at the altar?" "Why, I have been celebrating Holy Mass." He demanded to know what Mass is. I explained to him how the same Jesus, who was nailed to the Cross on Calvary, and who shed the last drop of His Blood for us sinners, does the same thing now on the altar but in an unbloody way. "That is what we call the Mass." Imagine my surprise when this man claimed to have seen what I had just described. When I asked him to tell me just what he had seen, he told me he saw me come from the sacristy to the altar and reading from a big book and going back and forth. "Then you bowed; you said something; and then you lifted up a round white object, when suddenly you disappeared and in your place, I saw a wonderful personage with arms outstretched; what beauty, what majesty! I can still see that face, those features, those eyes, the blood gushing from those wounds. His lips were moving as though he were talking to someone. And His body was shining like the sun. Then after some time, this wonderful personage disappeared and you returned."

That this man had indeed witnessed something extraordinary was proved by his conversion and subsequent fervent life. He was privileged to see with his eyes what you and I should see each morning with the eyes of faith. It is to stir up your faith and to enkindle your love that I give you these lessons. Each day your faith and love, like a flame, should increase and grow, so that you will never become accustomed

134

to a sort of routine of being there close to the altar during Mass. "Increase my faith, increase my love!"

Now, after all this, is there any miracle that can possibly be compared with the Holy Sacrifice of the Mass? Not one. Take, if you like, all the wonders wrought by Our Lord during His three years of public apostolic life; add to them the many miracles wrought by our Lady at Lourdes, the countless miracles of the saints: all this is like an electric light compared to the sun. The sun is Holy Mass, the only great, wonderful, marvellous miracle. The only first-class miracle.

In Europe I have known a poor little peasant girl who like Bernadette used to take care of sheep. I met her through the Archbishop who invited me to talk with her and to give my opinion about her case. He told me he had her case examined by five eminent theologians. They all told him she was a second Margaret Mary. She spoke to me simply, plainly and at great length, for she had confidence in me. She enjoyed an extraordinary privilege, that of seeing what goes on at the altar as you see me sitting here. For her there was no veil during Holy Mass. For her Mass was Calvary, as on Good Friday. And in her simplicity and candor she thought everyone enjoyed the same privilege as she. She was forbidden to speak to anyone about what she saw. There were miracles to prove that she really was what she seemed to be, a Margaret Mary. All this I learned from her.

We must be very careful about such things. There are too many sisters and ladies and girls who claim to have visions. 95% of those who say, "I see" are sick or the devil is there. There are exceptions, certainly. But in these cases Our Lord knows how to prove that it is not madness, not hysteria nor sickness, but that it is really He. How? By conversions and humility. I have met some of these prophetesses who are proud and far from bringing about conversions. If you tell them, "You are mistaken," and they get angry and excited, be sure the devil is there. When they told Margaret Mary, "You are crazy," she smiled and said, "Perhaps, why not?" But Our Lord proved she wasn't crazy, for he sent Father Claude de la Colombiere, who was a saint and a learned man, and who

135

soon let it be known he believed in the reality of Margaret Mary's visions.

Ordinarily, however, you must be extremely diffident; you musn't believe everything you hear about visions and stigmata. I receive hundreds of letters containing ridiculous, stupid, absurd things. If I told you some of these things you would laugh for three days and three nights!

THE MASS IN OUR SPIRITUAL LIFE

Now let us apply this marvelous doctrine of the Mass to our spiritual life, to our personal needs. With the lights of our retreat, we see important things are lacking in our souls. We are craving for many graces; to obtain those graces we have to become saints — humble, obedient. Ask for these graces, for this mercy of the Sacred Heart, *per Ipsum, cum Ipso et in Ipso.* Place these petitions on the altar with the consecrated host; place them in the chalice, in His Precious Blood. Then the Pontiff, Jesus, will say, "Abba, Father, behold!" Jesus is always heard because He is God as is the Father. He is praying *with* you, and *for* you — what a wonderful impetration! "Through Him, with Him, and in Him . . . . " Ask any favors you wish. I do not say health, no; but ask for those things that will make you saints, loving. Ask for the gift of love through Him. Oh, you will love this way of praying. I take Him to witness. If He does not give you that, then He is not God. He deceives you.

You have examined your conscience and you have seen your miseries, your failures of the past and present. How can you make up for all this? How can you make reparation for your violations of the Rule and your Vows? By doing penance? Taking the discipline in honor of the five Wounds of Our Lord? Wearing the hairshirt five times? Praying night and day? What good is all that to make up for one single sin? If you have committed one mortal sin in your life, you should be in hell. How can you make up for one single sin? By placing your repentance, your tears of sorrow *in the chalice.* Mingle them with the Blood of Jesus. Then the Redeemer, the Mediator, will say, "Father, here is My Blood — this is her repentance. My Blood! This is her atonement!"

You see clearly that Our Lord has spoiled you, He has overwhelmed you with miracles. You are so rich you could be crushed under the weight of these millions of graces. How can you be truly grateful? "Father, I am thanking for her," says Jesus. "Poor little thing, she cannot thank You. But through My lips she pays her debt of gratitude." This is *perfect* thanksgiving. Jesus is your thanksgiving, for your baptism, for your faith, for everything.

There is a hundred times more spiritual profit from the offering of one Mass than by the ecstasies of the saints. For what comparison is there between the ecstasy of a saint and your offering the Divine Victim with the priest? An ecstasy is a prayer, a private prayer; but Holy Mass is the public, official prayer of Christ — but Christ with *you* and you with Christ. Miracles and ectasies are silver, copper; Mass is *gold*.

Now I am going to let you in on a secret — the secret of my spiritual life. When I travel on the train, I say, ten, twenty "Masses of St. John" — Masses in honor of the Blessed Trinity. There is no prayer like that. I have but three devotions: My Mass, my breviary, my Rosary. The breviary is beautiful, but you cannot compare it with the Mass. There is no prayer like the Mass. As I travel, I offer my Mass on the altar of the holy Will of God, offering it in union with the thousands of priests saying Mass continuously, perpetually. I am tired, I cannot prepare conferences — I offer Mass instead. I said four or five Masses this morning. I do it the whole day. It unites my heart, my will with priests at the altar. When I awake during the night, the first thing I do is to take the shortest form of the Mass of St. John, *"Suscipe ... Offerimus ..." "Hoc est enim Corpus Meum" .... "Hic est enim Calix Sanguinis Mei ...."' "Domine, non sum dignus ..." "Corpus Domini Jesu Christi .... Sanguis Domini Jesu Christi, custodiant animam meam in vitam aeternam. Amen.!"* I hope to die saying Mass — between two consecrations.

You may have your private devotions, certainly. But that

all of them may become *divine,* priceless — the Rosary and the rest — put them as a drop of water in the chalice of your Mass . . . . in the morning and all through the day and night.

Now you might ask, "What do you mean by 'the Mass of St. John?' " I call this practice "The Mass of St. John" only to give it a title. It is really Jesus' Mass. What was the Mass offered by Jesus? The Mass offered by Jesus at the Last Supper was the most simple of Masses, the shortest of Masses, lasting but a few minutes. St. John's Mass, as He offered it for our Lady, was the same — short, simple, consisting however, of the same three elements, the same three prayers: Offertory, Consecration, Communion. The offering of the bread and wine; then: "This is My Body — This is My Blood." Then the Communion prayers — "Lord I am not worthy, etc." That's all. That is enough. That is Mass. All the rest is a frame. If at the altar I said only those prayers, my Mass would be a valid Mass. I can't do that because it is forbidden by the Church. But it would be a genuine Mass.

Learn these prayers by heart and then during the day you can live the wonderful grace of your Mass. You have a few moments free — say a Mass of St. John. You wake up at night — say a Mass. You come into the church for a visit or to make your adoration — begin with a Mass. "Receive, O Holy Father . . ." At the end of the day, offer a perfect act of thanksgiving, Holy Mass.

This is the *great* prayer, the most *wonderful* of prayers. I remember preaching in a big community in California. The Mother Superior said to me one day, "Father, I want to thank you. Yesterday after your conference about Holy Mass I went to the infirmary to see a poor sister who suffers terribly and who cannot sleep at all, especially during the night. She was smiling. "Mother, I have learned the secret of how to pass the night — the Mass of St. John. Thank Father for me for having told us about it."

Yes, pray the Mass of St. John during the day, but especially during the night, because as you know, night is the hour of crime and sin. Everywhere Our Lord is scourged horribly. But nothing consoles the Sacred Heart, nothing puts balm into the wound of His Sacred Heart, better than the Sacrifice you offer to the Trinity, through Him, with Him, and in Him.

May you live, and may you die, close to the altar, saying: "Glory be to the Father, glory be to the Son, glory be to the Holy Spirit — through Him, with Him, and in Him! Increase my faith, increase my love. Thy Kingdom come through the chalice!" Your life a Mass. That is sanctity, that is fruitfulness. You, the drop of water in the chalice, transformed into the Blood of Jesus after the Consecration. That is your share in the sacrifice.

CONSOLATION AT THE HOUR OF DEATH

Here is a consoling thought for all of you. When you are dying, in that decisive hour of agony, the enemy of souls will be alert. He is clever, he knows many things, he never forgets your sins. Then at that last moment, he might well say to you, "Do you remember, thirty or forty years ago, this and this, and that and that and the details? ... I have not forgotten ... sins, unfaithfulness, ingratitude, failures in your family life, unkind and useless words .... Now the inexorable Judge is going to pass sentence. He is Sanctity and you have not been a saint."

Well, not all, but most of that could be true. But you can say something to Satan that will vanquish him, if in truth you can reply to your enemy, "Yes, yes, *mea culpa, mea maxima culpa,* unhappily most of what you say is true, but ... " "But what?" "You know as I know that for ten, fifteen, twenty years, I have placed all those miseries, those failings, into the chalice every morning as a drop of water, I have drowned my miseries in the chalice." If you can say that, then you can be at peace. It is true, he may say, that your prayers, your penances have been inadequate. But you can reply that your prayers, your penances have become absorbed in the Precious Blood of Jesus, then he has to retire, beaten, defeated forever. He knows that this is the wonderful daily redemption. And if you could add, "I have done this ten, twenty times a day," angrily he will return to hell.

And there is something else. The devil could try to tempt you to despair by reminding you of your ingratitude in return for all you have received, "You have been ungrateful, you who have been overwhelmed with graces. And you have never given thanks the way you should . . . . " If only you will be able to reply, "I am sorry, what you say is true, I have been ungrateful. But I have drowned my ungratefulness, together with my miseries, my sins, in the chalice; I have thanked through Him, with Him and in Him, during Mass." If you can say this at the hour of death, you have nothing to fear from Satan. You will have silenced him, conquered him, forever.

* * *

To close, one final and interesting observation. Supposing I said to you, "The Church seems to have forgotten the greatest feast of all, the feast of the most Blessed Trinity." Perhaps you would say, "What do you mean, Father?" I answer, "Our Lady is a mere creature; the Mother of God, but still a creature; and yet she has splendid feasts with processions, flowers and high Mass: Immaculate Conception, Annunciation, Assumption, Immaculate Heart and so on. And St. Joseph, and your patrons, all have grand celebrations. Well, then, I ask what about the feast of the Trinity? There is nothing special — no music, no flowers, no special vestments. It is a Sunday like any other Sunday. It is true there is a beautiful Mass on that day in honor of the Blessed Trinity, but that is all. Has the Church forgotten that the feast of the Blessed Trinity is the greatest feast of all?"

We have been baptized in the Name of the Father and of the Son and of the Holy Spirit. For all eternity we will say, "Glory be to the Father, and to the Son and to the Holy Spirit." Then what about the feast of the Trinity? Ah, the Church has not forgotten. The mystery of the Trinity is so great, so marvellously great, that there is no liturgy worthy of the Trinity. What then is the real feast of the most Holy Trinity? DAILY MASS!

We estimate there are four hundred thousand priests in the world, more or less. This means four hundred thousand feasts of the Blessed Trinity each day. Who celebrates this feast? The King, the Pontiff, the Mediator, Christ. He is the *cithara*, the divine harp, vibrating, chanting "Hosanna!" and through Him, with Him, and in Him, the Church triumphant in heaven, the Church suffering in Purgatory, the Church militant here on earth.

All creation chants a hymn to the Creator. The birds and the beasts sing to the Creator; the trees and the flowers sing to the Creator; the sun, the moon and the stars sing to the Creator. Man, kneeling, chants the praises of the Creator; the angels sing His praises; Our Lady, kneeling, chants to the Creator. But, lo! there is someone else who is going to chant. Who? The divine Harp, Jesus! Where? On the altar, vested as Pontiff, with the mitre of thorns, Christ the King, Christ the Pontiff, Christ the Mediator. What does He say? Oh, what is that hymn of creation in comparison? All keep silent ... He is saying, "Glory be to the Father, and to the Son and to the Holy Spirit. Alleluia!" And the Church replies, "Hosanna, Hosanna, Hosanna!" That is Heaven on earth. That is Holy Mass.

Tomorrow in Heaven we will sing that hymn of creation with the archangels and angels, with the saints and the King and Queen of saints. Let us start here on earth with Christ in the Mass, the hymn to the Creator, to the Trinity, "Glory be to the Father and to the Son and to the Holy Spirit .... Through Him, with Him and in Him. Amen."

Chapter 12

JESUS IN THE BLESSED SACRAMENT

*"Jesus Christ is the same, yesterday
and today, yes, and forever."*[1]

HIS "HOUR" HAD COME, He had to leave His brethren and
return to the Father; "having loved his own who were in the
world, he loved them to the end."[2] What an excess and sublime
madness of love these words betray!

He was to be baptized with the baptism of blood, for
which He had longed[3] and His death was about to break the
chain which detained Him in exile with His "little children."
His love could not accept this separation. Up to that moment
His Heart had been victorious. From the bosom of the Father
to the threshold of death it had surmounted every barrier.
In dying He could not resign Himself to leave merely the
traces of His steps and the echo of His voice in the Gospel.
"My soul is sad, even unto death,"[4] He said. And why? Not
only, nor even principally, because we should be left orphaned and bereft, but for another reason a thousand times
more sublime and more beautiful.

During the thirty three years of His mortal life, His Heart
had taken deep root in this earth of His, His fatherland, His
mother's cradle and His own. Except for the Heavenly Father
all the objects of His love were here below: His home, the
Immaculate Mother, St. Joseph, His apostles, His brethren
and His friends. He drew from a human source the blood He

1 Hebr. 13: 8   2 John 13: 1
3 Luke 12: 50; *cf*. 22: 15   4 Mark 14: 34

was to shed. An eternal throne is His above — He is the Lamb of God. But having paid an infinite price for those other thrones of His, the crib of Bethlehem and the cross of Calvary — He could not leave forever the world where he had fought the great fight and won His victory of love, He, "the Lamb of God who takes away the sins of the world."[5] His Heart prompted Him to stay. He has no need of anyone, since He is God, yet He seemed to need our company. "Having loved His own who are in the world, (He) loved them to the end,"[6] unto that utmost limit which we call the Eucharist! His Heart conquered Him and forced Him to continue His pilgrimage as the companion of His brethren in body and in soul, in His humanity and divinity, until the consummation of the world.

In His daily life in Bethlehem, Nazareth, Samaria, Galilee, and on every page of the Gospel you find Him "meek and humble of heart,"[7] full of mercy and compassion. The holy narrative does not close with the death of Jesus, for the Gospel of His love is continued in the Tabernacle; Jesus, *the same Jesus,* is living today in His Eucharist. For the Jesus of Bethlehem and Calvary is also the living Jesus of the consecrated host. In both He is our Brother, the Son of God and of our Blessed Mother. He is the eternal Christ, ever dwelling with us and sharing our lives.

I have already spoken of His triple transfiguration, namely in the crib, on Calvary, and in the sacred host. The latter, which will take place until the end of time, is especially destined to transfigure our souls by a miracle of love. The altar stone is another cradle, the altar a new Thabor. The sacramental species, like swaddling clothes, bind Him, making Him helpless and, as His Blessed Mother bore Him in her hands and gave Him to the shepherds and the Kings, so the priest carries Him from the altar to the communicants. He is still more annihilated in the Tabernacle than He was in Bethlehem but He is the same Jesus. As for us we are in a sense more fortunate than the neighbors and passers-by who

---

5 John 1: 29   6 John 13: 1
7 Matt. 11: 29

could see Him, smile at Him and embrace Him; for, to quote Bossuet's beautiful expression, "we can devour Him out of love for Him while He devours us," and this thousands of times. Oh, how adorable is the helplessness of Jesus in the Blessed Sacrament! What a lesson in humility and abandonment He gives us in the host!

In the Gospel we read about Jesus, Child, Youth and Artisan at Nazareth. Here in our churches, His dwelling has changed its name and size; it is much smaller and is now called the Tabernacle; but, as in Nazareth, He is living in perpetual prayer before the Father ever interceding for us and saving us.[8]

Here, as in Bethany, He dwells in loving intimacy with His faithful friends; here we pour forth our peaceful tears and seek the Master's consolations. How many Magdalens, how many Lazaruses, have been brought to life by the secret, mystical virtue emanating from Jesus in the Blessed Sacrament.

Here, too, is Jacob's Well, and ever seated on its curb, is the eternal Watchman of Israel, that Savior athirst for souls, that Shepherd of straying hearts who once said to the Samaritan woman, "Give me to drink."[9] Here, to the brink of this well, come, consciously or unconsciously, a countless succession of souls with parched lips, yearning for happiness, athirst for peace. Here they find the "fountain of water, springing up unto life everlasting."[10] They drink of it and no longer thirst for worldly things, but are instead consumed with an unquenchable thirst, that of loving Him, the Love of all loves! Nothing is changed, neither the well nor the woman of Samaria, least of all Jesus!

Alas, the Eucharist perpetuates not only the divine Nazarene's moments of sunshine and victory, but also His sad hours, when the powers of darkness are loosed upon Him. Thus the Tabernacle is still the prison of that Holy Thursday, the gloomy dungeon of infamy where our Lord, abandoned

---

8 Hebr. 7: 25   9 John 4: 8
10 John 4: 14

to the mockeries of the guard, suffered all the insults, all the malicious taunts, all the outrages of which a brutal soldiery inflamed with drink is capable. Mark this, apostle of the Heart of Jesus: all the cruelties and insults inflicted on our King on that first Maundy Thursday are less than a single thorn in comparison to the terrible crown of profanations, sacrileges, loneliness, desertion, treacheries and hate which He has daily received during the twenty centuries of His imprisoned sacramental life.

Let us try to compare the deliberate and sacrilegious profanations of the millions of Judases who receive Jesus in the Blessed Sacrament on purpose to wound and despise Him — simply *because He is Jesus* — with the stupid and brutal ignorance of the high priest's palace guard. We shall see that the Tabernacle is far more a monument of living love and pain than was the prison in Caiphas' house. But the outraged Jesus is the same in both. This sacred dungeon of the Tabernacle will never fall into decay, and He who is constantly profaned will ever continue to be our Prisoner of love.

Among the dark hours of Jesus — *yesterday* and *today* — surely the darkest and most terrible are those spent during His Agony in the Garden and those of His Eucharistic life. He has ever before Him the same vision of sin, the same bitter chalice, the same lethargy of those who call themselves His friends, the same diligent activity of the undying race of traitors, ever on the watch and prompt to act. And here I would remind you, zealous apostles, of what Jesus Himself asked of His servant Margaret Mary in connection with this hour of Gethsemane, namely the *Holy Hour*. Be faithful to this homage of love and then seek out fervent friends to join you. Thus you will give a loving and beautiful denial to His complaint: "I looked for .... comforters, and I found none."[11] A complaint that is fundamentally the same as that in the garden: "Could you not, then, watch one hour with Me?"[12] Show real enthusiasm, make every sacrifice in order to multiply the number of those who, by day and by night, adore

---

12 Matt. 26 : 40   11 Ps. 68 : 21

Him in the Blessed Sacrament, at church and at home, and let this be done in a spirit of reparation and for the extension of the Reign of the Sacred Heart.

Our Lord said, "And I, if I be lifted up from the earth, will draw all things to myself."[13] Here He is perpetually lifted up from the earth, on the permanent Calvary of the altar in a never-ceasing and mystical immolation of love. May the ever-faithful God fulfill His promise to draw all things to His adorable Person, and may numberless souls ever be attracted to Him ever present in the Blessed Sacrament. He conquered on the cross. May the same Victim, the same Jesus, consummate His victory upon the altar.

* * *

His Heart, "yesterday, today, and the same for ever," never changes in its affection, its tenderness, its predilections. That which He loved yesterday He continues to love today. From the altar He gently calls the poor, the sad, the outcast. From the depths of the Tabernacle He is ever stretching out His arms to those who are hungering for justice and for *love*. From the host He is ever smiling and blessing the little ones of His flock, the simple of heart and the children, His great friends. The grace which has brought you here today shows that His Heart has not changed in any way. Yesterday He had His special friends. You, apostles of His Sacred Heart, are such today. He died for all, He calls for us all, but He does not show to all the affection He manifested to His little group of intimate friends. He loved Lazarus, Martha and Mary more than the multitudes whom He met upon the road; among the apostles He gave preference to Peter and James, but loved John with a special and greater love; so He loves you, too, and apportions to you a superabundance of grace and love, so that you in your turn may give these to others, as the heralds and the messengers of His divine Heart. Accept then, with humility and great generosity, a glory and a happiness which are not of your seeking, and endeavor to repay Him by corresponding with great docility to His designs.

13 John 12: 32

Since you are more intimate with Jesus than are many others — learn in this retreat the science of the saints: that is, "to know Christ's love which surpasses knowledge."[14] In real intimacy with Him, accept, like Margaret Mary, any confidences, desires or requests He may impart to you and may your absolute fidelity win for you the fulfilment of His promises. May you be ever able to repeat before the Tabernacle and with your last breath those words of St. Bernard: "I have found this Heart in the adorable Eucharist when I have found there the Heart of My King, of my Brother, of my Friend, that is to say, the Heart of My amiable Redeemer!"

---

14 Eph. 3 : 19

Chapter 13

APOSTLES THROUGH LOVE

*"Go you also into the vineyard
and I will give you whatever is just."*[1]

IF IT IS WRITTEN, "He who receives a prophet because he is
a prophet shall receive a prophet's reward,"[2] we can and must
believe that many souls will receive this "reward" for sharing
freely and lovingly in the sacrifices, labors and glories of
apostleship. This will be so with you, beloved apostles of the
Heart of Jesus, although, if I am to speak the truth, the only
reward you covet is the glory and victory of the King of Love,
while you yourselves remain in the shadow of oblivion as
useless servants whose task is done.

By "your task," I mean that you are the intermediaries
between the priest and certain social classes where a priest
can many times neither offer his sacrifices nor take any direct
action. In such cases, which are all too common in our day,
you can serve as a bridge to span the gap.

The priest can no longer do everything himself. The Catholic laity are no longer to be considered as benevolent spec-
tators, or beneficiaries of sacerdotal action. They often occupy the dangerous outposts on the battlefield. It is certainly
to be regretted that the priest should have a less prominent
position, since he is, by divine right, the *mediator* between
God and man, but from this evil God has drawn immense
good and glory, the participation of the whole Catholic body
in the apostolic action. It is very consoling to see on every

---

1 Matt. 20: 4   2 Matt. 10: 41

side ardent laymen and heroic women engaged in every kind of work, preparing the way for sacerdotal action and therefore acting as self-denying forerunners of the King of Glory, of the Sacred Heart of Jesus.

Our Lord's words may be applied to you whom I now address: "Lift up your eyes and behold that the fields are already white for the harvest. ... The harvest indeed is great, but the laborers are few."[3] Do you hear the voice of the divine Sower? He is pointing out the vast field which awaits your labor. He could, if He wished, do all Himself. Just as He created the material worlds without you, so, too, He can convert and sanctify souls without your co-operation. But such is not His will, and as He chose to solicit the free and loving co-operation of Mary, Queen of Clergy and Apostles, so He asks you to go forth in search of souls, to bring them to His Heart. I might almost say that He makes your co-operation a necessary condition of redemption, since it is very possible, and even probable, that not a few souls confided to your care would be lost if you refused Him your help.

A simple comparison will explain what I mean. Let us suppose that you ask me, a priest, to give you Holy Communion, and instead of opening the tabernacle I go back into the sacristy. Then, if our Lord does not wish to make good my culpable negligence by a miracle, you will have to go without Communion. The same occurs in the case of your mission. The poor, the ignorant, the children in thousands are unconsciously hungering for Jesus. The priest lacks the time and funds necessary to assist them. It is for you, zealous apostles, to step in and carry the message of love to those in outlying districts. If you neglect this duty and reject this honor through indifference or fear of bad weather, many a soul will live and die in ignorance of the love of Jesus. Through your fault, the divine Master will be deprived of incomparable glory, for Jesus entrusts Himself to you, and He would have gone wherever you chose to take Him. But if you really covet so great an honor, fear nothing, for He will say to you

---

3 John 4: 35; Matt. 9: 37

as to St. Margaret Mary, "Thou shalt never lack help until My Heart lacks power," which is to say, never!

CATHOLIC ACTION IS A DUTY

The apostolate is not a spiritual luxury and a work of supererogation, such as would be, for instance, to make a Holy Hour. It is a great and sweet duty. We cannot truly love our Lord and yet stand aside indifferent whether He is loved or hated, blessed or cursed by thousands of children who tomorrow will have a voice in public opinion and affairs. They will, indeed, have many voices, for most of them will found families that in their turn will live in hate, indifference or love, according to what those little ones are today in their schools or in their homes. Far be it from us to exclaim, "Every man for himself." "Am I my brother's keeper?"[4] Such is not the language of love. With a loyal heart and burning charity I would walk barefoot over live coals to any distance, if, by so doing, I could but bring a smile to the lips of Jesus and give Him even a single soul.

Traitors are always on the alert, evildoers are ever ready to use their influence and money to pay the price of the Just Man. Sinners daily renew His Passion. Shall we, His friends, whom in His mercy He has healed, pardoned and enriched, neglect our primary obligation of bringing souls to Him? I repeat that this apostolate is a necessity and a law of charity if we love Jesus as we ought. Good Catholics who do not understand this obligation may be classed in the category of "the devout," but only those afire with zeal can be admitted into the divine confraternity of great lovers. Thank God there are many nowadays who can repeat from their hearts the Savior's words to St. Margaret Mary: "Not being able to contain within My breast the flames which devour Me, I wish to communicate them to others." Let us train many souls in this doctrine of love, teaching them the lessons of the Heart of Jesus. In Catholic action we have less need of numerous workers than of great love.

---

4 Gen. 4: 9

Those who have no apostolic zeal are usually careless Catholics. In return for all our Lord has done for us, we ought to work generously for His glory and His reign. Humility is truth and the truth, beloved apostles, is that the Sacred Heart has entrusted His treasures to us, enriching us freely in a thousand ways. How are we to repay such liberality? I see but one way, namely, to give Him souls and families who will know, love, and serve Him. Would that we might say to Him in truth, "O Lord, in return for all I owe to Thee, and feeling my own poverty, I have tried to win hearts to Thee, that they may praise, bless and love Thee for me, in time and in eternity. I prepared that family to become Thy Bethany. I made Thee known there and spoke to them of Thy Heart. Today, parents and children love Thee and look upon Thee as their Friend. Thou art the Master of that home. So now, all that they give Thee, their love, their hymns, their gratitude, I give Thee, too. In my name they will pay Thee what I myself could never pay."

* * *

Why did our Lord, in His great wisdom, permit that there should be rich and poor? To save and sanctify the rich by obliging them to be generous and charitable to the poor. But woe to him who hoards his treasures for himself, heedless of the widow, the orphan and the needy, for one day those very riches will be his ruin.

It is the same in the moral order. Those that are rich in grace, those that have been given treasures of faith and love, must liberally share with the many who are suffering for want of spiritual light and help. God may withdraw His Heart from you, if, looking upon the apostolate as the privilege of priests or religious, you practise only comfortable and selfish devotions and keep your graces to yourself, instead of sharing them with your less fortunate brethren. In any case, you will force the King of Love to be very severe in the day of reckoning. But "blessed are the merciful"[5] and the apostles who in spite of difficulties and fatigues perform *this work of mercy*, for they shall in their turn obtain infinite mercy.

---

5 Matt. 5: 7

The apostolate is not to be compared to a voice crying in the wilderness, but to John the Baptist praying, loving, doing penance and *giving his very self to God,* before making prophecies and baptizing others. The apostolate does not principally consist in anything exterior, such as brilliant talent, soul-stirring eloquence, or great skill for organization. It consists above all in divine and heavenly energy, often hidden in a person as insignificant as a wisp of straw or a grain of sand. Yet people are always inclined to put their faith in what is showy and high sounding, hence many are deluded and deceived.

Then what is an apostle? *A chalice full to the brim of Jesus, and overflowing upon souls.* I do not believe in any apostle who lacks this characteristic. To convert souls, to win them to Jesus, to sanctify them, is pre-eminently a divine and supernatural work, and this cannot be obtained by human science and eloquence. In spite of the many learned scholars and eloquent preachers stones remain stones, that is, sinners are not converted, the indifferent remain indifferent, the good do not rise to greater heights. But let a true apostle speak one single word and *petra* becomes *Petrus,* and *Saul* is changed into *Paul.* The chief essential is a *deep interior life.* If you have not time for prayer, desist from the apostolate, and instead of cultivating other souls, water your own garden. You will then lose less time and you will expose yourself to far less danger.

Great apostles are frequently to be met in the cloister. This *self-imposed silence* is far more powerful than words. Only in heaven will they see how many souls they have converted. The world will not be saved by controversy but by immense faith. We must not forget that one drop of the divine blood far outweighs all human efforts. For myself, as I advance in life, I certainly believe less and less in my own activity and more and more in the *voice which speaks within.* But what I believe in most of all is the silent eloquence of the host! Hence my conviction that the most intense and efficacious apostolic action emanates principally from the sanctuaries of prayer and immolation. Satan must know this by intuition and by bitter experience, since he often raises up the most terrible persecutions against religious communities. A monastery where consecrated souls pray and live fervently has — according to St. Teresa — walls of crystal, and radiates more light and life than a thousand preachers who lack deep interior life. If, on the contrary, we possess it, we can exercise our influence at a distance by a sort of mysterious telepathy, preaching without the sound of words, baptising with fire, helping to a good death and deciding at the last hour the eternal destiny of countless souls.

I do not mean in any way to detract from the high importance and necessity of active ministry, but I do affirm that exterior activity becomes a mere feverish agitation, and even a danger to the soul, unless accompanied by a spirit of prayer, intense desire for sanctification and love of sacrifice. How many miracles would be accomplished every day if all consecrated souls were even one-tenth as saintly as the Little Flower in her hidden life of prayer and suffering. Then every religious house would be another upper room radiating invisibly, but none the less really, an outburst of spiritual life. St. Paul's epithet, "a tinkling cymbal,"[6] may be fitly applied to a priest who has nothing of the Trappist recollection, or to religious and laity engaged in active works but lacking the spirit of prayer which animates a Carmelite.

To be apostles and to glorify the Sacred Heart, we ought to meditate constantly on the fact that Jesus lived hidden in prayer and immolation for thirty years, in order to be the Redeemer of the world. At Nazareth, more than even in the Sermon on the Mount, Jesus is the Teacher of apostles, because there we learn from Him that preaching should be nothing but a spoken prayer, and also because not all apostles are called to preach, whereas there are and always will be many splendid missionaries *after the style of the Nazarene*, such as St. Teresa, St. Margaret Mary, St. Therese of the

---

6 1 Cor. 13 : 1

153

Child Jesus. All of them will rank among apostles after winning their thrones, not by their eloquence, but by their love.

THE APOSTOLATE OF LOVE

While treating a subject of such capital importance and interest, I should like, dear apostles, to insist on the fundamental theme and dominant idea of this retreat. Love much, love immensely, love even unto folly! This is the basis, the spirit, the crowning point of your apostolate. *Whoever loves much,* whether bishop or catechist, whether speaking from the pulpit, or lying sick in bed, is always a great apostle. What a comfort it is to know for certain that a life, often obscure and apparently useless when wholly transmuted into gold by love is always an apostolate in the home and even far beyond its limits. Take the case of a poor woman who spends her days in simple household duties, but who, like Mary in Nazareth, does her work with faith and love in our Lord's presence, and offers everything for His glory. She is, perhaps, anxious to convert her husband — long estranged from God. This will be granted her, and even if she does not witness his conversion here below, she will one day meet him in heaven, where together they will sing the mercy of the Sacred Heart. "Thou hast loved much," the divine Judge will say to her. "Thou hast loved for thyself and for thy husband; by thy love thou hast paid the double debt with interest; thus thou wert My apostle and so didst save thy husband." There will be many surprises of this kind in the abode where those who have loved much here on earth shall rejoice with Mary Magdalen and the Little Flower.

Such is the power of prayer in winning miracles of grace. I say "prayer," not the mere recitation of prayers, for real prayer is a sigh of the soul which rises to God and does Him violence in the measure in which it is a loving prayer. Pray much, but always with immense love. The great danger run by those who devote their life to active work consists in allowing themselves to be so much absorbed in it that they frequently neglect prayer, or hurry over it, or pray with a

154

heart full of petty interests. This is a very grave mistake. For the glory of the Sacred Heart, and to withdraw such an apostle from the edge of the precipice, his work should be suppressed, he should go into retreat and spend some time in recollection and prayer. Otherwise, while seeking to save others, he will lose his own soul.

Every tree, if it is to bring forth abundant fruit, needs good soil and water for its roots, since the abundance of sap and the richness of its produce depends on these factors. So we must first of all throw out deep roots into the Heart of Jesus, by means of great love and constant and fervent prayer, and it is only in proportion as we draw sap and life from Him that we shall bring forth beautiful flowers of virtue and bear fruit a hundredfold. Every other tree, rich though it be in foliage, is not planted by our Heavenly Father, and will one day be cut down and cast into the fire, for it cumbereth the ground.

THE REWARD OF THE APOSTOLATE

As I am addressing apostles of the Sacred Heart, I must draw your attention to an encouraging promise made by our Lord to St. Margaret Mary. The saint writes in her autobiography, "The divine Heart promised me, on behalf of all those who should consecrate themselves to it, that it would receive them lovingly, would assure their salvation, and *would take special care to sanctify them* and to make them great in the sight of our Heavenly Father, in proportion as they generously endeavor to promote the reign of its love in the hearts of the faithful." Our adorable Redeemer has therefore explicitly committed Himself to labor specially for the sanctification of those who accept all sacrifices with a view to making His divine Heart glorified by men.

Needless to add that this promise, far from exempting us from personal labor, emphasizes the duty of developing our interior life. But it is consoling to think that Jesus gives *a very special grace* to those who fervently endeavor to make known the mercies of His most Sacred Heart. By this promise He seems to say to you what He once said to St. Catherine of Sienna, "Think of Me, and I will think of thee"; or more clearly still, when speaking to His confidante of Paray-le-Monial, "Make Me thy only thought and I will think of thee and thine. Evidently My first care will be to make thee holy, for otherwise thou couldst not be the apostle of My love."

A zealous apostle thinks of nothing save the glory of the Sacred Heart. All petty interests are forgotten and everything is summed up in loving Him and making Him better known and loved. A delightful contest then occurs in prayer between this apostle and the King of Love.

"Dear child, thou seest how much I love thee; come near and ask Me what thou wilt, for thou hast stolen My Heart."

"To love Thee and to give Thee glory, O Sacred Heart!"

"Yes, my child, I understand and bless thy prayer, but hast thou no special grace to ask of Me? Speak, be not afraid, thou canst command My Heart."

"To love Thee and to give Thee glory, O Sacred Heart!"

"Thou speakest as My saints did. I wish to prove that if thou art Mine, I also am thine. Ask what thou wilt."

"To love Thee and to give Thee glory, O Sacred Heart!"

"I see that thou hast forgotten everything for My glory. Here is My Heart. I give it to thee, dispose of it as thou wilt with all its treasures. In this hour of grace, tell Me what miracle of love thou dost desire?"

"To love Thee even unto folly and to make Thee loved with the irresistible power of Thine own Heart. May Thy Kingdom come!"

If we think, speak and pray thus, Jesus will give us His Heart and help us to win souls. Then those words of St. Margaret Mary will be realized in a practical and admirable way. "Oh, that it were given to me to express what I have been taught concerning the rewards which His apostles will receive from this most adorable Heart!" These rewards are so surpassing, rich and great that the seer of Paray, like St. Paul, could not translate them into words.

While it is currently proclaimed that the cross is beneficial and meritorious, it has not been made clear enough that it also completes the work of prayer and *is just as powerful a factor in the apostolate.* A bitter trial bravely borne is not merely a source of personal merit, it may also be the means of miraculous conversions, for the spirit of sacrifice is an *apostolic virtue* which vivifies souls and helps them on the road to Heaven. Our Lord seems to have willed to make immolation the infallible secret of victory. Though a sinner has resisted all the exterior graces that come to him in the form of a good example, advice, or arguments based on doctrines of faith, suffering will bring him to his knees and overthrow his unbelief. A wife, a mother, or a child has won the victory by tears of love and years of prayer. I have frequently witnessed quite astounding conversions that testify to the truth of what I say. The cross wins the victory today as it did on Calvary.

We cannot all be as eloquent as Bossuet, nor conquer new worlds for God like Columbus. We are not all called to foreign missions, but all of us, whether we be young or old, priests or layfolk, rich or poor, can by our daily crosses redeem captive souls, restore sight to those whose minds are blinded by error and raise to life souls that are dead in sin. This is why I have started and organized everywhere the *Crusade of the Apostolate of Suffering,* begging those who suffer in soul or body to make a practical use of their crosses by offering them to Jesus for the extension of His reign. The members of this apostolate are taught that not a single tear shed for this intention is ever lost, and that they may win many souls to adorn the diadem of the King of Love by their sufferings patiently borne.

"Would you like to be My missionary?" said our Lord to a little girl of seven.

"A little thing like me a missionary! How could I be, dear Jesus?" she inquired.

"Yes, just because you are so little, child," He answered, "would you like to try?"

157

"Dear Jesus, I don't understand how."

"Dear little one, offer Me your daily Communions, your prayers and above all your sacrifices, everything that hurts or vexes you all through the day. Offer them with great love to win Me souls, and you will be My little missionary."

Do you understand the lesson, dear apostles? You can convert sinners, you can purify, make reparation, and save souls by offering your sufferings as apostles of love.

The Child Jesus often conversed familiarly with a little shepherdess of five. They would sit together on a stone beneath a shady tree for hours, watching the sheep that gazed near by, and Jesus would give her sublime lessons in virtue expressed in childish words. Telling her to put out her hand, Jesus placed in it a few crumbs of bread and, with a gracious gesture, invited the little birds that were twittering in the branches of the trees to come and eat therefrom.

When they had flown away, Jesus said to the little shepherdess, "Prepare yourself, for when you are older I will place, not in your hand, but in the chalice of your heart, *bitterness and sorrows*, and souls will be nourished by the example of your patient suffering. Prepare, dear child, for that great apostolate of the cross."

Another day, our Lord said to the same little shepherdess, "Can you guess how to make something very beautiful from two bits of wood?" As she could find no answer, Jesus said, "Bring Me those two sticks. See, they are quite like any others, though perhaps a little crooked." Then, making them into a cross and smiling, He said, "Look, can anything be more lovely now? Not even the angels could make anything more precious and more holy. Soon I Myself will fasten you to the cross and if, in spite of all, you love Me more even than you do today, and if you offer all for sinners, I promise by this cross to give you many souls and to make you an apostle of My love."

Thus, in the apostolic crusade, each of us can have a share of merit and glory, since we are all called to suffer and to mourn. What is most touching in this apostolate is that hum-

158

ble souls, the weak, the poor, the ignorant, are the favorites of our Lord. Even the youngest child and the most poverty-stricken may achieve what no orator can accomplish by his eloquence. Hence it is that as I go from place to place preaching the Reign of the Heart of Jesus, my one desire is to secure and strengthen its triumph by the generous offering of some humble souls, willing to be immolated as pure hosts for this intention.

At Lyons I had been preaching for six days in the cathedral and I had not met with one such soul. During my thanksgiving, I said to our Lord, "Dear Jesus, I wish You would send me a little hidden soul to consecrate herself like little St. Therese to love, pray and suffer, that You may reign in individual souls and in families. Give me that soul today, immediately, as a pledge of Your approval of this Crusade of Love." Hardly had I concluded my prayer, when the sacristan announced that a young woman was waiting to see me. She was a simple, working girl of about twenty years of age. "Father," she said, "I have heard about the Enthronement and I believe it to be God's work, but I know you want a soul like little St. Therese to love, pray and suffer. I have come to offer myself, if you will have me, to be consecrated in this way for the establishment of the kingdom of the Sacred Heart." I was silent for a moment, struck by the repetition of the very words of my prayer. When I answered that I would joyfully do so, she begged that I should return to the altar and offer her to Jesus while she would kneel before the tabernacle and devote her whole life to the Sacred Heart.

Blessed be the crucified King for teaching us that a hidden martyrdom of love is the greatest apostolate.[7]

7 For information on the Apostolate of Suffering write to the National Enthronement Center, Washington 17, D.C.

Chapter 14

APOSTOLATE OF THE SACRED HEART

"Make Me better known and loved"
(Our Lord to St. Margaret Mary)

MARY IS THE PERFECT TYPE and ideal of apostles and priests. Neither St. Paul, "the Apostle of the Gentiles," nor St. Peter, nor St. John were such powerful instruments in the hands of God as she, since the apostolate consists in giving Jesus to souls and souls to Jesus, and no one can ever do this as well as Mary, Mother of Jesus and mother of men. The more Mary possesses Jesus the more she gives Him to us. Thus, at the Nativity her Motherhood seems greater then at the Annunciation, and on Calvary where she consented to the death of Jesus, her maternity had something even more sublime. She went there as mother of her divine Son, she came down the mother of the human race.

Do not forget that we, like Mary, shall give Jesus in the measure in which we ourselves possess Him. He, in turn, will be the more ours in proportion as we give Him to others in an ardent and supernatural apostolate. This being so, let us now see what should be the dominant characteristics of apostleship in general and of the apostolate of the Heart of Jesus in particular.

A SUPERNATURAL SPIRIT

All zeal is not good, because all zeal is not holy and supernatural. Even in the organization and direction of good works we often find dross mixed with the gold; the work is beautiful

---

1 1 Cor. 1: 12

but the method of carrying it out is too human. Petty interests and personal preferences often hamper Catholic action. The gold must be purified of its dross. Let there be no contentions among us as there were in the days of the apostles when some said, "I am of Paul," and others, "I am of Cephas."[1] Let us all be apostles of Christ alone and prove it by our works, especially by *forgetting ourselves,* not trying to promote our own honor and credit, or that of our confraternity. We should even be ready to yield — no so much out of courtesy as in a supernatural spirit — to anyone who can do the work of God better than ourselves. Let us not say, " I was here first." Work done for God should never become a race. Our thoughts must soar above self-seeking and claims for preference. Such things hamper good works and do evil among the children of light.

Brilliant success in Catholic works should never be our primary goal. Let us trust the issue to our Lord, putting it out of our thoughts, at least in part. We should do this for several reasons; among others, because the true issue is a divine lottery, so to speak, depending neither on our zeal, nor on the co-operation of others. God gives success where and how He pleases, and very often He does not permit the result to correspond with the good work which has been accomplished. The fact that Jesus does not always reward zeal by grand achievements proves that such are not always in His eyes a sign of true success, a divine victory for Him. A great spirit of faith is needed to understand this and to prevent our feeling discouraged because our wings are clipped.

Also the Gospel promises and those made at Paray-le-Monial concerning the triumph of the King of Love should not be looked at — as too often happens — in the light of our human judgment, but only from a supernatural point of view. In this divine combat, apparent defeats are often great victories. As far as we are concerned, dear apostles, success ought to consist exclusively in His calling the souls whom He thinks worthy and in His crowning Himself with the glory which is His due, even though nothing accrues to us but disaster and confusion. Provided *He triumphs as He wishes, we should be satisfied.*

161

If you really seek the glory of the Sacred Heart, if you desire that glory above your own and above all your personal interests, however legitimate; if you are true and generous apostles, formed in the school of St. Margaret Mary, then I must emphatically say that you ought to *bless* our Lord for allowing contradictions and obstacles, for these very difficulties will more and more refine your zeal. In these hours of trial, when both good and wicked seem to have conspired together to ruin a grand and beautiful project which has cost you many tiring days and sleepless nights; when you see the hurricane wrecking the work which you had so long cherished, learn how to bless God Who opens and shuts the flood-gates of Heaven in His own good time. At such moments do not be too much troubled or alarmed. If you are tempted to accuse and condemn your opposers, control yourself, hasten before the tabernacle, offer your heart very lovingly to the divine Master and be at peace, for He cannot be indifferent to His Father's glory and His own.

Opposition has always been and ever will be the divine seal upon all works. Such contradictions come only when God wills they should and last only as long as He permits. Such storms have never ruined a work dear to God when the thoughts of the apostle were inspired by a great spirit of faith. We must confess with sorrow that this spirit is sometimes greatly wanting. It is not for lack of money or human support that many excellent works have no real life. So the apostles of the Enthronement should carefully avoid attributing an exaggerated importance to wealth and high patronage. In our work, money and influence are not all. Relegate them to the background. Jesus will provide. When the glory and love of the Sacred Heart are at stake, I beg of you, do not weigh the cost in money only. The saints never triumphed in this way.

THE SPIRIT OF FAITH

*"But lifting up their eyes, they saw no one
but Jesus only."*[2]

---

2 Matt. 17: 8

Our Lord said to St. Margaret Mary, *"I will reign in spite of My enemies."* This "in spite of" has given courage to many inexperienced and timid apostles who believed too much in the power of Satan and his followers. The power of the wicked comes from the weakness of the good. The issue of the fight mostly depends on the fidelity of our Lord's friends. "O you of little faith,"[3] Jesus said to His disciples. He might well say the same to those who tremble when menaced by the enemy.

It is a lack of faith that makes us long to see our work crowned as quickly as possible with striking and brilliant success and to desire that it should be known and published abroad that these grand results are to be attributed to us.

It is a lack of faith to expect to reap at eventide what we sowed at dawn and to seek for admiration and applause while professing purity of intention. Dear apostles, ask Jesus for a great and living faith that you may not betray His confidence, for He expects many victories from your spirit of faith.

I firmly believe that there is no such thing as failure in good works when they are undertaken and carried out by a true apostle. If by failure we mean the ruin of *our own plans,* however good, then there may be and even ought to be failure. God would not be what He is if He had promised to set His seal on any wild idea of ours, however honest and honorable our intentions may have been. If, however, my only purpose is the *glory of God,* I will not mind being disappointed in my projects. By upsetting them, God will not destroy the true spiritual results of my apostolate. The King of Love will be glorified and that is enough for me. The failure was mine and only apparent; the victory was His, a real, effective and complete one. Blessed be Jesus, the true Victor! I have come out of the combat humble and wounded; He has come out with palms and laural wreaths. Praised be for ever His Most Sacred Heart!

It is a lack of faith to be easily *discouraged.* Difficulties are so indispensable to divine works that if there were none

---

3 Matt. 8: 26

we *should have to invent or provoke them* in order to ensure the victory. We forget that Jesus does His best work in times of tribulation provided we believe that He is faithful and all powerful. During the early persecutions, bishops, priests and faithful were put to death by the thousands. The persecutors sought to destroy the infant Church. They might have succeded had those early Christians reasoned as we do and taken too much thought for the morrow, saying in their dejection, "If we die who will care for souls and for the altars? God has forgotten us. Woe to us! Woe to the Church!" But they did not speak thus, they died with a hymn of victory upon their lips.

If we could only believe as they did in the Savior's affirmation, "I have overcome the world,"[4] what miracles we should work in spite of exterior obstacles and our own incapacity and failings. Man has changed into means of communication even the greatest obstacles, such as the sea, the air, the mountains. How much more should our faith invent means of turning every difficulty to the glory of God. If we have labored for many a weary day and night without making any apparent progress in our works, we must humbly acknowledge that this may be because of our sins, and launch out into the deep with immense faith letting down our nets in the name of our Lord. Like the apostles, we shall then be rewarded by a miraculous draught.

Believe in the loyalty of the Heart of Jesus. He may well treat you as He did the woman of Canaan, making you ask and suffer refusal many times to test you, but His Heart cannot deceive nor be deceived. Knock once again and He will open to you. God has His own times. Let us hasten the coming of the hour of grace and mercy by believing with invincible faith. Do not stand arguing like St. Thomas, "Blessed are they who have not seen, and yet have believed,"[5] for they are the only true apostles and they alone will one day experience that the word of the Lord shall not pass[6] and that

---

4 John 16: 33   5 John 20: 29
6 Matt. 24: 35

164

His Heart, the fountain of mercy, is divinely faithful. Say to Him humbly again and again, "Jesus, I believe, but increase my faith."

THE SPIRIT OF BURNING CHARITY

"Lord, thou knowest all things, thou knowest that I love thee"[7]

God is charity. The Incarnation, the Redemption and the Church being the manifestation of that infinite love, all our duties are summed up in the first commandment of the law: "Thou shalt love the Lord thy God with thy whole heart and with thy whole soul and with all thy strength."[8] This love should animate our whole life. I insist on this point because, if we explain the law of God, the Redemption, the Eucharist, the sacraments and describe these marvels with no more ardor and conviction than if we were putting forward physical or chemical theories, people may understand and remember what we say, but they will go away as cold as they came. They will know a little more, but they will not have learned the one thing that matters, to love that God who is all love. What a difference it would make if we could speak and teach as the Cure of Ars did, as the Little Flower would have done. What a difference when our words, tone and gesture all betray a loving conviction; when, during a simple catechism lesson, our hearers feel that Jesus Himself is speaking through our lips.

We should always depict Him *as He is,* most lovable, meek, full of kindness and tender mercy, "patient and slow to anger" as Holy Scripture says. There is no need to exaggerate nor to alter a single feature of His true portrait when endeavoring to inspire souls with love for His sovereign beauty. He who created the Blessed Virgin so sweet, so compassionate, *so motherly,* has fashioned the hearts of all mothers out of the best of His own tenderness. If, then, the Blessed Virgin and our own mothers are patterns of loving kindness, what must He not be, He the eternal and infinite source of all love?

---

7 John 21: 17   8 Luke 10: 27

Moreover, by preaching *a very lovable* Jesus, a God of love, we at the same time emphasize His justice, for we show that because He is just He is also merciful. To limit the justice of God to the act of condemning most of His creatures to hell for mere trifles is contrary to justice and to that love which brought a God of charity down to earth to die as our Redeemer.

Inspire souls with loving confidence in God and you will give them wings. Treat others with that compassion and patience God shows to you. Remember that few people are really bad, but many are ignorant and all are weak. Therefore, *to be just* to souls and do them good, be kind and gentle, be "mothers" to those whose salvation may depend on you. In Jesus and for the sake of Jesus love the treasures which His Heart has confided to your care.

* * *

Now that you understand your mission as apostles, it will be easy to speak to you of *self-abnegation,* which consists in *giving yourselves wholly to souls* for the love of Jesus, as Jesus gives Himself to you.

I have met with many touching examples of such self-abnegation. I remember a little school girl who used to help me as secretary and copyist. She said to her mother, "I have promised to help Father in his apostolate, so will you, please, let me stay up from nine to ten, three evenings a week, to do some work that he has given me?"

"What work?" inquired her mother.

"I have to copy out some letters in four of five different languages. Please let me, mother." ..

"But why stay up from nine to ten?" asked her mother. "You could do the work on Thursdays and Sundays when you have no school. It might hurt your health to stay up so late."

"Yes," said the child, " I know the work could be done on those days, but I want to make a little sacrifice, even if it hurts my health. By love and sacrifice I may win back father's soul."

The lady, who was a good Catholic, felt deeply touched and gave consent. Three evenings a week, from nine to ten, the child lovingly copied hundreds of circular letters destined to make known the work of the Enthronement. This she did kneeling on her bare knees upon the floor, as a penance for the conversion of her father.

I shall never forget an old beggar woman who helped me at the outset of this Crusade. She often came to see me after having spent her day going from cottage to cottage in the pouring rain to speak of the Sacred Heart.

"But, my child, you are wet through. What are you going to do now?"

"Dry myself at a neighbor's stove."

"And have you had anything to eat?"

"A piece of bread . . . . but don't let's talk of that. What does anything matter when the soul is happy? I have succeeded in making Jesus loved."

In heaven many an orator of note will be put to shame by apostles such as these. Let us speak in schools and homes of Jesus and Jesus Crucified and we shall conquer many of them for the King of Love.

Chapter 15

CATHOLIC ACTION [1]

CATHOLIC ACTION, TODAY A WORLD WIDE apostolic crusade, had its official starting point in Italy under the personal high supervision of its founder the great Pius XI. This clever and saintly Pontiff personally wrote and traced its program — the social strategy of Catholic Action — and installed and codified the genuine supernatural spirit of this modern crusade.

Invited in 1925 to join the movement, I had the honor of preaching Catholic Action in 104 diocese of Italy under the guidance of the famous Father Gemelli, Rector of the Sacred Heart University at Milan. Father Gemelli, a former medical doctor and a convert from the extreme atheistic and socialistic camp, is today one of the greatest intellectuals in Italy.[2]

But now, what am I going to preach to this gathering of lay apostles, valiant soldiers of Christ the King?

Perhaps you are expecting to hear a report built on long experience and selected from my archives?

No! I prefer another theme, not less interesting and practical .... and far more inspiring: "The soul, the spirit, of Catholic Action," such as I have heard Pius XI expose it strongly and repeatedly to the leaders of different countries, and personally to me, in private audiences.

It's interesting to observe that while several times Pius XI modified and corrected the program and the tactics of Catholic Action according to what experience suggested, he

---

1 From the original notes of a talk given to men in California.
2 Father Gemelli died on July 16, 1959.

never modified a line or a word of what he had affirmed from the beginning concerning the fundamental Catholic ideal: the supernatural soul of this providential crusade!

I am then authorized to say when quoting the founder himself, "*Magister, Pontifex dixit.*" (The Master, the Pontiff has spoken.)

Now that master insistently affirmed that "A Catholic Actionist must necessarily be an apostle of Jesus Christ" — an apostle in the classical sense of the word.

What is an apostle? A supernatural agent and messenger whose heart must be a chalice filled with Jesus, but filled to the brim, overflowing Jesus from its superabundance. His exterior apostolic work must be then the spontaneous overflowing of his deep fervent Christ-life.

Yes, the Catholic Actionist must be the forerunner of the great King, preparing the way, and then building the City of God in the midst of a dechristianised society, under the guidance of the hierarchy and in constant filial touch with the bishops and the clergy.

Now it's clear that this social apostolate, so delicate and so important, presupposes in the Catholic Actionist a superabundance of faith, a solid piety, radiating, expanding from his own soul.

We read in the Gospel that a healing virtue radiated from the divine Master. So also, Jesus must radiate and heal and conquer through the Catholic Actionist when the latter realizes this statement of St. Paul: "To live, for me is Jesus Christ!"

It is clear as sunshine that just as the mystery of the Incarnation had to precede the glory and the redemptive grace of Christmas, so also with you: before you can succeed in causing Jesus to be born anew in souls, Christ must first become "incarnate" in each one of you, His apostles.

Listen to this lesson I once gave to a young priest. One day he said to me, "Father, I need your advice. I am really discouraged. I am an assistant in a parish where the faith is at a low ebb, and am working with the pastor and other assistant trying to help these people. For five years I've tried everything possible to win them over, but the results are nil. I can assure you I've tried everything and it breaks my heart to have to admit that there has been complete failure."

Once again he repeated, "I've tried everything. Please give me some advice and encouragement, for I really want to be a good priest and to save souls. Please tell me, what *do* I have to do to save souls?"

Expressly I made him tell me again that he had tried everything, without results. Then I asked him, "Have you ever tried becoming a *saintly* priest?" And when, surprised, he answered, "no", I told him, "well then you haven't tried everything! You don't begin with secondary things . . . . you begin with fundamentals, trying to be a saintly priest. First try this apostolate, and then one day, be it only in heaven, you will learn how faithful God is to His promises."

And what I said to this priest I repeat to you; a good, even a splendid worker, without that divine spirit, is only a "tinkling cymbal" says St. Paul.

A supernatural work supposes the competence and the grace of a "supernaturalized" instrument.

We must not be like a "channel" that lets all the water pass through . . . . and keeps only the humidity. No! We must be reservoirs, pouring out great volumes of water in all directions, but always full!

Once more, allow me to give the great Pope Pius XI as my authority for this doctrine. On October 19, 1934, I was received in private audience prior to leaving for the Far East to preach retreats to missionaries in many mission lands. At the end of the audience, the great Pontiff made me kneel down and then placing both hands on my head he recited the *Veni, Creator Spiritus,* (Come Holy Ghost, Creator blessed,) after which he said to me, "Now go, Father Mateo, and preach *sanctity,* the only secret of divine success."

Now I wish to confirm these lofty, unshakeable principles with the facts of experience.

I take as a typical case Italy where Catholic Action was

170

born and where it developed into a vigorous, transforming Pentecost of graces which were badly needed both in big cities and in country areas. The spiritual success, the profound revival of fervent and deep Catholic life, has been wonderful, as well in the risky foundation and continued existence of the Catholic University of Milan, as in the evangelization of the rough population in the big industrial areas and in the steep jagged mountain areas of Calabria, Sicily, and Sardinia.

I preached everywhere, and everywhere I've been the witness of a powerful, conquering Catholic reaction, so really powerful that Pius XI, ordinarily so calm and well-balanced by nature was deeply moved and struck — I may even say "surprised"; "The Sacred Heart is with us," he said, "the Sacred Heart is clearly manifesting His Will, His intervention in Catholic Action is a miracle! Then go ahead."

But now let us stop for a moment and look for the reason of all this, because this extraordinary success certainly had a cause; behind this triumphant movement there must have been a moving power. What was it? A partial reason at least is to be found in the splendid activity displayed because of a fixed method, a well-organized program.

For months at a time I've travelled by day and night with hundreds of leaders of Catholic Action. I've assisted at their "missions" given in schools, in halls, in the open air, even in theaters, to rich and poor alike. All this was indispensable because nothing solid is done in the Church, nothing lasting without catechising, without Christian doctrines and principles.

But please note well: all this activity, admirable as it may be, is not by itself the corner stone of the sanctuary. This activity is certainly part of the foundation, but to it must be added an indispensable element, the messenger, the *apostle himself!* The best proof of this is that the same principles presented by two different Catholic Actionists produced blessings of grace and life in an entirely different degree in those who heard them.

With great confidence then, I stress this point: these apostles, these Catholic Actionists of whom I have been speaking were trained in the school of strong piety and spiritually. They loved Our Lord with a flame of love that makes me blush! They loved their adorable Master with a great spirit of sacrifice and self-denial. All of these leaders — about two thousand, the majority my personal friends — were daily Communicants. All made their meditation every morning — and all had their monthly recollection. Believe me there lies the whole secret of their outstanding apostolic success. As in the case of Our Lady, so in their case, the Kingdom of God starts, bursts forth from within! Apostles, in order to give life, must have something of the contemplative in them — they must be men and women of prayer.

Lately I've been in India where I arrived at the conclusion that Francis Xavier, that giant of marvellous activity, was, in the jungle, a contemplative and a man of prayer, greater than many Trappists!

Years ago I knew in Madrid a phalanx of 75 apostles of Catholic Action, young, between 20 and 35, engineers, lawyers and business men, who together every Thursday spent the whole night in Adoration! Their leader was a distinguished lawyer and famous writer, saintly, simple, joyful as a child, a warrior for Christ, a crusader of old.

We sometimes think that the race of saints is almost extinguished or, at least that if saints still exist, they are exclusively cloistered monks. No! happily no! both statements are wrong. For example there is the case of Dr. Necchi a celebrated specialist in mental and nervous diseases and God's instrument in the remarkable conversion of Father Gemelli. He died some twelve years ago and already his cause has been introduced in Rome. He was one of the most conspicuous leaders of Catholic Action in Milan, a personal friend of Pius XI. I knew him well.

Another outstanding apostle of Catholic Action was Giorgio Frassetti, who died at the age of 15. He was followed in North Italy by hundreds of Catholic students who called him the "jolly good fellow, the smiling and singing saint." Yes, sanctity is a permanent reality in the Catholic Church in every state of life.

In Europe, in America, everywhere, in the field of lay-Catholics the best Catholic Actionists are the supernatural souls, men of prayer, deeply in love with Jesus in the Eucharist. Mere active workers are not lacking but what are lacking are genuine apostles, Eucharistic souls, men of prayer!

All true apostles are wonderful workers but not all workers are wonderful apostles because the pentecostal soul of Eucharistic Action is sometimes lacking.

Before closing allow me to give you with great conviction two practical councils: one concerning Eucharistic fervor . . . and the other about fervent, very fervent Christian homelife.

First of all Eucharistic fervor. Yes, in the measure you passionately love the Sacred Heart in the Sacrifice of the Altar in that measure will you be an apostolic power in the Christianising of America! It's easier to go to Mass every month than a few times a year. It's easier to go every week than once a month. And far more easy every day than once a week!

I've preached everywhere that there are too many novenas to Saints. Better to change them into Novenas of Masses and Communions!

Second, thoroughly Christian home-life! You the best, the leaders, strive strongly to lead American families back to the venerable old traditions, especially the family Rosary. Celebrate, for instance, with a simple family gathering at home the First Friday and the Feast of the Sacred Heart. Jesus must be a King and a Friend at home, the center of the hearts of parents and children. Catholic men, rebuild "home sweet home" — Catholic homes — with the Sacred Heart as your King and your adorable Friend!

Society is and a country is what families are!

Now you understand why the saintly Pius X said to me: "No, I do not permit the work of the Enthronement of the Sacred Heart in the home, I command it!"

I have just mentioned "home," the rock on which the

173

Catholic Church is built. Alas, a deadly neo-paganism, ending logically in the fatal crime of divorce is by far a greater, more ruinous, national disaster than wars with all their horrors. Divorce is not only an awful plague, but the summary of the seven plagues of Egypt!

Catholic leaders: just as there are wise, strict regulations for public hygiene, a barrier must be found to stop this devastating raging fire that could provoke a rain of avenging fire from above. Remember that divorce is a deadly poison against family and country before being a social, a legal blasphemy against Christ's positive law!

Allow me to close this meeting with a most comforting statement made by this foreigner working hard for your dear country — and sincerely admiring more and every day the extraordinary qualities of the American race. I don't know if I have succeeded in conquering you Americans, but you have certainly conquered me! Believe me then if I dare say that you Americans are made of very rich stuff .... rich enough to match the best Catholic Actionists I've met elsewhere. Americans, you are capable of being apostles performing heroic deeds for Christ, for the Church, for America! But to accomplish your redemptive mission you need an "elite" of leaders passionately loving Our Lord in their private lives, leaders in the virile style of a Frederic Ozanam, apostles with the strong faith of a Dr. L. Necchi; pioneers of the Gospel with a manly christian conviction of Garcia Moreno, the martyred Ecuadorian statesman! Catholic ardent patriots with the iron tempered Christianity of an Engelbert Dolfuss, the Austrian Chancellor killed by the Nazis.

Once more: the rich metal to forge these leaders, these giants of Catholic Action is to be found in the Christian American home.

Through the Eucharist transform your lives into a radiating power .... and you'll transform the home into a tabernacle of peace, of prayer, of Christian happiness.

With the greatest conviction I end this lecture by applying to you the words addressed by Pius XI to hundreds of Catholic Action leaders of all nationalities: "In this hour of dreadful and stormy crisis we have a great hope. The hour of the Sacred Heart has come! Catholic men, hold aloft the banner of the Sacred Heart, in it lies the assurance of a promise for victory!"

For peace and for home and for the Church and for America let us go and fight the battle for Christ, the King of truth and justice, the King of Love and mercy: may His Kingdom come within you, and through you!

Chapter 16

THE SIN OF FRIENDS

*"I was wounded in the house
of them that loved me."*[1]

WITH THE GREAT REVELATIONS AT Paray-le-Monial, reparation
has assumed a prominence which it did not previously
possess. Reparation is always implied in the teaching of the
Sacred Heart, and, given the abnormal and unstable situation
created by sin, it is also inseparable from perfect charity.
Indeed we cannot here on earth fully love God without *ex-
piating* the offence which sin inflicts on Him, without *giving
consolation* to His Sacred Heart, which is wounded and sorrowful unto death because of sin, and without *making
amends for,* or repairing, as far as lies in our power, the evils
caused by the rebellion of sin. In other words, reparation is
a love of compassion, of satisfaction and of penance for the
irreverence committed against our Lord.

Leaving aside for the moment considerations relative to
great sinners, the executioners of our day, who with cruel
hate scourge and crucify our Lord anew, I prefer to put
before you another sin, crueler even than the point of the
spear with which Longinus pierced the Savior's Side, I mean
the *indifference and coldness of those who call themselves
our Lord's friends.* This is the sin which hurts Him most. It
pierces His adorable Heart, not because it is graver than that
of the wicked, but because it is a hand of a friend that scourg-
es Him, because it is a heart on which grace has perhaps been

---

1 Zach. 13: 6

poured in abundance that wounds Him with ingratitude and disregard. And in this sense we may say that one drop of gall from such a loved one is bitterer to Him than all He suffered during Holy Thursday night.

When speaking of the offenses of His own people, of those of His household, of His friends, He said to St. Margaret Mary, "This is what is most painful to Me." For this sin He asked of His confidante and apostle a special act of reparation. We certainly cannot shut our eyes to the thousands of very grave transgressions by which the sacred majesty of God is outraged, especially in our large modern towns, which are so many Ninevehs and Babylons. But I have abundant reason for saying that many of these transgressions would not be committed if we — *the children of His predilection* — love Him as we should. Let us not begin by mourning and making reparation for the sins of the wicked, but rather for the slackness and apathy, the indifference of those who, like ourselves, are the work of infinite love.

Oh! if we but loved Thee, Jesus, as we love creatures, when we squander our affections on them! For it must be admitted that in spite of our pettiness we all have a reserve of nobility hidden in the depths of our souls, a store of generosity, much unsuspected courage and self-abnegation. In time of danger or misfortune these treasures are suddenly discovered. We know how to love when we want to do so, but we rarely desire to love Jesus ardently. He is so neglected that we shut our hearts to Him, while we open them wide to others far more exacting than He is. Poor Jesus!

During the war I witnessed among soldiers and nurses innumerable acts of the most amazing heroism which — though performed but yesterday — will soon seem to have been fabulous and legendary. How often, when wondering at their marvelous patriotism and their exuberant martial spirit, I have felt my soul oppressed by great sadness, for I thought within myself, "Never in my life have I done for Jesus the thousandth part of what I am admiring in this soldier or this nurse, and I am a priest and call myself an apostle!" One's country, the national honor, the family are sacred ideals which always call forth noble sentiments in the solemn hour of danger, and Jesus who created these exquisite feelings, Jesus, the most lovable of kings, fails to touch us, fails to incite us to doing splendid deeds of virtue. His country, our heaven of tomorrow, is less alluring to us than this earth on which we live.

I am not addressing the indifferent or unbelievers, but the virtuous. I believe in their sincerity. I know they have true and sterling faith, but I fear *they do not love with all their hearts*. Can you otherwise explain the fact that in many countries where neither the faith nor competent Catholic organization is lacking, the hosts of Satan have made a formidable advance? They have been able to plan the paganizing of society, and they are actually realizing it with complete impunity, or almost without resistance. I am convinced that good people disapprove of this disgraceful state of affairs, yet they take no step against it. They should erect an insurmountable barrier against the enemy and organize a firm resistance; *they should be ready to die rather* than see their churches, schools and homes desecrated by the enemies of Christ. In these hours of trial and danger, their hearts should awaken, but they remain unmoved and indifferent when our Lord's rights and interests are involved, for Jesus is not loved. Our faith is languid. Our love is measured out grudgingly to a God who loves us without measure. That is a great sin which much retards our spiritual progress and that of the souls among whom we labor.

* * *

Without ardent charity the true Christian spirit gradually dies out or brings forth but a scanty harvest, for no other virtue can produce, or make perfect, what love alone begets. Wherever I go, I meet with complaints among superiors and inferiors. Whether listening to them in the convent or in the world I draw my own conclusions, namely, that as the love of God becomes cooler, people become more and more unhappy. I may declare with St. Paul that the whole perfection

178

of the law — whether in social or in religious circles — consists in love and love alone.

LACK OF SPIRIT OF SACRIFICE

The unanimous opinion of the clergy and all who deal with souls is that the spirit of sacrifice is dying out among the rising generation and the idol of self is being set up in its place. "Self" rules supreme. This is only logical, for there is but one Master of self-abnegation, namely, Jesus Christ! The cross is the only forge in which the metal of personality can be given a Christian shape. Either we passionately love that Master with His cross, or we replace Him by the idol known as "Self." And we cannot forget Self unless we greatly love Him who alone can overcome our selfishness. Those who really love our Lord always rejoice in their suffering whatever they may be.

LACK OF ZEAL

The needs of the Church are growing, but apostles do not come forward to meet them in sufficient number. Many of the faithful take no interest in their brethren's souls, and although the movement towards the Heart of Jesus has drawn many to join the ranks of the apostolate, there are others who resist and care nothing for the interests of our Lord. This is because, in spite of all their pious practices and retreats, they have not really grown in the love of Jesus. They are content to vegetate, satisfied with refraining from all that is not really wrong. If we wish to increase the number of true apostles, rather than the number of workers, let us teach the heart to love.

LACK OF EUCHARISTIC FERVOR

There is no doubt that since the days of St. Pius X we have gained much in Eucharistic spirit and fervor. What that great pope did for the God of the tabernacle will endure and continue to develop. Nevertheless, we have not profited as we might have done by the impetus given by Pius X. His decree relative to Holy Communion has not yielded the results it should have produced. The words of Pius X, " I desire that the faithful partake frequently of Holy Communion," can only be realized by love; the fact that we are invited to the banquet is not sufficient, *there must be hunger for Jesus!* There must be *love* before, during and after receiving Holy Communion. Let us draw ever closer to Jesus by putting our whole confidence in Him. Intimacy with Jesus should be more widely preached and we should train ourselves in self-abandonment to the Heart of Jesus, exciting within our souls a great hunger and thirst for sacrifice and souls, *all for love* of *Jesus*. Real lovers of Jesus cannot let even a single day pass without receiving Him in the sacred host.

SCOURGING BY FRIENDS

Here I should like to bring to a close this talk on reparation. But it would be cowardice on my part if, when speaking of *the sins of friends*, I were silent about that one which provokes sorrow and righteous anger in our late Holy Father, Pope Pius XI. I refer to the great sin of *immodesty*, of *shamelessness among many Catholics* and even, as this pope said, among the *pious* and *devout*.

I am certain that the indignation of the Vicar of Christ exactly reflects the deep wound inflicted in the Sacred Heart, a wound rendered crueler by the fact that so few have obeyed the pope by changing their behavior in this matter. This canker is eating away the best elements of Christian society, insensibly perverting and paganizing families which are by tradition Christian and religious; immodesty and frivolity mask a true carnival of sin.

I fear the wanton disregard shown by many Christians for the pope's grief — and for his explicit pronouncements on decorum in dress — will bring a curse on those who are still grieving the Sovereign Pontiff. I hope that I am mistaken, but I feel that I am not. Woe to those women who incur the responsibility of many a grave sin by their immodest clothing! Woe to those mothers who tolerate these abuses in their daughters and let *their little ones go about half dressed*, thus accustoming them to a nudity which the Church condemns, and who — on the pretext that their children are innocent — *culpably disobey the pope and bishops.* If such mothers only knew what they are laying up for themselves later on! But they foolishly imagine they know better than their pastors. Today they smile, careless of the consequences; tomorrow, alas! their tears will choke them!

I am not alluding to evil-minded, worldly people; I am lamenting an inconceivable aberration on the part of persons who are actually frequent communicants. May our Blessed Lord pardon them! How are we to explain this incredible blindness, this tenacity in following indecent fashions, in a professedly good Catholic woman? Is this depravity on her part? No, but she *loves herself* much more than she loves Jesus Christ. Hence the absurd anomaly of her wearing an immodest dress and yet displaying a medal of the Immaculate Virgin or bearing within her heart the sacred host.

Ah! Jesus, did they but truly love Thee with the passion of a bride for her newly-wedded spouse, or the rapture of a mother for her little babe, they could never thus offend Thee. A wife who truly loves her husband will never dress in a manner displeasing to him. But how few fear to offend Thee, Jesus, the Love of loves.

O Immaculate Queen, of thy mercy work a great miracle in *Christian homes* for the glory of Jesus and to close the gates of hell to many souls. Tear away the thick wall which blinds so many women to this evil which the Roman Pontiff deplores so bitterly. But above all, O sweetest Mother instill in their hearts a passionate love of Jesus that will lift them above the follies of the world which incites them to set even the lowest passions before Thy Jesus, His Heart and His law.

* * *

As you see, I have but one idea: "to make Jesus loved." This is my solution to all difficulties. Christ loved and much loved is the infallible and divine panacea for all evils. You may remember the simple and profound words of the Little

181

Flower: "For my part, I do not want to be little, mortified and humble that I may learn to love. That is not my way. I wish to love in order to be little, I wish to grow in love that I may be mortified, I wish above all to love much that I may be very humble." The surest method and the shortest way in the spiritual life is to begin by love, to go on by love, and to reach the crowning point by love.

Beginning with ourselves, dear apostles, let us make reparation for our want of true love and meditate upon the first commandment of the old law and of the law of grace: *Thou shalt love the Lord thy God with thy whole heart and with they whole soul and with all thy strength.*

Love, and you will be good Catholics.
Love, and you will be faithful friends of the divine King.
Love, and you will be His heralds and apostles.

Spare us O Lord!
Increase our love!

Chapter 17

MOTHER AND QUEEN

"To Jesus through Mary."

THE LESSON OF THIS RETREAT would be incomplete and the King of Love Himself would reproach me if I did not speak to you, apostles of His divine Heart, of Mary the Mother of fair Love. "Before all ages, in the beginning"[1] she was intimately and inseparably united to the Word in the divine plan of the Redemption. He was the Redeemer, she the Immaculate co-Redemptrix. Let us then respect and adore the design of the Most High by keeping the Hearts of Jesus and Mary perfectly united. To Them be honor and glory for ever and ever!

My road to reach the Holy of Holies, to the very heart of Jesus, to the most intimate recesses of that sanctuary of justice and of love, is perfectly mapped out for me. The necessary and direct road is Mary. No one goeth to the Father save through the Son, "nor does anyone know the Father except the Son, and him to whom the Son chooses to reveal him."[2] So, too, we may say that no one goeth to the King unless led to Him by Mary, nor doth any one know the King but he to whom His beauty is revealed by the queen. Through her the Word came to us from the bosom of the Father. The Word could have chosen a thousand other ways, or no way at all, for neither bridges nor intermediaries are necessary to the purposes of God. It was His explicit will that, just as God was to come to men through Mary, so

---

1 Sir. 24: 9   2 Matt. 11: 27

redeemed humanity should also go to God through her. No Christian worthy of the name will choose any other road than Mary, the one planned out by Him who called Himself "the Way."

To be unwilling to pass through the arms of the Immaculate Queen in our soul search for God and for His Son would be to presume to rectify what He Himself accomplished in the stupendous miracle of the Incarnation. By eliminating Mary we would neither straighten the road, nor shorten the distance between us and God, for, to suppress the Mother of Jesus, the divine intermediary, is not at all the same as abolishing the royal antechamber in the palace of the King. Mary is the sanctuary itself, wherein He dwells. Since the Annunciation, she has occupied such a position between God and His creatures that anyone seeking to avoid her intervention, or to eliminate this "gate of Heaven," will lengthen the road and be exposed to the grave risk of never reaching the final goal.

In Bethlehem, the shepherds, kings and even Joseph received the adorable Baby from Mary's hands. She took up her Treasure and, after tenderly embracing Him, *lent* Him to those who had been so happy as to receive a special summons to the crib. When they had caressed and adored the Child, they returned Him to His mother's loving arms. For many years, Jesus did nothing of importance without asking Mary's leave, if only to give her another proof of His filial tenderness and love. The words "He was subject to them,"[3] cause Mary to stand out in bold relief. Like a queen she commands, decides, directs, and Jesus is obedient to her.

It is the Will of God that the voluntary dependence of Jesus on Mary and Mary's queenly right of giving Jesus to us should still subsist and be rendered more sublime by the glory of Son and mother. Though Mary holds so high a place in the heavenly hierarchy and is unique among all creatures by virtue of her divine maternity, yet she is but a creature. Mary of Nazareth, our sister, one of our own flesh and blood.

---

3 Luke 2: 51

Therefore we may call ourselves the kith and kin of that sweet queen who reigns in heaven surrounded by angelic hosts.

"Thou, O Queen Immaculate, art the bridge set by God Himself between the paradise we have lost and the paradise we hope to gain. May Jesus come to us by thy hands and may thy arms, O Queen and Mother, bear us to the depths of His adorable Heart!"

Jesus is our perfect model of filial love for Mary, for, except His heavenly Father, no one was so dear to Him. The first words lisped by the divine Babe were surely, "Mother . . . . Mary," and they came from the depth of the God Man's Heart. He loved her as only God could love the most holy and matchless of creatures. "You are beautiful, my beloved, and there is not a blemish in thee."[4]

Jesus loved her with the gratitude of God, because by her "Fiat" she gave Him what He lacked as God, the power to suffer and to die. Jesus loved her with the gratitude of a Son who drew His life from her and slept peacefully in her loving arms. His Heart enjoyed the tender caresses and watchful care which Mary lavished on Him, the Son of God and her own Son!

Jesus loved her during those thirty years of closest intimacy, when the Hearts of Son and Mother were united by the continual converse of their souls, by that passion and secret agony which throughout their lives crucified them both. Jesus loved her on Good Friday and gave His Heart to her on the Via Dolorosa to strengthen and comfort her! How He loved her when He fixed His dying eyes upon her and entrusted His Church and all mankind to her in the person of St. John.

Thus you see, dear apostles, that we have learned the love of Mary in a good school, that of the Heart of Jesus. We cannot be mistaken in loving what He loved and as He loved. By thus imitating Him in the love He bore His mother, we are drawn into a closer intimacy with His most Sacred Heart and we give Him great joy and glory. Let us therefore love

4 Cant. 4: 7

to repeat the "Salve Regina," with a slight and very beautiful variation: Not only "after," but "during this our exile, show unto us the blessed fruit of thy womb, Jesus, O clement, O loving, O sweet Virgin Mary."

MARY, TEACHER OF APOSTLES

We have seen that no one can teach us to love Mary as well as Jesus, for no one knew or loved her as He did. We may add that Mary, more than any other, will lead us to the knowledge and love of Jesus. She alone can break the seven seals of that mysterious and divine Book, the Word of God. Neither the prophets nor the saints ever read in it as she did. She is the "Seat of Wisdom" who bore within her the Sun of Uncreated Light.

We are overcome with amazement on reading how little the apostles understood of all our Lord had taught them. Though they had been eyewitnesses of so many astounding miracles, we find them at the beginning of Passion week, and even after the Resurrection, wanting in trust and little enlightened by what they had seen and felt. Truly "they had eyes and saw not; they had ears and heard not."[5] Then came the great light of Pentecost which gave them new strength and so enlightened their minds that the veil which shrouded the mystery was rent and the scales fell from their eyes. Awestruck and happy, they trembled at the great revelation made to them by the Paraclete. Only then did they fully and entirely grasp that they had lived on familiar terms with the Messias, the Son of God.

We can imagine their astonishment, their stupefaction, when they saw and understood what the Holy Spirit was revealing to them about that Jesus who had been their Friend and Master. They had fled from Him in terror, Judas had betrayed Him and the Jews had cruelly put Him to death. He had lived in their midst, He, the Desired of nations, the Redeemer of Israel foretold by the prophets. He was the Word, the Son of God, born of the blessed Mother whom

5 Ps. 113B: 5, 6

186

they had hitherto appreciated so little. For if they were blind to the lessons taught by the miracles, still less did they understand those to be learned from the silence and modesty of His mother. But, on the day of Pentecost they turned with profound respect and tender veneration to Mary, who presided over them in silence — though yielding the place of honor to Peter — and who from that hour became the tabernacle and living oracle of all the secrets of God.

Before the apostles dispersed, they must often have gathered round their Queen, plying her with questions, begging to be told the secrets which she kept hidden in her heart. Conscious that a great part of that treasure belonged by right to the infant Church, she, tenderly, modestly and with great wisdom expounded to the astonished apostles *what she alone knew.* Thus the apostles and evangelists learned many things which no one otherwise could ever have known, or even guessed, such as, for example, the whole mystery of the Annunciation. Some of them are to be found in the Gospels, but others have only been handed down to us as the traditions of the Church. Mary sought to satisfy, as far as possible, the evergrowing eagerness of the apostles to know the tiniest details about Bethlehem, the flight into Egypt and the sojourn there, the thirty years of obscurity, subjection and intimate life of Jesus at Nazareth. If Mary had kept silence those secrets would have been lost to us. No one but the angels were witnesses of what was said and done in that cottage, and perhaps the angels, from the very fact that they were angels, saw and understood less than Mary did.

Enlightened by the Holy Ghost and instructed by Mary, the apostles carried with them — when they dispersed — the flame of charity, quickened and intensified. Many a time the thought of Mary helped them to face a thousand obstacles, dangers and even martyrdom. John, the beloved of the Heart of Jesus and Mary's special favorite, kept, even more than the other apostles, a fresh and loving memory of the Virgin Mother's teaching and affection.

Dear apostles, draw near to the mother with filial love

187

that she may lead you to her Son and open wide the entrance to the Sacred Heart. She will lead you by paths known to her alone, paths along which she led the saints, till she brings you to the full and intimate knowledge of the Word made flesh. Draw near her in your Communions and beseech her to give you her divine Child, so that, in your turn, you may give Him to souls. How easy it is to give Jesus when we have received Him from Mary's hands.

MARY, MOTHER OF MERCY

Though Jesus belongs entirely to Mary, there is something in Him which belongs more specially to her. It is *His Sacred Heart*. What St. Francis of Assisi, St. Gertrude or St. Margaret Mary knew of that adorable Heart is but a drop compared with what she knew of that abyss of love and mercy. For if our Lord resembled His Blessed Mother in features and in beauty, how much more likeness must there have been between the Heart of Jesus and the Heart of Mary? We call her "Mother of fair love" and "Mother of Mercy." She is the mother of Him who is the Love of loves. He himself created His mother in His own image, making her the most loving and gentle of all creatures, so that her Immaculate Heart perfectly reproduces our Lord's own charity.

She loved Him as perfectly as any human creature could. She loved Him as a spotless virgin, as a spouse chosen out of myriads. Mary loved God as a mother, because the Word who had clothed Himself in mortal flesh, was in very truth her Son. Resting on her heart, He smiled upon the world, looked out on it with infinite compassion, and from her arms gave it His first blessing. Weeping on the altar of her heart, He offered Himself to the Heavenly Father as an infinitely merciful Redeemer. Thus, if Jesus is the God of mercy, Mary is the altar and throne of mercy, reproducing the infinite compassion of the Heart of Jesus, teaching and dispensing lavishly the doctrine of merciful love. From the heart of Mary you will learn to be kind, compassionate and merciful to others and the Mother of fair love will bless your apostolate and answer your prayers for the good of souls.

I remember, as a boy of twelve, I was very friendly with a pious Catholic family who had a protestant relation living with them. He was extremely bigoted and at that time was very ill. During the May devotions which were daily held in the house, we made his conversion our principal intention. One evening while we were thus engaged, we heard the sick man's bell ring violently. Hastening to his bedside, we found him in his agony. We at once began to recite the rosary, begging that he might be converted before he died. After a few moments, the invalid opened his eyes and gasped, "I wish to die a Catholic; I wish to be baptized."

You can imagine our astonishment and joy! A servant ran to the Church, but all the priests were out on sick calls. It was evident that he had not long to live. So one of us baptized him. At that very moment the dying man smiled and said, "I am so happy. Say a prayer to the Blessed Virgin." He asked for her picture, which he clasped and kissed, shedding many tears. We then slowly recited the "Salve Regina," and he, struggling for breath, made a loving effort to repeat the whole prayer after us. When at last we got to the words "O clement, O loving, O sweet Virgin Mary," he raised the picture to his lips, gave it one last kiss and yielded up his soul to God.

THROUGH MARY TO JESUS
IN THE BLESSED SACRAMENT

"Show thyself a mother," a girl once said to the Blessed Virgin in a moment of anguish and Mary answered with gentle sadness, "First show thyself my daughter." May we never have to merit a like rebuke from Mary's mouth. We must thoroughly understand what it means to be the children and disciples of such a mother. It is a praiseworthy homage to place flowers on Mary's altar, but she would much prefer as a proof of filial love a fervent and loving communion. She knows that the manna of the Eucharist glorifies the King, her Son, and brings profound and enduring good to souls. The more true love for Mary progresses and intensifies, the

189

brighter will glow the Eucharistic flame. Devotion to Mary and love of the Tabernacle should be one and the same thing.

It must be our aim to convince families of the Sacred Heart that Mary is the tabernacle of tabernacles and that we should approach her immaculate Heart with true devotion, begging her to give us the blessed Fruit of her womb, Jesus. By so doing, we pay the highest possible homage to the Blessed Virgin and, at the same time, honor and adore her divine Son in the precious monstrance of her most pure Heart. Thus, to the great joy of our Lord, of the Blessed Virgin and of the Church, all the feasts of Mary, including the May devotions, will soon bear the Eucharistic stamp. This has already been partly accomplished. Our Lady of Lourdes is instilling this doctrine of true love more and more deeply into the hearts of the multitudes who throng to honor her, and we hope to achieve still more by our Crusade for the Social Reign of the Sacred Heart. Love of Mary is the best preparation for the triumph of Jesus in the sacred host.

The devotion to Mary is in perfect accordance with the Gospel and with the whole spirit of the Catholic Church. It is summed up in the following prayer: "Holy Mother, I love thee because thou art the Mother of Jesus and my Mother. I come before thee to protest that I love thee with my whole soul, with all the tenderness of a child for its mother. I implore thee to open the tabernacle so that Jesus may come to me through thy hands. He is thine, give Him to me, O Mother, and grant that He may be mine in time and in eternity."

Chapter 18

THE PRIME MINISTER
OF THE KING OF LOVE

DEVOTION TO THE POPE

After speaking of Mary, the Queen of fair love, let us at once turn our thoughts to the Roman Pontiff, the living voice and the very image of Jesus Christ in the Church.

The pope is one of the richest gifts of Christ's most merciful love. Recall that beautiful scene along the Lake of Tiberias, when after receiving a threefold profession of love from Peter, the divine Master makes him His representative on earth, the dispenser of His power, investing him with that full authority to which kings as well as their people are subject. His dignity far surpasses all human grandeur. The Vatican, that summit ever colored with the divine majesty, is the Sinai of the new Law whence God dictates to the new Moses — the pope — His sovereign Will.

Apostles and friends of the great King, lend me an attentive ear, a docile heart. The devotion to the pope, so important, so eminently Catholic, is not sufficiently known.

The King of Glory and His august vicar must be loved, I should say, with a selfsame love, venerated with a selfsame veneration; both must be obeyed with the same unlimited, perfect obedience. Not that we wish to confound God with His representative, but because the honor bestowed upon the Sovereign Pontiff is rendered to Jesus Himself. Has He not said, "He who hears you, hears me; and he who rejects

191

you, rejects me"?[1] And may we not add with as much certainty "He that honors and loves you, honors and loves Me"?

Fear no exaggeration, for the Gospel testifies most explicitly that the pope is, by right divine, our visible Jesus upon earth.

This reminds me of a private audience with which I was gratified by the Sovereign Pontiff and the answer His Holiness made to one of my remarks. "Holy Father," said I, "I always request prayers for the pope, for I unite the Eternal King and His vicar in one same love. I often preach the devotion to the pope, whom I consider as a kind of second Eucharist."

His Holiness suddenly interrupted me and said: "Oh! you do well, my son, and you are quite right in saying that the pope is as a second Eucharist. Unfortunately the beauty and necessity of devotion to the pope is not always understood. You, my son, spread this devotion wherever you preach the King of Love."

Yes, dear apostles, the pope is a visible Jesus, concealed beneath a thin white veil as in the sacred host; another Jesus, a living, authentic Jesus is truly present under the cover and disguise of Peter. The name changes: we call him Pius, Benedict, John. These are external accidents which disappear and change: the substance remains immutable. It is ever Jesus to whom the Father has given as a heritage, all nations of the earth[2] and a name which is above all names.[3]

From this true and beautiful symbolism, let us now draw some practical conclusions. To the pope, this Eucharist of the Vatican, we owe the greatest, the most profound respect, the highest honors, as a homage of our intellect; to him we owe an immense, devoted, tender and filial love, as a homage of our will. To prove our submission, our steadfast obedience, our unswerving devotion to the pope, we should be ready, as O'Connell, the great Irish hero says, to waive

1 Luke 10: 16   2 Ps. 2: 8
3 Phil. 2: 9

all personal interests, and if necessary seal our loyalty with our blood.

Happy, a thousand times happy are you, dear apostles, whose enlightened faith enables you ever to distinguish Jesus beneath this thin white veil. Happy are you who well nigh confound what our Lord seems to have confounded and blended together on earth — His own self and the pope — whether in the attribution of His power, "Whatever thou shalt bind on earth shall be bound in heaven,"[4] or in His formal demand of perfect submission to the appointed Shepherd of His Flock, "Feed my lambs, feed my sheep."[5]

If Jesus has promised heaven in reward for the good done to a little child;[6] if He has condemned the scandal given to this little one who represents Him,[7] how much richer must be the blessings He bestows on the families that honor, serve, console and obey His own vicar on earth. On the contrary, what wrath do they not bring down upon themselves who, in thought, word or deed, dare to profane this second Eucharist, the pope?

A mountain, the Vatican, distinguishes us from those outside the church, for the touchstone is and ever will be Peter. His authority soars far above and beyond all human discussion and control. It is indeed the pope who, in the face of all human authorities, all existing tribunals, may apply to himself, in the full sense of the word, the categorical expression of St. Paul, "He who judges me is the Lord."[8] Yes, the only Judge, the only tribunal to which the Sovereign Pontiff is accountable is the tribunal of the Most High, the tribunal of the King of Kings. In the meantime, while on this earth, his commandments have the character of "supremacy" for all true Catholics. Hence the axiom: "Rome has spoken, the question is settled." This is truth which shall remain eternally.

---

4 Matt. 16: 19
5 John 21: 15, 17
6 Matt. 18: 5
7 Matt. 18: 6
8 1 Cor. 4: 4

Dear and zealous apostles, teach this beautiful doctrine, spread it around you, weary not in explaining that the Holy Father's slightest desires are sacred to his children, to Catholics true at heart and worthy of their title. Especially stress the point that his formal orders are inviolable laws which cannot be transgressed, without sin. This you know full well is a fundamental principle of our faith and of religious discipline.

Promote true love for the pope wherever the Sacred Heart has been enthroned as King of the family. By this sublime term "love," I wish to imply all that the immortal Pontiff, Pius X, implied when he wrote the following words: "When people love the pope, they do not discuss his orders; they do not question the extent of their obedience, nor in what matters they are to obey. When people love the pope, they do not pretend that he has not spoken clearly enough, as if he were obliged to whisper in each one's ear that which he has oftentimes expressed so clearly in words and encyclicals. One cannot cast a doubt upon his orders under the pretext so commonly adduced by those who are unwilling to obey, that it is not the pope who commands, but those who surround him; one cannot limit the ground on which he may and ought to exercise his authority; in matters of authority, one cannot give the preference to persons whose ideas clash with those of the pope, however learned these may be, for though they be learned, they are not saints." Such are the very words of the great Pope of the Eucharist.

*   *   *

Families of the King of Love, you His intimate friends, do you wish to know a secret that shall ravish His Sacred Heart? — Love the Pope with an immense, filial love. Love him with that supernatural affection made of a profound gratitude, a perfect, integral submission that will stand any proof. To the love which is due to the Vicar of Christ, we may apply the ringing words of St. Paul: "Neither death, nor life, nor angels, nor principalities, nor things present, nor things to come, nor powers, nor height, nor depth, nor any other creature will be able to separate us from the love of God"[9] and of His sweet visible Christ, His *alter ego,* the pope.

I have spoken of the pope as a second Eucharist. Consider therefore, that if the Eucharist, the God-Man, is at an infinite distance above all creatures, yet the voice of the pope has the right to assure us of that divine Presence in the consecrated host. This is a sublime right which marks the transcendency of the papal authority. Hence it is that all heretics have begun by rejecting the cornerstone, Peter, accusing him of going beyond his power, of trespassing on the domain of philosophy, science, history, politics, etc. ... And once they have broken away from his authority for one or the other of these reasons, they have logically thrown overboard the treasures of our faith which we call Catholic unity, the Holy Eucharist, the sacraments.

I close these reflections, so important, and no doubt, so interesting to all friends and promoters of the Reign of the Sacred Heart, by relating the little anecdote that gave rise to the title of this chapter.

At the audience which followed the reception of the famous autographed letter of His Holiness, Pope Benedict XV, which officially entrusted to us the work of the Enthronement, as I was thanking the Holy Father for this great and unexpected favor, he said to me, "Do not thank me, my son, do you not say that you are the apostle of the great King Jesus?" — "Yes indeed, Your Holiness, that I wish to be with my whole soul!"

"Well then," replied the pope, "you preach the King, I am His prime minister; it is I then who am to thank you for what you do for the King of Love."

Dear apostles of the King of Love, may Jesus confirm the word of His prime Minister, may He confirm it for you and for me in life and in death. May He confirm it by the richest blessings of His adorable Heart.

---

9 Rom. 8: 38-39

PART II

AT HOME WITH THE SACRED HEART

Jesus, King and Friend of the Family

Chapter 19

THE ENTHRONEMENT OF THE SACRED HEART IN THE HOME

THE ENTHRONEMENT IS THE OFFICIAL and social recognition of the rule of the Sacred Heart of Jesus over the Christian family, a recognition affirmed, outwardly expressed and made permanent by the solemn installation of the image of that divine Heart in a conspicuous place in the home, and by the Act of Consecration.

The God of infinite mercy said in Paray-le-Monial: "Being Myself the fount of all blessings I will distribute these abundantly wherever the image of My Heart has found a place, to the end that It may be loved and honored." And further: "I will reign in spite of My enemies and all those who attempt to oppose Me."

The Enthronement then is simply the realization, not of this or that one of the requests made by our Savior to St. Margaret Mary, but the complete and integral realization of all of them, calling forth the fulfillment of the splendid promises with which the King of Love has enriched them. Note that we say "integral realization" of all the requests made in Paray; for the supreme end of the Enthronement is not, and ought not to be, to further a new pious practice, but to *sanctify the home*, and convert it into a living and social throne for the divine King.

REBUILD THE WORLD ON THE HOME

Truly, in order that the world may be transformed and saved, it is absolutely necessary that the Nativity should be not only a great feast, but a living and lasting reality; in other words, that Jesus, our Emmanuel, should be really and truly *dwelling among us,* His brethren, who are much more weak than evil. Let us not deceive ourselves; in order to bring about the day, be it far or distant, of the Social Reign of Jesus Christ, proclaimed and revered as King ruling by Sovereign right throughout the whole of human society, it will be necessary for us to re-fashion the society of today from its very basis, that is to say to rebuild it on the model of Nazareth. Every nation is worth what its family life is worth, for a nation has ever been, either in holiness or corruption, that which the home is. There has never been any exception whatever to this rule.

In this connection, I remember what a great convert once said to me: "Father, you cannot exaggerate the importance of the crusade which you are preaching. I know what I am speaking about: the Freemasons, of whom I was one for so many years, have but one single aim, and that is the *dechristianizing of the family.* Once this object is attained, in whole or in part, they may safely leave in the possession of Catholics all the cathedrals, churches and chapels. Of what importance are these buildings of stone when they have taken possession of the sanctuary of the home? In the measure in which this sectarian strategy is successful, the victory of hell will be secure. It was thus I reasoned, and for this I worked, Father, when I was in the ranks of Freemasonry." Alas, what the Gospel says will always be true, that "the children of this world are in relation to their own generation more prudent than are the children of the light."[1]

The great evil, the evil of evils, in our society today is that the sense of the supernatural, of the Divine, is lost. But there is assuredly a remedy for it, and that is to take again the road of the Gospel, and return to Nazareth. The Eternal Wisdom willed to found the redemption of the world on the corner stone of the Holy Family. In it the Word, Jesus, our Brother, commenced His work of redemption. By no other

---

1 Luke 16: 8

way than this ought we to try to save the modern world; we must mold it after the pattern, so simple, yet so sublime, of Nazareth.

How eloquently men have described and illustrated by photographs the hideous destruction of churches and shrines in what was the immense field of battle in the Great War! Cathedrals, monasteries, chapels were razed to the ground in the inevitable swaying back and forth of armies. How much more appalling is the moral ruin of this thrice holy sanctuary which is the home. Basilicas and cathedrals, however magnificent and venerable they be, will not redeem the world, but holy families will do so. This is logical, for the *family is the source of life and the first school of the child. Hence, if the fount is poisoned, the nation will perish.* Our purpose then, in this campaign, is to *inoculate the home,* and the principle of education in the home, *with Jesus Christ* and the sap of His divine love in such a way that *the tree may finally be Jesus Christ Himself* in the blossom and fruits it bears.

JESUS IS KING AND FRIEND OF THE HOME

The Enthronement, then, properly understood, is Jesus King of Love, coming to the threshold of the home and asking for His place in it; one which belongs to Him by divine right, the same which He was offered in the villa of Bethany. And it is a place of honor because He is the *King*[2] who, at no distant time and by His loving conquest of the families, will reign over the whole world. It is also a place of intimacy because He wants to be in very truth the Friend.[3] In a word, the Enthronement teaches us how to dwell with Jesus in our homes.

Alas! How little Jesus is known! and consequently how little He is loved! ... The majority of those who call themselves Christians fear Him, and keep far from Him. ... If not with their lips then by their works, they say to Him: "Remain in Your Tabernacle, O Lord, that we may live our

---

2 John 18: 37   3 *Cf.* Cant. 5: 16

family life as we wish, without Your intruding too intimately upon it. Do not come too close to us, do not speak to us, or we shall die."[4]

Thus did the Jews speak to Jehovah, thus do His children go on speaking to their Father and Shepherd! We persist in not seeing in Jesus our Savior who is so sweet, so accessible, so gentle and so simple, the King of Love, who "... found delight in the sons of men,"[5] who in His mortal life rejoiced to lodge in the house of sinners, [6] or to preside at the Marriage in Cana,[7] showing us in a thousand enchanting and marvelous ways that the delight of His Heart was to share our life with all its difficulties and joys.

THE FRIEND OF SINNERS

We plead our unworthiness! What an absurdity! As if Zacheus was worthy, who out of curiosity and for no other reason, put himself in the path of his Savior. As if such persons as the woman of Canaan, the woman of Samaria, Simon the Pharisee, and so many other sharers in our fallen state were worthy. No, not one of them was worthy; but they believed in the merciful love of the Master and accepted in all simplicity of heart His divine condescension. Happy those unfortunates whose afflictions attracted and moved the Heart of the Redeemer! For, with Him, salvation, peace and conversion entered those houses and those souls. "Today salvation has come to this house."[8] And what a Pharisaical pretext is *respect!* It is indeed effrontery and insolence, when the God of all Majesty strips Himself of His kingly robes, calls us, holds out His arms, and offers His hand, that we should presume to read Him a lesson by maintaining our distance, as if we would say: "Remember that Thou art God and King, withdraw Thyself apart." There are thousands and thousands of pseudo-Christians, who in spite of the Redemption, pretend to serve their Redeemer by establishing between

4 *Cf.* Exod. 20: 19   5 Prov. 8: 31
6 Matt. 9: 11   7 John 2: 2
8 Luke 19: 9

Him and them valleys, mountains, abysses, and all this out of respect!

True respect is a manifestation of love, and not a matter of etiquette, at any rate with Jesus. By His explicit will, respect is not a keeping at a distance, since He annihilated distance by His Incarnation and in the Eucharist. But in so doing He exacted, nevertheless, an adoration more complete and more perfect than that which *the Jews rendered Him trembling at a distance.* How many Christians there are whose baptism is but skin-deep, who in their souls are Jews, and live in a stage of exaggerated fear; who if Jesus should speak and say to them, "My little children," or "My friends," would die not of emotion and love but of terror! As for me, I can but say over and over again, "Let Moses and all the prophets be silent; let them hold their peace, however sweet sounding their voices, they do not impress me, for my soul yearns to hear but Thee, Jesus, who hast the words of eternal life and of love. Let me hear Thy voice, that I may preach Thee, the true Jesus, the Love of loves, the Son of God and the Son of Mary."

I remember a gentleman who considered himself to be a good Catholic saying to me: "What! expose in my room an image of the Sacred Heart of Jesus? Never, Father! What a want of respect! It would be the height of absurdity!" What would that bright specimen of a Catholic have done if he had seen with his own eyes the King of Kings conversing with sinners, seeking the confidence and intimacy of publicans and of so many other people by no means respectable or distinguished? This is but disguised *human respect* and hidden pride. As if the Jesus, whom the bride and bridegroom of Cana invited to preside at their wedding feast, could not feel Himself honored and in His place, in the living room of a Christian family. Is He not the King of Kings?[9] How sad and true it is to say that after twenty centuries of Christianity "Love is not loved!" We do .not sufficiently preach the love of Jesus Christ, and yet this love is not weak sentimentality. It is a love full of fire and life.

9 Apoc. 17: 14; 19: 16

And all this comes, in part at least, from people not reading, still less meditating on the Gospel, where every page expresses our Lord's desire for familiar intimacy with man. Do you think they were afraid of Jesus, those little ones of Galilee who, fascinated by His look, threw themselves into His arms, and rested on His Heart? When they were dragged from Him by force how quickly they returned to Him, attracted as by a magnet to the bosom of the Master. He can never be known and loved with passion, if our faith and piety do not lead us to live in close intimacy with Him. How can we love Him with a deep and personal love when we see but a distant and distorted image of Him? *On the contrary, who is there who having once seen His beauty will not hold all else as dull and miserable?*

JESUS AT BETHANY

Call to mind a scene which I venture to term a Gospel one, though we do not find it there textually. Let us call it *the first four visits of Jesus to Bethany.* If you read with your heart you will surely admit that the picture has a happy reality although the frame may be somewhat ornate. Something of the kind, and still more touching, must have happened in Bethany.

The first time Jesus came as a visitor, Mary was as yet a wandering and erring sheep, and He was received by Lazarus and Martha with a certain reserve not exempt from a legitimate curiosity. Close to them was the famous Nazarene whose miraculous deeds were being talked about everywhere. They kissed His hand and listened to Him. Who could He be? A rabbi? A prophet? Lazarus and Martha certainly felt flattered by this honor and their interest was roused by such a great personage. Something mysterious which emanated from His whole person had secretly touched and conquered the inmost fibers of their hearts. So it came about that when bidding Jesus good-bye at the threshold of their home they were carried away by an emotion they had never felt before and said, "Master, come back to Bethany. Do not forget us."

And Jesus, with a smile which gave them a glimpse of heaven, promised to return.

See Him on His second visit. There were flowers, there was expectancy as for a feast. Lazarus and Martha could scarcely control their joy. The Nazarene was approaching; with loving impatience they went out to watch for His arrival. *The respect they now felt was much greater than on His first visit, for love was beginning to dawn in their hearts.* This time they were not merely content with listening to Him; they had sufficient confidence to ask Him questions, so the conversation was almost familiar. How simple-hearted and good the Master is, they said to themselves! How sweet and yet impressive is His Majesty! His look refreshes and enlightens, His words transfigure and His Heart enraptures. This time, when He went away, Lazarus and Martha could scarcely restrain their tears, and both with one accord implored Him with simplicity and humility to return again, "From now on, it will be difficult for us to live without Thee; come back to us, Lord; this home is Thine, look on us as *Thy friends!*" And Jesus was touched and said to them, "I will gladly be your *Friend,* and, since you love Me, Bethany will be the oasis of My Heart."

What an outburst of joy and feast of love there was when Jesus returned for the third time! We may call this the loving welcome of the Enthronement. Lazarus and Martha had counted the hours to His return. Since the day when Jesus had promised to return as their friend, their life had been one of unbearable loneliness and longing. Nothing could calm their anxiety, nothing could make them smile. The one golden dream, or rather the one reality was Himself. Jesus had taken them by storm. At last, He for whom they had longed approached. They ran to meet Him; they fell at His feet and kissed His sacred hands. In real ovation of love and tenderness, they called Him with holy audacity *Friend,* and talked to Him with the holy familiarity of disciples who knew themselves to be favored, understood and loved.

Suddenly when the dialogue was at its warmest, there was

205

a hush; Lazarus drew yet closer to the Master, and throwing himself at the feet of his divine Friend, broke out into sobs.

"Why weepest thou?" Jesus asked him.

"Thou knowest all things," answered Lazarus.

"Yes," replied Jesus, "I know all things; but since we are true friends, speak, confide to Me thy whole soul."

Then while Martha hid her flushed face in her hands and wept in silence, Lazarus explained. "Master, we are two, but we *were* three in this house. Mary, our sister, covers us with grief and shame. They call her the Magdalen. We love her so much and she is now the dishonor of Bethany. Jesus, if thou art our Friend, restore her to us cured, saved, and purified."

Jesus, mingling His tears with theirs, replied, "Your sister shall return, she shall live and Bethany shall be happy!" When He took leave of them that evening, at the threshold of their home, Jesus blessed His two friends and repeated, "Mary will return to the fold for My father's glory and Mine."

The Gospel narrates the rest: the resurrection of the Magdalen, how at the Savior's feet she broke the alabaster box — symbol of her repentant heart — and anointed her Redeemer's head and feet with precious perfumes. And when the Lord returned for the fourth time to the house of His friends, the first to come out to greet Him, singing Hosannas, was Mary Magdalen. From that time on, in that sanctuary restored by the Prince of Peace and King of Love, the three lived for many years as inseparable as they had been before. But now the Heart of Jesus had strengthened the bond between the brother and sisters.

The Lord well knew the bitter grief that weighed upon this home. Nevertheless to relieve it He waited till the afflicted brother and sister wept upon His Heart, and confided their tribulation to Him. He waited till He was the King-Friend of Bethany, and only then did He work the miracle as a reward for their love, their friendship and their trust.

I repeat, these scenes are not met with in the Gospel, but is it not true that something similar and still more beautiful must have taken place in that favored household? Is it not true that you better understand now the beauty of the enthronement? What is there strange in the fact that the King of Bethany, ever constant in tenderness, should daily ratify by wonders and prodigies, what we have just asserted concerning the confidence of the true lovers of the Sacred Heart of Jesus? Happy the home which says when welcoming Him: "Stay with us,"[10] while the doors are, as it were, locked on Jesus, Who finds Himself bound forever with the bonds of love.

BETHANY REPRODUCED

The great need of our times is the reconstruction of Nazareth, or if you prefer, the reproduction of the family of Bethany, the home of the true friends of Jesus. I say "Bethany" because Nazareth, in its sublimity, will be unique throughout all ages, whereas in Bethany are creatures of our own condition, cast in our mold of clay, and therefore this home is wholly and perfectly imitable. And how many homes have, as Bethany had, what we can never imagine in Nazareth, souls like Magdalen's, and prodigal sons. Call to the Master, hearken to Him, treat Him as an intimate Friend, and you will witness resurrections even more marvelous than that of Lazarus, and conversions as wonderful and touching as that of Magdalen.

Unfortunately Jesus is too often refused admittance even in homes which make profession of Christianity. You will find Him, the King of kings, seeking a shelter and begging for love and compassion on the threshold of a home which so sorely needs Him! And if, here and there, He is occasionally admitted, there is more formality than love in receiving Him. He is not a friend, but merely a passing guest, a stranger to whom a formal courtesy must needs be paid. In such homes — and they are many — Jesus has to content Himself with empty forms and, so to speak, crumbs of love, He whose Heart is aflame with infinite Charity.

The moments we can devote to God in church are few,

---

10 Luke 24: 29

207

for our duties compel us to live our daily life at home. Unfortunately most of our religion is limited to those rare moments, and when we return to our homes we find them untenanted by Him who should be the center of our lives, the Lord and Friend of our homes. This is a very grave error, for we neither live, nor struggle for existence, nor suffer, nor in all probability do we die in church. We live, struggle, suffer, and most likely die in our own homes. In them, therefore, we ought to *live in close fellowship* with Him, our Cyrenean and the companion of our exile, so that, on the last day, He may be, not the inexorable Judge, but the King of Love and the devoted Friend. Indeed the very pagans had some sort of glimpse of such a need and that is why they invented their Household Gods. For a long period also, the early Church allowed fervent Christians to keep the Blessed Sacrament in their homes.

We are reviving and realizing something now of this most beautiful and consoling presence of our Lord by the Enthronement of the Sacred Heart in the Home. We certainly do not pretend to compare the symbol of love with His real and substantial Presence in the Consecrated Host. However, by means of the Enthronement, Jesus really enters the home to have a part in and guide the whole life of the family. His love becomes the soul of both parents and children and His Heart their shrine.

Great and close relations exist between the cult of the Sacred Heart and that of the Blessed Sacrament. In our crusade also, the link between the two tabernacles — the altar and the home, the Eucharist and the family hearth — ought to be close and intimate; in both of them, wherever the spirit of the Enthronement exists and is understood, there is the same living King and Friend, Jesus. Our object in fact is to form thousands and thousands of Eucharistic families by means of this crusade; then He will truly be the Master, the *King*.

"I HAVE LOST FAITH IN MIRACLES"

What does this Prince of Love do in a home which is really His own, as were Nazareth and Bethany? To use St.

John's words, I might say that if I were to write all that I have seen and felt of the mercy and loyalty of the Sacred Heart, "not even the world itself, I think, could hold the books that would have to be written."[11] If there is, indeed, anything that perplexes me in the pulpit, it is to make choice amongst the innumerable marvels I might relate and which no one can gainsay. My eloquence consists solely in that I can say I have seen mountains moved, I have heard the stones cry out, that is to say I have seen so many struck to earth like Paul on the road to Damascus!

It is because of this that I one day said to His Holiness Pope Benedict XV: "Holy Father, I am losing faith in miracles, for in order to believe it is necessary not to see, and I am daily seeing and feeling marvels." The most common case is that of a mother, daughter, or wife who, having made the Enthronement with fervor and lived according to its spirit, has wrested from the Lord a miracle of mercy: the stupendous and apparently hopeless conversion of a beloved one. To take one instance: I keep in the archives of the Work, among a thousand other trophies, the diploma on parchment of a Freemason of high rank, master of his lodge! God only knows the number of those who after him have been caught in the nets of this Work.

Would you like another example and a most moving one? It concerns the father of a family whose wife prayed and did penance for his conversion. She one day heard a sermon on the Enthronement, and said to herself, "This is my only hope." But how was she to proceed, what steps was she to take, since her husband was a lapsed Catholic? Suddenly a happy idea crossed her mind. Her birthday was drawing near and both her husband and her daughters were preparing for her feast. She would seize the favorable occasion with boundless confidence in the Sacred Heart. Having offered fervent prayers and sacrifices for the success of her plan, she approached her husband and begged, as proof of his affection, that she might be allowed to enthrone the Sacred

---

11 John 21: 25

Heart in their house on her birthday. To her great surprise, he gave his consent, but he warned her that he would not assist at the ceremony. The first part of the miracle was accomplished; but Jesus never does things by halves.

The day arrived; the ceremony was carried out with great love; and mother and daughters begged for the soul of the master of the house, promising in return to lavish love on the faithful Friend of Bethany. When everything was over, the husband entered the room out of curiosity and looked at the picture. Here, radiant with love, was Jesus, the King of his house! He lowered his eyes as if dazzled, paced up and down the room and looked at it again. This time he was struck to the heart. Thinking his emotion might proceed from overstrung nerves, he sought to crush his feelings by leaving the room for some fresh air. But attracted as if by an irresistible magnet he reentered. In spite of himself, he raised his eyes to the picture: There He was, He the Conqueror, offering him His Heart! With tears in his eyes, he drew aside his wife and stammered. "Whom have you let into the house? For hours there has been someone in the house, I tell you. I do not see Him, but I feel Him. *There is someone in the house.*" The mother called her daughters and they renewed their entreaties. At the end of the prayer, the father was on his knees behind them.

That very evening, his confession made, this new Lazarus, brought to life again, praised with his family the mercy of the King of Love.

THE FULFILLMENT OF HIS PROMISES

These facts excite our surprise and admiration; yet we should feel no astonishment, for however extraordinary they appear to us they are nothing but the faithful fulfillment of the promises made by Jesus in favor of the friends and apostles of His divine Heart. He Himself said:

"I will touch the most hardened hearts.
I will establish peace in their families.
I will bless all their undertakings.

*I will grant them all the graces proper to their state of life.
I will reign by My Heart."*

After these and other wonderful promises, if there were
to be no miracles in the homes of the Heart of Jesus, in those
which are truly His, it would be the greatest disappointment
to me; but I shall be spared this because God is true, entirely
worthy of our trust — and Jesus is God!

Therefore, receive Jesus into your homes as a *King* and
a *Friend*. He is a King, as He Himself said with sublime
majesty to the cowardly Pilate, and He desires that every
family and every nation should recognize and proclaim His
Kingship over human society. Jesus asks and exacts this of
you because He is King by right of Creation and Redemption:
Jesus of Nazareth. He asks it of you as an act of reparation,
and a consolation to His Heart. See Him stand at the doors
of countless houses, rich and poor, crowned with thorns, His
hair wet with the dew of the night, begging and imploring
to be admitted, asking for a shelter from the tempest that
has broken out against Him in the world. He has been ousted
by parliaments and courts of justice, banished from laws and
schools, and even sometimes from His very churches. Behold
Him wandering like a pilgrim, travel stained, sad and desti-
tute, on lonely roads, loaded with insults, offended by the
outrages heaped upon Him by ungrateful traitors. Hearken
to Him: He is knocking with His wounded hand and saying
to you: *I am Jesus, be not afraid, I am the King of Love.
Open to Me!*

"Poor Jesus!" Have compassion on Him, at least you, who
call yourselves His friends. Give Him shelter, for the mob
in its madness is pursuing Him with stones, shouting with
raucous voices: "Away with Him, He is guilty of death. Crucify Him! We will not have Him to reign over us." To make
up for this blasphemous cry throw your doors wide open
and say: "Lord, we love Thee and we beg Thee to reign
over this house. Be Thou the *King*." And be assured that
this hospitality which He asks of you with divine persistence
will be the greatest of blessings to you; He wants to enter
for your good.

He who calls at your door is the great, the unique Consoler. Have you, perhaps, no tears to be wiped away, no griefs for Him to soothe? Why ask such a question which serves but to re-open many a wound? Who can tend these wounds? Do you still believe in the healing power of creatures? You know that He, the God-Man, the Man of sorrows, has reserved for Himself the gift of bringing consolation. No one will ever be able to pour balm on the open sore in the heart of a mother, widow, or daughter, mourning for a loved one, no one except Jesus. What a long training is needed to be able to heal the wounds of the body. Is there no sublime, divine Red Cross to heal these hearts which have been rent with grief? Certainly, there is the loving Reign of the Heart of Jesus in the home. During the dark hours, He redoubles His knockings and calls to you again and again. "Do not delay," He says, "for I know there are desolate hearts here. Open to Me quickly, for I am Jesus."

Out of compassion for yourselves, open to Him and admit the Cyrenean of all your crosses. Open to Him, the Friend of Man, who is ever disinterested and true, who will never change, never betray you, and never die. Open your Bethany to Him, for it is never too late for the Friend Jesus. How sad it is that so many should mourn and suffer far from that Friend! For tears without Him poison the soul, and afflictions without Him are a foretaste of death. If He had been there, as Martha said, in our hours of bitterness, we should have found honeycombs in the open desert and flowers growing among the rocks. But we will not believe He calls us to a life of intimacy with Him. We look at Him from afar, and then, like the apostles who saw Him walking on the waters of Genesareth, we take Him for a phantom. But John, His beloved disciple, knew Him at once: *It is the Lord.*

We must live *close* to Jesus if we are to know Him as He is. It is by daily contact that members of a family learn to know and love one another. It should be the same with our older Brother. He wants to comfort us, but above all to save our souls. Even if we were saints we should need this help to work out our salvation. When you choose Him for your King in spirit and in truth He will overwhelm you with graces.

* * *

THE CEREMONY OF THE ENTHRONEMENT

Now let us say a few words about this simple and beautiful ceremony. Choose an image as beautiful and artistic as possible; set it in the place of honor in the house, for, behind this standard the divine King will come and take possession of the home, to remain forever in it as the adorable Friend.

And here I wish to say that love and a living faith will give the Enthronement a note of eagerness and enthusiasm which constitutes its proper character. For here there is certainly no place for cold and formal ceremony.

Let the parents and children assemble at this solemn hour. Friends and relations may also be invited, they will form the court of the King and learn a lesson of social adoration. All gather around the "throne" of the King. The father, mother and children stand nearest to the priest, who stands facing the image of the Sacred Heart. After the priest has blessed the picture or statue, the father or mother will solemnly install it in the place of honor prepared for it. This is the symbolic act of *Enthronement.*

Then all stand while the Apostles' Creed is said as a proclamation of the faith of this Christian family. At this point the priest will address a few words to those present about the ceremony, after which all kneel while the priest recites the official Act of Consecration. An Our Father and a Hail Mary then said for all the absent members of the family (whose photographs have been placed around the throne). Here follows a prayer of thanksgiving; an act of homage to the Immaculate Heart of Mary; the blessing by the priest and the signing of the family document.

But this pious ceremony is more than a consecration, for, in the Enthronement there is, in addition, the acknowledgment and social acclamation of the *Divine Kingship* of Our Lord. There is, too, the hosanna of love and reparation, the "Hail, King!" of the family, in the name of the great fatherland, the nation. This is why we use the word Enthronement. And precisely because you are receiving the King of Kings, display all the pomp you possibly can, so that Jesus may not reproach you as He did Simon the Pharisee: "I came into thy house; thou gavest me no water for my feet.... Thou gavest me no kiss.... Thou didst not anoint my head with oil..."[12]

GIVE HIM ROYAL HONORS!

You would not receive an important personage, a victorious general, say, or a papal legate, except with great honor and solemnity, but when Jesus comes, because He is silent and humble you put Him in some back room. Such indifference must surely wound His Heart. Receive Him royally like the King that He is. For Him alone the place of honor! Tepid faith and lack of love invent strange reasons about the inconvenience of receiving this Sovereign where the bishop or the king would be admitted. The real reason is often fear of having to change one's way of living and obeying the laws of God. *He can and should preside over everything,* and that which cannot be said or done in His presence, cannot be said or done *either in the house, or in the street.*

Give Him the seat of honor, the first place, the best room you have in the house. Make reparation in this way for the outrages of Herod, and that of so many of the great and powerful who relegate Him to the background or try to eliminate Him completely. St. Margaret Mary says on this subject: "He desires to enter with pomp and magnificence into the abode of princes and kings, in order that there may be rendered to Him as much honor as He suffered outrage and humiliation in His Passion."

But Jesus wants to reign just as much among the lowly, the poor, and the simple. See how gladly He returns to His

12 Luke 7: 44-46

214

favorite friends, the humble — He Himself the humblest of them all, stripped of all appearance of grandeur and majesty, with no more power than that of His wounds, and His Heart for His only wealth. See Him calling at the door of some hovel, or laborer's hut — He, the Artisan of Nazareth, born in a stable. "Open to Me quickly," He says, "for I have known, as you do, the gloomy uncertainty of what the morrow will bring, the hardships and anxieties of the poor. Out of love, I willed to be born and to live in poverty." No one has ever loved the lower classes as did Jesus, the adopted Son of Joseph the Carpenter; hence His longing to win them to Him by His Heart, and to make them happy by His Love. He wants those — for whom in His divine compassion He multiplied the five barley loaves and two fishes[13] — to know how different it is to suffer, to labor, and to endure hardships, when they have Him as a Compensation for their privations and a Consoler in their tribulations.

Oh! enthrone Him, the Poor One of Nazareth among the poor, His friends. How sweet it is for Him to preside over a frugal meal, in the cottage of some working people and to find Himself surrounded, as in ancient times, by hungry children and parents out of work and who need to be consoled. He will make these simple hearts understand why He said: "Blessed are the poor in spirit.... Blessed are they who mourn...."[14] He will make them realize that the matchless treasure is Himself, His Heart.

---

13 John 6: 9   14 Matt. 5: 3, 5

Chapter 20

BEHOLD, THE GREAT KING IS COMING!

FORTUNATE ARE THOSE who are prepared to receive Him!

Happy are those families who possess these priceless treasures — a Christian home, and the Sacred Heart King of the home. What a grace it is to know your home is the palace of the great King; that the adorable King is really the sovereign in your family.

I said, "happy families," and I stress the term, *really happy families*. But, is it possible to have happiness here on earth? Certainly! We have been created to be happy. Sin, it is true, destroyed the original and perfect happiness of our first parents, but Christ came to restore all things. And the first thing he brought back to us was peace, the essence of happiness. Once more then, Christian happiness is possible. It is a wonderful Christian reality. The greatest proof is the saints — millions of them — from Our Lady to the Little Flower, and so many others, all supremely happy.

Allow me to contradict the pagan assertions of those who do not follow the Gospel of Christ. In this matter they are absolutely wrong:

Happiness is not wealth — so many rich families are unhappy, so many poor homes really happy.

Happiness is not youth — youth is a springtime that passes and vanishes forever.

Happiness is not a brilliant position or title — this is merely a facade that one day will crumble into dust.

Happiness is not pleasure — sensual pleasures are like intoxicants that poison the system.

Happiness is not the absence of the cross — it is the presence of the crucified Master in a soul and in a home.

Hell starts where Jesus Christ is absent; Heaven starts in a home filled with His delightful presence.

When I preach the Sacred Heart, Prince of Peace, to the Christian families, I am inviting them to receive into their homes the Sacred Heart of Jesus. This is exactly the same request made by Jesus to Zaccheus the Publican: "This day I must abide in thy home!" When the invitation is accepted, then will be heard the same words Jesus spoke to the converted Publican, "This day salvation has come to this home!"

The beautiful ceremony is but the starting point. Behind the banner — the picture or statue — is the King of Love. A Christian home life is the Enthronement lived — the hidden Jesus blessing the home by His presence. Once more, I insist, with Him you can be truly happy. When Jesus is absent — never! That is the reason true happiness is so often lacking in home life: Jesus' spirit, Jesus' Gospel are not the ruling spirit — the Lord Jesus is not there. Such a home is a cemetery where peace is buried. On the other hand a home like that of the Little Flower is radiantly happy in spite of many trials and heavy crosses.

Invite Him to your home then, lovingly. Receive Him royally. Enthrone Him as your adorable King and faithful Friend. And when He crosses the threshold of your home He will say to you, "Peace be to this house and to all who dwell therein." Because you have carried out His divine request to be invited to your home, He keeps His promise to bless your family and all its undertakings, to sanctify your joys and sorrows, to console you in all your trials, to keep your family united and to give to it true peace and happiness.

But of course, if a Christian home is the palace of Christ the King, His Sacred Heart in the Eucharist must be the source of that peace and happiness. So, when I ask you to enthrone the Sacred Heart in your home, at the same time I urge you to go more often to Mass and Communion. Thus will be united the two tabernacles of the King — that of the church and that of the home. And the common bond will be the Sacred Heart of Jesus ruling in the living throne of the family, and from His Eucharistic throne in church.

If you are responsive and generous, in the name of the Sacred Heart of Jesus, I promise peace and conversions and true Christian happiness! "Come, Lord Jesus!"

* * *

LET US NOW STRESS A FEW IMPORTANT POINTS so that the Enthronement may yield as much glory as possible to God. Our Lord certainly can and will perform miracles when His purpose requires them. He has wrought marvelous ones already, at the outset of the work, in order to mark the providential nature of the Enthronement. But the All Wise God does not perform unnecessary wonders. The work as now established will of itself bring forth fruit a thousandfold, if organized and directed in a fitting manner, and will continue to work miracles of grace without our urging God to grant them, provided we cultivate this tree of life confided to our care.

If the Enthronement is to produce the marvelous fruits we have referred to, the ceremony must, as a rule, be *well prepared*.[1] When you are about to introduce the King of Love into any home, you should first send a forerunner to see that the importance of the act is fully realized by the family, and that they are ready to perform it with all the piety it requires. When a king is to visit any of his subjects, it is customary to make sure beforehand that the prescribed etiquette will be observed, so the reception will be worthy of such a guest. In the same way, where the Enthronement is not understood and where the members of the family are ignorant of the obligations it entails — however light and pleasant these may be — the King of Love may be exposed to a certain want of respect and reverence.

The ceremony may, in a way, be compared to the reception of the Holy Eucharist. A pious Catholic is not satisfied with being in a state of grace; he makes careful preparation

---

1 See Appendix 1

218

by prayer and meditation so as to derive all possible profit from so great a Sacrament. So, too, it does not suffice for a family about to enthrone the Sacred Heart to be good and pious; all should be informed that, as a consequence of the homage rendered to the King of Kings, He must be given the rightful place of honor in daily life. Exterior display, such as setting out of flowers and lights in the room where the image is honored is advisable too, but, the real lights and blossoms are the hearts of parents and children.

We often find that the poor and unlettered have an extraordinary grasp of the mysteries of faith. In Rotterdam a zealous parish priest asked me one Sunday, after High Mass, to go with him to enthrone the Sacred Heart in the homes of dock laborers. In one of these houses I noticed a fellow about thirty years old who seemed very touched by the prayers the priest was saying. When the ceremony was over, I inquired the reason for his emotion, and the workman replied in a trembling voice, "How can I help being touched to see my King and God coming to this humble cottage as a Friend who wants to stay with us and help us to live as He would have us do." I was much struck by the reply, but I should mention that, for more than a week, promoters of the work had been going from house to house preparing these people to receive their *King and Friend.* It means hard work, but this is the only way to obtain consoling and satisfactory results and to assure that the Reality is there under the symbol and not the image alone.

I insist on this point. You must prepare very carefully for the Enthronement, as if you were scattering flowers in the path that Jesus is to tread, or erecting triumphal arches and spreading carpets in His way before the entrance to that house. The Enthronement should be a reproduction of the triumphal entry into Jerusalem, and when it is over the homage must be kept up by a more fervent Christian life, a life of love.

* * *

The triumph to be obtained for Jesus must not be calculated by the number of homes where the Enthronement is performed. We do not want a superficial and illusive victory but a deep, intense, lasting one. One household permeated with the true spirit of the Enthronement and determination to make Jesus the King and Center of the family life, will give Him far more glory and consolation than five hundred homes where the ceremony has been performed with much outward manifestation of piety, but with little love.

Try to *intensify* the Christian life of the family so that the home may be a real Bethany in spirit and in truth. Go back ten times and more, if needs be, to that house where you have gained some influence and explain the meaning of the work. Thus, by gentleness and unfailing patience, you will bring about the spiritual transformation of the family. Never weary of stirring up the sacred fire, and encouraging piety, frequent and fervent Communion and family prayers. See that Jesus the God of Truth and Love is given a throne built on sure foundations.

A story is told of a crippled soldier who was a socialist before the Great War and later became an anarchist seemingly possessed by an anti-social and anti-Christian spirit. A zealous apostle of the love of Jesus decided to transform his miserable home into an *abode of light;* so, plucking up her courage, she went there and found the soldier sunning himself outside. She greeted him kindly and talked to him some time without receiving a reply. At last he cried out, "Go away! Down with the clergy and the rich!" Controlling herself, she gently sought to make him listen, but in vain. He shouted at her and threatened to use violence. "Very well, then," said the lady quietly, "I will go, but I shall come back tomorrow at the same time." Next day the same frantic invectives greeted her, but she returned patiently day after day till the soldier, at last, called out angrily to his wife, "Look here, rid me of this person. She has been annoying me with her visits for several days and intends to keep on coming. Just let her talk to you instead."

So the wife came and sat down beside the lady. The anarchist remained there, as if suspicious of what might be said. The children, too, soon crowded round. They sat on the ground and listened curiously to the first catechism lesson of their lives. Going straight to the point, the promoter spoke at length of the love of God their Father; then, fondling the little ones, she rose to go. But the soldier, to her surprise, begged her to stay a little longer, and when at last she left they all exacted a promise that she would return every day. Later, she brought someone with her to instruct the children, while she herself taught the soldier and his wife who often commented, "How beautiful! Why were we never told all these things before? How happy we might have been!"

After about six weeks, the parish priest was called in. He could hardly believe his eyes on finding such a change. A few days after, the children were baptized in the parish church, and *the whole family received Holy Communion for* the first time. That same evening the Enthronement was solemnly performed in their home — one more Bethany was won for the Heart of Jesus. With tears in his eyes the erstwhile anarchist said, "Without knowing it, I have always hungered for our Lord whom I received today in Holy Communion. He has come this evening to stay with me, in our home, till I die. I was wretched because I was longing for Jesus; now, with Him I need nothing else."

This is the way, dear apostles, to carry out the Enthronement campaign and to ensure a complete victory for the King. In ordinary things what is worth doing at all is worth doing well; how much more so in all that concerns the glory of our Lord.

A question rises here. Can the Enthronement be carried out if there is a notorious sinner in the house? A careful distinction must be made. In a family, there may be a soul that has strayed from the right path; one who, though good and worthy in other respects, does not love our Lord and neglects his religious duties. But if his wife and children are fervent Catholics the ceremony may be performed, and perhaps Martha's faith and Mary's love will constrain Jesus to raise the Lazarus to life. It is quite right and even advisable that our Lord should come not only as King but as Physician, provided that the other members of the family make up for the love the head of the household refuses to give to Him. If they want a conversion they must deserve it and pay dearly for it. Every work of mercy is preceded, as on Calvary, by appeasement of the justice of God.

Let us here remark that the Enthronement must not be regarded as a reward — this was a prevalent error, at one time, on the subject of Holy Communion. It is a *means* of bringing Jesus to many a home that has need of His great mercy. However, in a home where real scandal is given and where there is no desire for amendment, the Enthronement cannot be performed. There is an immense difference between the two cases. Jesus entered the house of Simon the Pharisee and of publicans, since it was for such He had come down from Heaven.

I once visited a house where the Enthronement had been made. The picture of the Sacred Heart, in a rich gilded frame, had been placed upon the grand piano, and beside me stood the master of the house who had only *consented* to allow the ceremony at the request of his wife and children. He had neglected his religious duties for over forty years. I had determined to make an attack upon him and had asked him to see me that evening without giving a reason for my visit. So there we were, not two of us, but *three*: he — I — and between us, Jesus. In the midst of our conversation I suddenly cut him short with: "I have made up my mind not to leave this house without giving you absolution."

"What did you say, Father, absolution?" he inquired, smiling, as though he took it for a jest.

"Yes, certainly, absolution, but of course after hearing your confession in this very room."

"And you really mean it?" he asked with a good-humored laugh.

"I do," was my answer. "I am perfectly in earnest. Look at this picture of Our King. It cannot lie. It means that Jesus is the only Master of this house, that He rules here, and all obey Him but you. So kneel down and I will hear you on the spot and give you absolution."

He stopped laughing and changed his tone; there were no more excuses. He stood on the defensive, said he would think it over — perhaps some other day — for anything so serious he must have time to think.

"If the Angel of Death were to visit you tonight would you tell him to come back in a month because you need time to meditate and prepare yourself? Well, it is not Death but Life that comes today. It is Jesus. Do not drive Him away. Kneel down and I will help you." He hesitated a moment. Then, conquered by the King of Love, he fell on his knees, and I began the examination of conscience. He made an excellent confession and, some days after, the wife and five children with this Lazarus who had risen from the dead received Holy Communion together. "For the Son of Man came to save what was lost,"[2] said the Master. "It is not the healthy who need a physician, but they who are sick."[3]

"I desire mercy."[4] "I bear and offer in My Heart infinite mercy, accept it." "Behold, I stand at the door and knock."[5] If you receive Him with faith, trust and love, if you pay off the debt of the one you beg Him to convert, you will understand the words He addressed to Zacheus: "Today salvation has come to this house."[6]

＊ ＊ ＊

You have often heard me deplore as the great fault of our days that Jesus is not really known even in Catholic circles. He might repeat the words He said to His apostles, "Have I been so long a time with you, and you have not known me?"[7] To remedy this, when you visit homes, advise the families *to read and meditate on the Gospel.* Great benefits will thus be derived from our crusade, for the Gospel is an immense help to those weak in religious instruction. Its pages often conquer and captivate even those who are far from being pious, and no other book has such power to stir and touch the heart.

Many have a craving for a whole library of pious books.

---

2 Matt. 18: 11
4 Matt. 9: 13
6 Luke 19: 9

3 Matt. 9: 12
5 Apoc. 3: 20
7 John 14: 9

We cannot censure this praiseworthy desire, but sometimes along all this Catholic literature the one great book — the Gospel — is left out; and this is much to be regretted, for those who have not nourished their minds and hearts with our Lord's own words lack something that can never be replaced.

We shall have made an enormous stride towards rechristianizing the world when, by means of the Enthronement, we succeed in restoring the grand principles and traditions of Catholic family life, and when we persuade parents to read the Gospel aloud to their little ones at home. There we find the simple sublime picture of Him who holds the solution to all problems of the family and of society, Jesus Christ our Lord, in whom alone are light and peace. No one ever spoke as He did, He who is the Word of God. When He is absent, no one else can give us the words of eternal life.

Chapter 21

CHRISTIAN FAMILY LIVING

THE ENTHRONEMENT PRESUPPOSES, as we have seen, a sincere *homage of social adoration* to Christ the King and a loving dependence on Him. This homage is more important today than ever, seeing that the modern crime is social and national apostasy. It is impossible therefore to insist too much on this Christian act of faith and reparation which is implied in the suggestive title and the whole work of the Enthronement.

But this homage, for all its beauty and eloquence, constitutes neither the whole spirit nor the sole program of our crusade. In the home which acclaims the Heart of Jesus as its King of Love, the Enthronement ought to be the beginning of a *new life*, far more intimate in faith and much more ardent in charity. Thus, far from being a mere formality, the consecration is *lived*. I mean that by virtue of a great Christian and supernatural spirit, the Heart of Jesus will become, little by little, the divine soul of the family, whose one law will be that of the Gospel, and whose sole happiness will be to obey the Master of the house.

SHARING FAMILY LIFE

This means sharing our family life with Jesus to whom a throne has been offered precisely in order that He may remain and abide with His friends, blessing everything in the house from dawn to twilight and from the cradle to the grave. How much easier it is to live and struggle, to keep a bright face in spite of our sorrows, when Jesus is the Center of the beloved home, when He presides over it as a Friend, Confidant and King. Everything is ennobled and sanctified in this enviable Bethany because Jesus shares the family joys and sorrows. *He really lives* in such a home, and the family lives by Him and with Him.

Unfortunately this is not the general conception of the Christian life in a home. Many make their whole devotion consist in reciting vocal prayers. There are plenty of families which are more or less "devout," but only a few where Jesus is looked upon as a Friend. This reminds me of a scene in the episcopal palace at Bologna. I had just given a lecture on the Enthronement and its spirit to a large and distinguished group of ladies. I was about to descend from the platform when the Archbishop said to me, "Wait a moment, Father, I have a word to say. You have just preached to us a great truth, but let me add the final amen. On the great feasts, my cathedral and the churches are filled by enormous crowds, and, notwithstanding this, I do not see that my people are improving or becoming more sincerely Christian. And this is due to what you have said: Many people think they have done all that is required when they have attended Mass or taken part in a religious ceremony, but, on returning to their homes, they do not find Jesus in them. Our Lord is not the life of the family; the house is far from being a tabernacle; and this is a great fault of Catholic family life. What is missing is the Bethany-Home."

And now let me insist on this same idea and illustrate it by a series of very beautiful incidents, which are not only interesting in themselves, but will also explain better than any sermon what I understand by the Heart of Jesus, *King and Center, the Divine Soul, the living Friend* of the home.

The incident which I am going to relate occurred during the World War. One day a mother, a woman of wonderful faith, received an official telegram which told her of the death of her eldest son. It was a terrible shock, but conquering her emotion, she ran to the living room, placed the telegram at the feet of the King of Love and then calmly called her little ones and the servants. She asked that the throne of the Sacred Heart should be adorned with unusual splendor. She herself helped to beautify the shrine with flowers and candles. Then she bade all sing with her, and herself led the singing. After the hymn they recited the Credo and the act of Consecration. It was only then, after the family had, so to speak, presented arms to the King and made open acknowledgment of His presence in this great grief, that the mother took up the telegram and read it to her children. "Your brother," she said, sobbing, "has gone to heaven to the arms of his King. His Will be done. Long live His Sacred Heart! May His Kingdom come!" They wept, of course they did, but peacefully and on the Heart of Jesus. This is not the grief of flesh and blood, but a glorious, a meritorious one. This is how we should lovingly suffer with Jesus.

A very different picture now, but with the same fundamental idea. It was the yearly day of the distribution of prizes, and six boys came home from school laden with medals, books and certificates. They proudly made for their father's room expecting congratulations and presents. On seeing them coming in, their father said, "Do not come in here first, follow me!" He led them into the living room where the King was enthroned. "Now," he said, "go and place your prizes before this divine Master, and say to Him: 'We love Thee; Thy Kingdom come!'" The six boys obeyed joyfully, and recited with their father an act of consecration. "Now," he said, "let us go to your mother so she also may congratulate you; but never forget that in this home the One who rules, and must never be forgotten whether in trouble or in joy, is the Heart of Jesus."

And now a still more touching story: I was once celebrating the marriage of two young people who were very poor, and they asked me to enthrone the King of Love in their cottage that very day. "Promise me," I said to them, "to treat Jesus as a Friend, as if you really saw Him. His Heart will bring you happiness in spite of the troubles. which are sure to come for you."

A few years later the young man came and called for me. "My little wife is dying," he said. And in fact she was most

227

grievously ill, but at peace and breathing a sweet and infinite calm. The only treasure to be seen in that poor little home was the picture of the Heart of Jesus, which I had presented to them and enthroned on their marriage day. After hearing her confession I was rather surprised that in so bitter an hour such a heavenly peace should reign there; so, wishing to find out the reason, I said to her, "Before going to heaven, tell me, my child, have you been unhappy since your marriage?" She opened her eyes wide in great surprise, and, raising herself up, said to me, "What! you who on our wedding day committed us to the King Jesus, and brought Him to us to be the Friend of this little home, you ask me if I have been unhappy *with Him?* Never, Father! not for one second! No doubt we have had to suffer, we have had our struggles also. That is quite inevitable. But could we be unhappy with Jesus, the King and Friend of poor people, and especially of this cottage?" And then taking her young husband by the hand she said to him, "And you, what have you to say? Have you been unhappy?" In a broken voice, yet in words which were almost a canticle of the soul, he answered, "Father, we have had a hard struggle; such is life; but as she has said to you, with Jesus our Friend we have been happy — so happy! He is the Master, He comes to take her away; but soon He will come for me, and then, in heaven, we shall be united in happiness with Him, just as we have been happy with Him in our little home!"

The sublimity of these ideas and words needs no comment. These two poor people had understood and marvelously *lived* the idea and the spirit of the Enthronement. In their wretched dwelling they had made of Jesus their King and their inseparable Friend; their God and their All. These two simple folk knew more of the Gospel than very many devout and learned people. In that home there were always *three*, Jesus and His two intimate friends.

Now for a letter from a poor country woman: "Father, since I made the Enthronement in this poor cottage I consider that I am the tenant of Jesus, for on that day I handed everything over to Him: my flowers, my fowls, my husband,

228

everything is His. Since then I have lodged in the palace of the King. I know His Heart has accepted my offering, because from that day He has completely changed my life. We no longer live for ourselves, but in Him and for Him."

I have often told the story of a poor servant girl who wrote to me: "Two weeks ago I listened to your lectures on the Enthronement. Today I was married and at the end of the meal which the rich call the wedding feast, I send you these few lines. We poor people have invited the Divine Friend of whom you talked to us so much, He whom they invited at Cana, and my husband and I have made the Enthronement in this solemn hour, beseeching Him, as you told us, to be the Master and the Friend, not for an hour, but for our whole lives. Father, bless us and confirm our consecration. The Sacred Heart will be our only King and Friend in joys and sorrows. Our little house will be His, and He will be ours."

I cannot reproduce here the whole of the ill-spelled letter, scribbled in pencil, but marvelous in its doctrine. Do you know what I did with it? I sent it to His Holiness Benedict XV, saying to him: "Your Holiness will like to see how a poor servant girl is capable of understanding the Gospel which your Holiness has commissioned me to preach." I am certain that the Holy Father, on reading that ill-written letter, must have smiled with joy and probably wept with emotion.

A last touch to the picture. The head of a very noble family, an excellent Catholic, determined to have the Enthronement made on the following Friday. But our Lord had decreed otherwise. He was suddenly taken dangerously ill, and died on Wednesday. But before dying he said to his wife that he did not wish to quit the house for the cemetery until the gap which he would leave had been filled by the Heart of Jesus. "After this bereavement," he said, "He must be more than ever the Master, the All of my house!" The cruel moment of the last farewell came. The coffin was about to be taken away from the house, when, to the surprise of all, the widow came forward surrounded by her children and said, "One moment; do not take it yet." She advanced bearing

229

a picture of the King of Love in a rich frame. She set it up over the coffin and then said, "His last wish was that he should not be borne to the cemetery until the Enthronement had been performed. I invite you to join me and my little ones in carrying out his desire." Thereupon they all recited the Credo and the prayers of the Ceremonial. Then she said, her voice broken with sobs, "Now you may bear away the body, for he will remain among us in the Heart of Jesus!" How easily suffering is borne, how holy and calm are our tears when He is in the home!

One fearful night, and only a few moments after a terrible earthquake, I went in search of a family where I had enthroned the Sacred Heart and I found my friends quietly standing amidst the smoking ruins of their house while the earth was still quaking. "Father, we have lost everything," the mother said to me, " . . . everything except the peace and happiness of which you spoke on the day of the Enthronement. Bethany can never die, for its soul, its peace and its happiness is Jesus!"

It is needless to add that if you have carried out the Enthronement in your homes in this spirit, you will not forget the very beautiful petitions made by our Lord to the friends of His Heart, petitions to which He has attached magnificent promises. Among others, the loving and solemn celebration of the First Friday, frequent Communion in a spirit of reparation, and the practice of the Holy Hour. And lastly, the great and beautiful Feast of the Sacred Heart of Jesus, which you will celebrate with a very fervent Communion in the morning and an intimate feast at home in the evening. Above all if there are children, mark the importance and beauty of this day by some family festivity. By this means the Feast of the Sacred Heart of Jesus cannot fail to become *a true family tradition* among fervent Catholics. Unite the altar and the home on that Friday in a holy demonstration of joy, and at a suitable hour when the whole family is gathered, renew before the image of the Sacred Heart the homage of the Enthronement.

I will close by reminding you that it is the Pope's desire

that this work, which he calls providential, should live, be organized, and expand. The Vicar of Christ considers it urgent and of the greatest importance; for the Enthronement ought to succeed in uniting in one single stream the fountain of natural life, which is the home, and the inexhaustible fountain of grace and divine life which is the Sacred Heart of Jesus. Let us generously fulfill the Master's demands formulated at Paray, and He will fulfill with an *excess* of mercy His divine promises.

Chapter 22

THE FEAST OF THE KINGSHIP
OF OUR LORD JESUS CHRIST

THE HOLY YEAR OF 1925, so rich in blessings and graces for all true lovers of the Sacred Heart, was brought to a close by the institution of the Feast of the Kingship of Our Lord Jesus Christ. Pope Pius XI solemnly and officially proclaimed that Christ was the King of Love; a divine King Who ruled through His Heart. This truth was emphasized when the Holy Father ordered the Act of Consecration of the human race renewed on the Feast of Christ the King.

This marvelous gesture of the Supreme Pontiff was received with an ovation of faith by the whole Catholic world, and welcomed with intense joy by those who were fighting under the banner of the "Social Reign of the Sacred Heart." In 1924, I had presented to the Fathers of the Congregation of the Sacred Hearts assembled in Chapter a petition for the institution of this feast. We all signed it. The work of the Enthronement can indeed take credit for having educated public opinion in its favor. Hence, I may justly claim for the apostles of the work that glory which is rightly due to them, as the Pope benevolently acknowledged in his encyclical: *Quas Primas — On The Kingship Of Christ*. It was also most encouraging to the director-general and national directors to receive, as they did from every quarter of the globe on New Year's Eve, 1925, innumerable messages of sincere and affectionate congratulations. All alluded to the establishment of this feast, regarding it as the logical consequence of the apostolate accomplished by the Crusade of the Enthronement of the Sacred Heart of Jesus and as a world-wide Enthronement carried out by the Supreme Pontiff to mark the close of the Holy Year. And, indeed, the meaning of the word "Enthronement" has never been brought out so fittingly as on that day in St. Peter's portico.

Recall to mind the beginnings of the work. The Crusade of the Enthronement started an intense spiritual movement, perfectly in harmony with the idea of the Social Kingship of our Lord, an idea which logically proceeds both from the nature and organization of the work. From the very dawn of the Crusade, we have always taught that Jesus, King of Love, must reign in family life and in society. And, though many applauded the idea, others opposed it, saying that the term "Kingship" was inopportune and imprudent and they regarded as a rash innovation the title adopted for the Work: *Social Reign of the Sacred Heart of Jesus*. We call it "Social" for, though in the case of each individual we insist on the necessity of a deep interior life which should be essentially Eucharistic, we do this with a view to reforming the whole of society and bringing all men to the Feet of the King of Kings. It was, from the outset, our most cherished hope to see Jesus Christ one day acclaimed King of Kings, Master of legislators and Ruler of peoples, a divine, victorious Monarch, through the Scepter of His Heart.

We have always opposed Modernism which tries to dethrone Jesus and banish Him from the life of the family, society and nation. We ever do our utmost to shun this evil and to encourage solemn acts of reparation for the terrible war that is now being waged on God. Christ must not be deprived of His social rights by the shameful cowardice of His so-called friends and the malice of his enemies. His title must be accepted by individuals and families.

His empire must also extend to Parliaments and laws, though many would think it *prudent* that He should remain mute in the Tabernacle, mute in Parliament and mute before the abuses of modern society. To us, therefore, accrues the immense satisfaction and glory of having boldly preached

233

this divine and social Kingship, with its inherent consequences. We have often been bitterly criticized, but always favored with the Holy Father's blessing and approval, and encouraged by a flow of countless graces.

The word *"Enthronement"* is eminently suitable as proclaiming the Social Kingship of Jesus Christ and is now used by the very people who at first opposed it. The homage we ask of families clearly implies *royal honors,* since we claim for the Sacred Heart the most honorable place in every Catholic home, the throne which by right belongs to Him as King. We do not impose any particular picture of the Sacred Heart, but we have always recommended the copy of the celebrated painting, commonly known as Garcia Moreno's in which the Heart of Jesus is shown with the emblems proper to His Kingship.[1] This representation of the King of Love has found its way throughout the entire world and may now be seen in homes of every kind, from native African huts to magnificent homes in Europe and America, everywhere proclaiming the sublime ideal of our Crusade, as expressed in St. Paul's famous words, *"He must reign,"*[2] and by the words of the Lord's prayer, "Thy Kingdom come."

The ceremony of the Enthronement has also been carried out in Catholic schools, in factories, clubs and business offices. It gradually invaded official groups and organizations. A start was made by celebrating the Enthronement in public establishments such as hospitals and barracks; then came the turn of public committees and municipal governments and lastly parliaments and royal palaces. At the end of the First World War, to show her gratitude to the Heart of Jesus, Belgium made an act of homage to the Sacred Heart, which, if not official, was extremely solemn. The King and the Episcopate presided.

But the greatest of all was an act which is perhaps unique in history as an official national protestation of faith and

---

1 Copies of this picture may be obtained from the National Center of the Enthronement, Washington 17, D.C., or from one of the local Centers.
2 1 Cor. 15: 25

adoration. I refer to the Enthronement carried out in Spain on May 30, 1919, on the Cerro de los Angeles by that great Catholic Monarch Don Alfonso XIII and his entire government. I had the undeserved honor of being appointed to preach a triduum in the historic church of San Jeronimo el Real, in Madrid, in preparation for this official Enthronement.

Early in 1925, I wrote to the Holy Father concerning our campaign: "If liturgically and officially this feast is a new one, the homage which it involves has already been practiced for some time past in many countries, thanks to the work of the Enthronement." What an honor it is for us to see our humble efforts crowned and our most ardent wishes realized by the Holy Father's encyclical in which our Lord is explicitly called *the King of Love*. Moreover, the consecration of families and societies to the Sacred Heart is recommended as the most excellent means of acknowledging the Kingship of Christ. Finally, the Supreme Pontiff has ordered that on this new feast day the act of consecration of the entire human race to the Sacred Heart of Jesus should be publicly renewed, using the formula wherein are several times repeated the words *"Be Thou King!"*

And now let us note that the spirit of this solemn and beautiful feast is the same as that of the Enthronement. Some seem to imagine that Christ is to rule only in private life. They would like to suppress, or blot out, those pages of the Gospel which show His inalienable and divine right over society and over nations, over all authority and governments. This right has been proclaimed anew before the whole world by the Vicar of Christ in his encyclical. He desires above all that this Kingship should come to be not only recognized, but *lived up to* practically by all the faithful, and our work can help to bring this about, as it helped in the establishment of the Feast.

We must aim at strengthening and developing true Catholic ideals in the family, since these are the only possible basis for the true restoration of the rights of Christ. A more profound study of the Gospel will lead us to know and obey ever better the precepts established by *Christ the King*, and to regulate the standards of our social life thereby, for if we frequently repeat the ejaculation "Thy Kingdom come!" we must accept the obligations it entails.

The moral strength required for the fulfilment of these obligations is especially acquired in the family, the root of the social tree and the source and sap of the life of the nation. Hence, we must firmly maintain that the home is really and truly the foundation stone of the throne of Christ the King, and only good Catholic families can form the crown which society will later place at His divine feet. Lively and intrepid faith, Eucharistic fervor, sanctification of our daily actions, faithful observance of the laws of the Church, all virtues, in short, depend on the intensity of the love for the Heart of Jesus as *center and Lord* of the family.

Apostles of the Enthronement, it is for you to make the Kingship effective in the families which your zeal has already conquered for Christ. Quicken in them the spirit of faith and see that the spirit of love burns more and more fervently, so that Jesus may be in very truth the King and center of their supernatural life.

Forward then, ever forward! The more the King is loved in families as the Friend of Bethany, the more secure will be His sovereignty over nations.

PART III

"WATCH ONE HOUR WITH ME"

Chapter 23

NIGHT ADORATION IN THE HOME

"Watch one hour with Me"[1]

For a long time past I have had a great desire to suggest to you a very simple and beautiful way of giving glory to the Sacred Heart. What I am going to ask will not be possible in all families where this book is read. But when a little group of true Bethanies have given the example, others will follow their lead. What I propose is *to organize Night Adoration at home in* the same spirit of love and reparation which inspires you when watching before the Blessed Sacrament.

Two classes of families might undertake this work. In the first class I include those who, unable to attend the "Holy Hour" in Church, make it in their home before the picture or shrine of the Sacred Heart. This should be done *once a month,* on the eve of the First Friday, if possible. The children and all the household should be present. As a rule the Holy Hour may be kept at any time of the evening up to midnight, according to circumstances. We have already enrolled many such families. May the Divine Heart shower blessings on these faithful Bethanies. We congratulate them with all our heart and pray that the number of these homes in which the agonizing Heart of Jesus is loved and consoled may be increased. Our promoters must endeavor to secure for our Lord many living tabernacles, so that He may not justly repeat His sad complaints, "I looked for sympathy, but

---

1 This was the first appeal for Night Adoration made by Father Mateo (1927)

there was none; for comforters, and I found none."[2] "Could you not then watch one hour with me?"[3]

In the second class — composed of large and very fervent families — I propose to organize *Adoration throughout the night,* in the sanctuary of the home, from ten in the evening till five in the morning.[4] Would it be too much to ask *each member of the family for one hour of Night Adoration every month,* and this without having to leave the house, when unfortunately it is very common, even among good people, to give up almost a whole night's rest to frivolous, not to say dangerous amusements? While Judas watches to betray the Son of Man and finds plenty of accomplices to watch with him, shall the apostles, the intimate friends of the King, always be overcome by sleep?

Night Adoration in church has made marvelous progress within the last few years, and is producing graces more abundantly than any other work has ever evoked. We look with admiration upon those thousands of sentinels who keep their watch in the dead of night before the Blessed Sacrament. But there are many others who for various reasons cannot leave the house at night to join in adoration in the church, and these, I know, will be glad to adopt my suggestion.

Wherever Nocturnal Adoration has been established, it is noteworthy that the most fervent in this vigil of love and sacrifice are nearly always those who at the end of the day are utterly tired out by work and who, in many cases, have to walk miles to the church. If this can be done, surely my plan also must be acceptable. And do you not think that within ten years or so the number of Night Adorers before the Blessed Sacrament will be gradually doubled and trebled by the recruits trained in the bosom of the family?

There will, of course, be difficulties, but certainly they are not insuperable. For instance, it is not at all unusual for anyone to sit up late not only for worldly reasons, but when there are family gatherings and rejoicings. Often this is done

---

2 Ps. 68: 21   3 Matt. 26: 40
4 The hours are now from 9 p.m. to 6 a.m.

through a motive of charity, such as caring for the sick. Consequently, if a little rest can willingly be foregone for the sake of a friend, if fatigue can be endured to watch and tend an invalid, would it not be possible to do as much for Jesus who is so forsaken and so insulted?

I know very well that I can only expect a few to take up a work which entails such self-denial, and it is to these chosen few I appeal, ardently calling them in the name of the divine Mendicant of our hearts. Fervent families, souls that are afire with passionate love for Jesus, generous souls, meditate this appeal before the tabernacle, and may Jesus in the Holy Eucharist pour out His heart into yours, telling you Himself of His immense sadness, when, especially during the dark hours of the night, Satan goes about the world inciting men to evil. Jesus wishes to forestall the enemy and to kindle in your hearts the fire of His love. But He waits until He is invited and welcomed to the sanctuary of your home; then He will come and allow Himself to be made prisoner, entrusting His Heart to you and flooding with graces your dwelling thus transformed into a house of prayer.

How beautiful it will be to see a family, at the appointed time for Night Adoration, light the candles before the picture of the Divine King and begin the vigil. As each hour passes, the adorers, like well-drilled sentinels, replace one another, one watching whilst the others take their rest. Close to the Master's Heart, they pray for the whole family, for the absent, the sick and for the prodigal sons. What a sweet, peaceful and delightful night, not in spite of, but precisely because of the hour of sleep sacrificed to the Beloved in remembrance of His agony in the garden and His loneliness in the tabernacle.

Do not join the number of those who in every pious enterprise look not at the immense benefits, but at inevitable difficulties and petty obstacles. The example given by Night Adorers will be contagious; from one lamp many others will be lighted, and the fire will quickly spread. As for me, I am launching this idea with great hopes of success, for whenever I have stretched out my hand begging for love, I have always had the undeserved good fortune of receiving a generous and loving response. Why should I be disappointed on this occasion? I will go from door to door and knock in the name of the King and for His glory. Dear Bethanies, come out with lighted torches to meet Jesus Crucified and prove to Him that your house is really His abiding place.

How many prodigal sons would thus be brought home again! How many who are spiritually blind would recover their sight! How many that are paralyzed would be cured! What graces would be poured out on holy souls in reward for this monthly adoration in the home! This covenant of love between Jesus and His friends would one day be repaid by miracles of mercy, for our Lord never lets Himself be outdone in generosity.

The idea is launched; it has started as a dart of fire from the Heart of Jesus. He awaits your answer. Give it to Him in a fervent thanksgiving after Holy Communion. Then write to me, that I may know I have not begged in vain for Him who is athirst for love. Tell me you are enrolling yourselves in one of the two classes, that of the Holy Hour, or that of Night Adoration. I look forward to your letters with deep emotion. With your names, I will make a list to be offered every morning during my Mass and, as an acknowledgment, I will send each one of you, through the secretariat, a picture as a souvenir to remind you of your promise.

"I have sown in Thy name, Jesus!

May Thy Heart now reap great glory!"

❈   ❈   ❈

The preceding pages were written in my annual Circular letter in 1927. By the grace of the Heart of Jesus they met with the most flattering success. That is my reason for publishing them in this book, which is to be read and meditated in Bethanies of the Sacred Heart. It will also be of the highest interest, for the glory of the King of Love and the spiritual benefit of His intimate friends, to insert herewith two articles which give accounts of the new triumph won by the King and Friend of Bethany. They can but increase the splendor of such a victory and bring in new recruits.

KNOCK IN THE NAME OF JESUS,
AND IT SHALL BE OPENED UNTO YOU!

I knocked at the doors of those homes where Jesus is enthroned as King, and I asked for one more homage of adoration and reparation to His divine Heart. I suggested that they should make their monthly Holy Hour *at home* when they found it impossible to go to church. I even asked for a whole night of adoration before the altar of the Sacred Heart. A wonderful surprise awaited me. Truly, I only expected that a few doors would be opened, but, for once, the touching complaint of Our Lord: "I have sought for one who would sorrow with Me and I found none," has been proved untrue, and He can exclaim, "Rejoice with Me, ye Angels, for I was sorrowfully seeking for one soul who would sympathize with Me, and lo, I have found many. I called timidly at some doors, and whole families are willing to spend the lonely hours of the night watching with Me. Congratulate Me, ye angelic choirs!"

When Mary knocked at the doors of Bethlehem there was "no room" for her and her Divine Son, but, as little Therese would have said, she had no Blessed Virgin to go before her, as I had, to prepare the way. Love of Mary has opened many a home to Christ the King, and letters in response to my appeal have reached me from all quarters of the globe. Here are some of the answers:

1) I have just read the Review in which, under the inspiration of the Sacred Heart, you suggested the idea of Night Adoration and the Holy Hour made at home. As you so kindly ask for a reply, so that you may know whether or not your words fell on deaf ears, I hasten to assure you that, in my home, where the King of Love is already enthroned, we received your proposal with great joy. We are not a large family — just myself, two children and one servant. We, therefore, arranged that the servant shall take from 10 to 11 p.m., then each of the children will take an hour, and I will take the rest of the night till 4 a.m. But the children protested against not sharing my watch till early morning,

and I would be grateful for your advice about allowing it. When winter comes, will it not be injurious to them to keep their promise? Please decide for me. I only presume to trouble you because the children keep saying, "Mummy, ask the Father, and whatever he says will be sure to be what Jesus wishes."

I wrote back that great prudence would be necessary during winter, and that she must wrap up her little ones very warmly during their night watch, so heroically undertaken — but she must remember that Jesus also suffered. In summer and winter alike, He feels the bitter coldness of those for whom He died. That is why I decided in favor of these fervent children. May the Sacred Heart bless their home very abundantly.

2) I was much moved on reading your suggestion that Night Adoration should be made in the sanctuary of the home with the same spirit of reparation with which it is carried out in church. My answer must be mailed this very day — I pledge myself to make the Holy Hour on the eve of every First Friday, before the picture of the Sacred Heart. For the past two years, I have spent almost every night at the bedside of my dear ones — my husband was slowly dying, and my children have also been ill. If I could thus watch beside them without any ill consequences regarding my health, I can surely give up one hour a month to honor the Sacred Heart. This is my intention and moreover, I will do all I can to propagate this devotion, so that many families may console Jesus in a spirit of reparation.

3) Father, after reading your touching appeal, I write to ask you to inscribe my name in the list of Night Watchers at least up to midnight, for, as a rule, I am entirely alone. Send me your blessing, Reverend Father, and believe that I am more than happy to be able to respond to the desires of the Sacred Heart.

4) Please put my name upon the altar while you offer the Holy Sacrifice and promise our divine King for me that I will make the Holy Hour and prolong it until I am over-

244

come with sleep. Tell Him that henceforth I am more than ever His and every beat of my heart is offered to Him.

5) I already make the Holy Hour every month, but henceforth I want to be more generous, and so I pledge myself to watch the whole night in adoration on the eve of every First Friday. *What is one night a month?* I will ask Jesus to give me the strength to do it and I will sympathize with Him and console Him all through the night, for I want my home to be a real Bethany where the divine Pilgrim always finds a couch strewn with flowers of love and trust ready for Him.

* * *

Are not these extracts sufficient to show what a strong, though unseen, spirit of reparation is to be found in the world today? But there is something still better. In my circular, I purposely abstained from addressing religious communities — they already have their own devotional practices mapped out. Nevertheless, I have received letters from many fervent communities. Here is one from a convent where my unspoken wish was at once understood and acted upon:

Reverend Father, your recent circular, addressed to the true Bethanies, moved my soul to its depths. I thought of the consolation given to the Heart of Jesus by the generous and loving Night Adorers, and I said to myself: "I, too, am the mother of a family, since, in spite of my unworthiness, Jesus has confided to me the care of a whole community."

Four of our sisters watch each night by the sick and dying members of Christ our King. Why should we not offer this work in union with the families making their night adoration, with the intentions of furthering the Social Reign of the Sacred Heart? What would you think of this, Reverend Father? These night watches are rich in merits, each sister being responsible for about thirty invalids — and what invalids! Most are near death's door, many in great danger of losing their souls. Every moment, someone is calling for help. May Jesus, our King and Divine Healer, deign to accept our efforts, and every step we take in attending to the sick.

May they learn to glorify Him in their sufferings. Henceforth, our turn for the Night Watch will be eagerly awaited. We leave to Christian families an hour on Mount Thabor spent in the peaceful intimacy of their homes, our vigil shall be kept on Mount Calvary. Tell me, Reverend Father, whether you approve of my idea — the extension of Christ's Kingdom besets me.

Enclosed in this letter was a list of the special intentions assigned to each hour:

9 — 10 p.m.	Children and young people.
10 — 11 p.m.	Families where Christ is enthroned as King.
11 — 12 p.m.	The pope, priests and religious.
12 — 1 a.m.	Missionaries and heathen peoples.
1 — 2 a.m.	Heads of governments — reparation for sins of revolt against lawful authority.
2 — 3 a.m.	Worldly families.
3 — 4 a.m.	The poor, the sick and the tempted.
4 — 5 a.m.	Students for the priesthood and novices.
5 — 6 a.m.	Catholic schools and their staffs.
6 — 7 a.m.	The enemies of Holy Church.
7 — 8 a.m.	Bad Catholics, heretics and schismatics.

As each hour chimes, the sisters say five times: "Most Sacred Heart of Jesus, Thy Kingdom come," and once: "Most Sacred Heart of Jesus, may You be known, loved and imitated."

This letter is in itself a splendid offering to the Heart of Jesus and many other fervent communities will be thus encouraged. Listen to one more — this time from a convent of contemplative nuns:

Yes, Reverend Father, your dart was well aimed and has pierced the hearts of all of us. This very night Jesus gathered His first fruits in our Night Adoration from 11 p.m. to 5 a.m. Thank you, Father, for having explained to us so well the desire of Jesus. What greater happiness can there be here below than to find out what our Divine King wishes and then give it to Him? Jesus has certainly smiled upon us and His smile is the omen of victories to come — the triumph of His

Sacred Heart over many homes that will be transformed into tabernacles of adoration, reparation and love.

You will be as deeply touched as I was on reading these lines and in the name of the Divine Beggar of hearts I thank all those who have given Him so much consolation. Encouraged by their generosity, I hold out my hand a second time, knocking at the doors of those whom Jesus loves and who have not yet given Him this great consolation. The world continually asks of its votaries nights spent in pleasure and frivolity, if not in sin. Shall it triumph over souls for whom Jesus has died? Whom will you choose, Jesus or Barabbas? Answer me, you who call yourselves friends of Christ the King.

Dear apostles, now that you realize what Night Adoration is, I would ask you to meditate on two most touching scenes.

The first is one which I have endeavored to retrace in several of my Holy Hours: Our Lord is being outraged by a violent and drunken soldiery. The King of Glory, seated on a bench of mockery, is being treated with brutal fury, according to instructions given by the priests and Pharisees, and probably under the very eyes of His most bitter enemies. With satanic joy they are revenging the anathemas He has launched against those who are hypocritical and proud. After having covered Him with a purple robe, they bend the knee mockingly before Him and spit upon Him. *Rebellious flesh and pride* are here taking a cruel and sacrilegious revenge on the Master Who has imposed on men the new precepts of *purity and humility*. Bathed in His blood and quivering with pain, Jesus holds His peace.

The second scene is that of Paray-le-Monial. Contemplate, in the little Chapel of the Visitation, the King of Love complaining gently but bitterly of the ingratitude and perfidy of His children, showing St. Margaret Mary His wounded Heart, and begging for love and reparation. Behold Him, fleeing as it were from the storm of hate and sin and begging a shelter in her heart. His faithful servant witnesses anew His sorrow in the Garden of Gethsemane; she listens to the gentle complaints of His adorable Heart. But in the vision at Paray, feeling Himself to be understood and loved, Jesus asks for consolation and reparation and begs His confidant to extort from Him pardon for those sinners who, by their sins of flesh, are scourging Him.

Alas! these two scenes of divine suffering, that of Jerusalem and that of Paray, are ever being re-enacted. Bethanies of the great King, listen, but from afar, to the sounds issuing from those dens of vice where the triumph of Venus is acclaimed. See those crowds assembled in theaters where the sins of society are deified; stand outside some of the public places of amusement, dance halls, theaters, night clubs, and count, if you can, the human stream of so-called Christians, many of them Catholics. With hardly a twinge of remorse, they look upon immodest sights and accept them as a necessity of the social life of today.

Poor Jesus! They hiss and mock Him, crying with the Jews, "Away with this man!"[5] Poor Jesus! He is one living wound; from the crown of His head to the soles of His feet there is nothing whole. He scourged Egypt to liberate Israel, and now Israel, or, rather, treacherous and ungrateful friends are scourging Him — their King. In His bitter passion, He looks for friends and entreats even His torturers to have compassion on Him, but above all upon themselves and their own souls.

He also turns to you, Bethanies of His Divine Heart: Open to Me, He says, open quickly to your King, to the One Friend who is always sincere and faithful. Have pity on Me, those of you at least who are My friends, for I am wounded with love and mortal agony. Do not keep me waiting. I am wounded with love and mortal agony. Do not keep me waiting. I am Jesus!

In my circular letter of June, 1927, I ventured to interpret that cry of divine anguish, and the appeal resulted in a magnificent triumph for the Heart of Jesus. *Praise be to Thee, O Christ!*

What is the secret of this triumph? Among other reasons, I find one which is at the same time a consoling lesson for

---

5 Luke 23: 18

all the apostles of the enthronement. For the past few years, our work acted as a preparation for this new demand of love and sacrifice. By His presence in the home, the King Himself has inspired many hearts with a great desire for loving reparation. He first whispered in secret the appeal which the circular put into words. In fact, many of those who asked to be enrolled wrote to me: This idea corresponds exactly to an earnest, though undefined, desire of my own, to a longing I could not express, and which has been haunting me for some time.

The appeal was marvelously well understood because it was opportune. A few years ago, perhaps, we should not have met with the generous response which has been coming in from all sides. What immense glory this homage of love and adoration brings to the Heart of Jesus! Truly it is a proof of real love; often of heroic love, wherein routine has not the least part. It is impossible not to be deeply moved on reading letters which contain such phrases as this: "Please give me a difficult hour for my adoration, one that nobody wants. If possible, that from 2 a.m. to 3 a.m." Other souls, filled with the same thirst as Jesus Himself, are not satisfied with the minimum I asked for, *one hour a month,* but beg for an hour a week. And these are more numerous than one would think — there are even some who make their hour of adoration every night.

You have no doubt read and deeply appreciated the encyclical[6] of His Holiness Pius XI on reparation, and you must have realized the necessity of consoling the Heart of Jesus. You cannot better put into practice our Holy Father's desire than by carrying out Night Adoration in the Home, and we could not have better interpreted the Holy Father's wish had we organized this work after his encyclical. Read again and ponder over that magnificent letter and you will find, even in tiny details, that we are in perfect harmony with the sovereign pontiff's views and advice.

I would emphasize here, after his example, two grave sins,

---

6 Miserentissimus Redemptor

for which the Night Adorers should make reparation in a special way: First, *the revolt of pride,* which is a lofty attitude of want of submission; that *"non serviam,"* "I will not serve," which is so opposed to "the obedience unto death, even unto the death of the cross" of the Son of God. Secondly, the *sin of sensuality,* which is met with in the drawing rooms of "distinguished" people, at the seaside — and even in our churches — under the form of immodest fashions very often patronized by careless Catholic women who, by their shameless clothing (or lack of it), are real "sowers of mortal sin," "ticket-sellers for Hell!" Most of the gravest sins are caused by this revolting indelicacy and these fashionable Catholics heap up for themselves a crushing weight of responsibility against the hour of justice. They sow death along their path, they will reap divine vengeance.

It is needless to say that, in our crusade of Night Adoration, we do not want *even one* of those who think themselves pious while they scandalously disobey the pope and their bishops, stifling their conscience and preferring pagan elegance to the love of Jesus and to the dignity of Christian womanhood. We want to make reparation for those, who, more like Eve than like Mary, have set aside, along with their modesty and sense of delicacy, one of God's most binding commandments. No, we want none of these; Jesus turns away His face from them. We will not have one such in our ranks. The Immaculate Virgin could not bless us if we did, for the tears she is today shedding on those who think themselves to be — but are not — her children are still bitterer than the tears she shed at La Salette. This crusade aims precisely at making reparation for the sins of "friends"; at saving those who, loaded with graces by the Heart of Jesus, nevertheless pierce that divine Heart with the sharp lance of their pride and worldliness.

You will have already gauged, no doubt, what this adoration will bring to your families in grace and mercy. It could not be otherwise! Do you think you can make sacrifices in reparation, and console so lovingly the agonizing Heart of Jesus without drawing down upon yourselves His richest

250

blessings? Many families devoted to His Sacred Heart know this today by experience, and in reading these lines tears of gratitude well up in their eyes.

Apostles of the Sacred Heart, take to heart this campaign which is the splendid crowning of your work. Seek out, zealously but discreetly, yet another *living lamp* willing to watch lovingly while the Master falls beneath the blows of cruel, ungrateful men. Sin gives Him no respite, let there be no respite in our reparation. Let us vanquish hate by love.

Chapter 24

A MESSAGE TO NIGHT ADORERS*

"O night more beautiful than the dawn!" (St. John of the Cross)

FORTUNATE ARE YOU MOST FAITHFUL SOULS, for you have taken to heart the sad complaint of the Savior agonizing in Gethsemani: "My soul is sorrowful unto death... Watch and pray with Me!"

So great was the sorrow that filled the Heart of the Savior, His veins burst asunder and He fell to the ground, covered with a bloody sweat.

"And there appeared an Angel from Heaven, strengthening Him."

Faithful adorers, outdo the consoling Angel! Offer to Jesus a chalice of consolation; but together with your love put into the chalice the tears of your own bitter sorrows — something an Angel cannot do.

Love the Lord Jesus with the generosity of a friend and with the courage of an apostle. Watch and pray with Him, joyfully sacrificing an hour of your well-earned rest.

He Himself told us He has at His disposal legions of Angels. Yet it was not these He invited to watch with Him, but us, for whom He agonized and for whom He died on the Cross. Humbly kneeling at His feet let us freely acknowledge we are sinners, that we have gone astray. Especially, let us weep over the greatest offence of all: our ingratitude! Like Veronica, on Calvary's sorrowful Way, let us offer to Him loving reparation and consolation.

---

* Written in 1957 from Valparaiso, Chile

Think this over: the darkness of night hides from our eyes — but not from the eyes of Jesus — the horrible crimes and sins by which a pleasure-seeking and materialistic people unceasingly scourge Him! And how many of them are members of His own household, as He Himself sorrowfully revealed to St. Margaret Mary!

Judas is ever on the alert. And following him come an ungrateful crowd of sceptics and the impure — a veritable army. Worse still are His hate-filled enemies who plot to crucify Him again: peddlers in sex, anti-religionists, freemasons and communists, furiously demanding the elimination of Jesus Whose moral code and Whose Church annoy and exasperate them. That is why they cynically insist on their freedom to sin, on their inconceivable right to damn themselves!

* * *

Night adorers, it is impossible for us to empty or dry up the hate-filled bilge of these modern Sanhedrins; nor can we wipe away the gall forced upon Him by the lack of love and the indifference of so many baptized who follow Him reluctantly and against their will. But we can, during our night watch, offer Him our love — a love marked by gratitude and perfect contrition.

Some there are, we know, who will consider this appeal a pious exaggeration. But you, His faithful friends, think otherwise. You know that what I have just proposed in His name was first requested by our divine Savior Himself. Moreover, is it asking too much to sacrifice one hour once a month, when a mother considers it her privileged duty to watch entire nights beside the bed of her sick child? When doctors and nurses do the same? When a soldier passes the entire night on guard duty for the love of country? Are we to be denied the privilege of giving to the Lord Jesus a fraction of the time we give to members of our families, to our friends, through love and loyalty?

Isn't it strange — and sad — that worldly-minded Catholics who recognize and admire the beauty and heroicity of the sacrifices made for family and country, take quite another attitude towards those made for the crucified Master? No wonder a Saint sadly exclaimed: "Poor Jesus! He is the only One who loves us with a love worthy of that name... and the only One Whom we serve with bargaining and stinginess, fearing one thing only... exaggeration!"

* * *

For your consolation and encouragement, read these words which follow. Jesus would have the right to inflict martyrdom on every one of us without promising any recompense, for as God His authority is absolute. But this isn't the way He acts. By a happy experience I declare categorically that a grateful Jesus royally recompenses this night watch especially by granting the much-needed miracle of the conversion of a prodigal son or a sinner in the home.

Take courage, you mothers whose hearts are breaking because that oldest son, so talented, has quit the Church and has become an unbeliever, choosing to exercise his free-will and ignore His Savior. There is still hope! And you wives whose husbands have turned their backs on Christ and the Church and who, despite the fact they consider themselves honest and upright men, are inwardly spiritually dead. How many of these corpses have I not seen rising from their tombs because their mothers, their daughters, their wives with the faith and love of St. Monica, have paid the price for their conversion, not only by their tears, but by their sacrifices and their prayers.

If there is a prodigal son or daughter, a wife or husband, a brother or sister, in your family — take heart! Lift up your eyes to Heaven; weep with the sorrowful Mother, pay the ransom, then one day you will join her in a hymn of thanksgiving for the wonderful spiritual resurrection of a loved one. Peace and confidence! Enkindle in your soul the fire of a great Eucharistic fervor through frequent — even daily — Mass and Communion, but of course without neglecting your duties. Go to Mass and receive Communion for those who never go. Lovingly and generously light the lamp of nocturnal adoration in your home by becoming a night adorer. Watch at night for those who sleep the dangerous sleep of mortal sin on the very precipice of eternity. With this divine money purchase the everlasting happiness of your loved ones. Through your Eucharistic love, by your penitential adoration, satisfy the justice of the just Judge ... and He will be their Savior!

Then in that decisive hour when death comes knocking at your door, this same Judge to Whom you offered your arms in the hour of His agony during your night adoration; this same Jesus Who never forgets, will in His turn come to you and in your own hour of agony will extend His blessed arms to you. Supported by these arms, and in the fiery Chariot of His merciful Heart, you will leave this land of exile for your true country, there to continue for endless centuries your adoration in an ecstasy of everlasting joy!

Chapter 25

TWO HOLY HOURS*

I

THE CRUCIFIX

WITH THE ANGELS AND SAINTS IN PARADISE let us pray:
Glory be to the Father and to the Son and to the Holy Ghost . . .
We love Thee Jesus, because Thou art Jesus!
We want Jesus to reign over us!
Most Sacred Heart of Jesus, Thy Kingdom come! (5 times)

In union with Our Lady of Sorrows let us fix our eyes on the Crucified Master dying on Calvary.

With her let us adore and kiss Jesus' Wounds as she did on Good Friday evening when His Sacred Body, torn to pieces, was laid in her arms.

She is now close, very close to us because the altar is really another Calvary.

Ah, never forget that Jesus, the King of glory keeps in Heaven and will keep for all eternity His Wounds shining as so many suns.

And in the tabernacle is the same risen, glorious, loving Jesus, still our Victim as on Calvary. Never forget that all of us, as well as the Jews, opened those wounds.

Let us now fervently adore them in union with Our Lady.

And first Jesus' adorable Head cruelly lacerated by the

---

* Preached by Father Mateo in San Francisco. Taken from the original manuscript.

crown of thorns! Ah! that painful crown proves that He really is a King of love and mercy.

In reparation for this mockery of His Kingship:

King omnipotent, crowned with thorns, we bless Thee!
King of Truth, crowned with thorns, we adore Thee!
King of Justice, crowned with thorns, we praise Thee!
King of Wisdom, crowned with thorns, we glorify Thee!
King of Mercy, crowned with thorns, we trust Thee!
King of Love, crowned with thorns, we love Thee!

That diadem of shame and suffering atones for the most grievous sins of pride.

Yes, pride is the sacrilegious insult to the humility of His birth at Bethlehem and to His unspeakable annihilation in the Blessed Sacrament. In the Eucharist the glorious Son of God, Splendor of His Father, has not even the form, the appearance of a man.

Now, pride, insults and outrages all these wonders of His wisdom and love. How many so-called intellectuals pass scornfully by, despising Him as did the Sanhedrists and Pontiffs on Calvary!

Not long ago a stateman said, "We must not tolerate a Gospel that preaches the madness of adoring a so-called God who died shamefully on a cross!"

Oh, let us protest against this blasphemy with a strong faith and a burning love! Let us offer atonement for countless proud and haughty Christians who insult Him by their pride.

Receive this prayer, O Lord, and save the great number of souls who are on the brink of the abyss:

Convert them, Jesus, by Thy divine Heart!

Convert the proud, the unbelievers who deny the existence of God, Creator of heaven and earth and of all things.

Convert them, Jesus, by Thy divine Heart!

Convert those unfortunates who deny the marvel of Thine Incarnation and who do not wish to acknowledge Thee our Brother by Thy human nature.

Convert them, Jesus, by Thy divine Heart!

Convert all those who, by spreading these denials, make them the pass-word to combat Thy Gospel and Thy sovereign rights.

Convert them, Jesus, by Thy divine Heart!

Convert the blind, who, seduced by these insidious doctrines, apostatize and deny Thy love.

Convert them, Jesus, by Thy divine Heart!

Convert those who, with infernal rage, undermine Christian institutions; those who have sworn Thy ruin in that of Thy Holy Church.

Convert them, Jesus, by Thy divine Heart!

Convert those who, out of hatred for Thine adorable Person, work to make Thy Cross vanish from the conscience of the child, from the soul of the people, and from the heart of the family.

Convert them, Jesus, by Thy divine Heart!

Convert those who, under cloak of science, and with hypocritical delicacy, work to eliminate Thee without violence from every walk of life.

Convert them, Jesus, by Thy divine Heart!

Convert those who, by deplorable ignorance, pay no heed to Thy words, and live in apparent tranquility far from all faith and the inspirations of grace.

Convert them, Jesus, by Thy divine Heart!

Finally, Jesus, convert those thousands of souls who, in far-off lands, live, act, and appear to rest peacefully in the shadow of paganism, heresy, and death.

Convert them, Jesus, by Thy divine Heart!

* * *

And now fix your eyes on Jesus' Eyes veiled with a torrent of bloody tears!

Those adorable Eyes illuminate the eternal Jerusalem, and their beauty enraptures the Angels and the Saints!

Those Eyes are veiled with tears because they contemplate Christian life turned into a pagan and sacrilegious comedy.

How many baptized Catholics seem to forget altogether the Precious Blood shed to save them. Jesus in agony, saw them caught up in the whirlwind of vanity and worldliness. They are not always wretched and wicked but extremely weak. They live as if they had no soul — intoxicated with pleasure, and very often in a state of mortal sin, in grave imminent danger.

Jesus a God died for them all, and they do not live for Him, nor with Him!

Oh, let us have pity on them lest they perish!
For our sins, for those of our relatives and friends,
Pardon, divine Heart!
For infidelity and profanation of holy days,
Pardon, divine Heart!
For impurity and public scandals.
Pardon, divine Heart!
For those who corrupt childhood and mislead youth.
Pardon, divine Heart!
For deliberate disobedience to Holy Church.
Pardon, divine Heart!
For crimes in homes and for the faults of parents and children.
Pardon, divine Heart!
For attacks committed against the Roman Pontiff.
Pardon, divine Heart!
For disturbers of peace in Christian society.
Pardon, divine Heart!
For abuse of the Sacraments and outrages to Thy Holy Eucharist.
Pardon, divine Heart!
For vile attacks by the press and for the machinations of secret societies.
Pardon, divine Heart!
Finally, Jesus, for the good who falter and for. the sinners who resist grace.
Pardon, Divine Heart!

* * *

The unfortunate criminals who died crucified suffered the torture of an unbearable, feverish thirst.

Jesus' Lips are burnt with that thirst. "Sitio" "I thirst" cries He. He dies athirst of love, athirst of souls.

"My little ones, quench my thirst. Come, give me your hearts. Oh, love Me!"

Alas! as response the pagan soldier applies gall and vinegar to Jesus' Lips.

But still worse many ungrateful children offer Jesus the gall of religious indifference! For one loving soul there are 10,000, nay, 100,000 for whom Jesus counts for nothing in their lives.

"Why did He die for men who didn't want Him; who needed Him not? That's foolish!"

Let us repair this rank ingratitude:
We love Thee, Jesus, for your ungrateful children.
Forgive them, Jesus, for your Father's glory!
Convert them, Jesus, for your Mother's honor!

And what sorrow for the dying Savior athirst of souls to contemplate the army of selfish Christians who could, and who ought to help in the work of the Catholic apostolate, who have certain qualities and means to be apostles in one way or another. But no! They have time and devotedness and enthusiasm for business, for friends, for family, but not for Jesus, nor for souls. And look around you at the immense crowd, the many ignorant, sickly souls abandoned, adrift, at the mercy of a wicked propaganda!

How the wicked are zealous to set satanic fires, to organize the apostolate of irreligion, to foment and kindle hatred.

Alas! Catholic apostles, men and women, boys and girls, are badly lacking everywhere. Let us be like the apostle Thomas, who cried out in an hour of danger, "let us go and die with Jesus and for Jesus!"

To obtain a generous love and zeal, let us pray:

We love Thee, O Jesus; grant us the grace to deem it an honor to be rejected by the world for the sake of Thine ignored Heart.

We love Thee, O Jesus; grant us the grace to deem it a happiness to be humiliated for the sake of Thy despised Heart!

We love Thee, O Jesus; grant us the grace to deem it a privilege to be disregarded for the sake of Thy outraged Heart.

We love Thee, O Jesus; grant us the grace to deem it an honor to be scoffed at for the sake of Thine afflicted Heart.

We love Thee, O Jesus; grant us the grace to deem it an honor to be despised for the glory of Thy Divine Heart.

We love Thee, O Jesus; grant us the grace to deem it a favor to be insulted for the triumph of Thy bruised Heart.

We love Thee, O Jesus; grant us the grace to deem it a favor to be forgotten in order to console Thy Sacred Heart.

We love Thee, O Jesus; grant us the grace to deem it a favor to be one day persecuted for the sake of Thy wounded Heart.

We love Thee, O Jesus; grant us the grace to regard it a delicious bitterness to be calumniated for the reign of Thy Sacred Heart.

We love Thee, O Jesus; grant us the grace to consider it a glory to be betrayed in a holocaust of reparation close to Thine immolated Heart.

We love Thee, O Jesus; grant us the grace to consider it a favor to be hated in union with Thine agonizing Heart!

We love Thee, O Jesus; grant us the grace of choosing as a real privilege to be condemned by the world as a homage of reparation to Thine ignored Sacred Heart!

O! we entreat Thee to grant that we may receive lovingly our rightful share of the outrages and agony of Thy Eucharistic Heart.

*　*　*

Now look at those adorable Hands that showered blessings; that cured the sick; those adorable Hands kissed by the happy mothers and their little ones; those adorable Hands that Our Lady pressed upon Her heart at Nazareth, with love and adoration; those adorable Hands that took the bread and the chalice, that distributed the first Communion to the Apostles at the Last Supper.

Look, oh, look at them pierced, streaming with Blood, streaming mercy and salvation, even then, especially then, tender, beautiful! Ah, those two awful wounds repair the abuse of grace! Those bleeding Hands weep over many privileged but unfaithful souls. Yes, souls privileged in their Catholic education; souls who heard many a merciful call; who, during a retreat, during a mission felt that Jesus loved them very dearly, but who also realized that Jesus was expecting a generous gift of their hearts in return. And like the rich young man in the Gospel, they sadly turned away.

In the name of those who abuse Divine Mercy, to spare them a rigorous justice — to make up for that dangerous sin, let us pray:

By Thy Hands pierced because they blessed and pardoned us,

Convert all sinners, O Sacred Heart!

By Thy divine Feet pierced through and through because they left on earth, imprints of peace and mercy,

Convert all sinners, O Sacred Heart!

By Thy Lips which spoke the language of mercy and felt a burning thirst for our sickly souls,

Convert all sinners, O Sacred Heart!

By Thy divine Eyes, illuminated with the light of Paradise, which shed so many tears to wash away our faults and obliterate them forever,

Convert all sinners, O Sacred Heart!

By Thy Sacred Body which became one living wound to give life to a world transgressing Thy divine Law,

Convert all sinners, O Sacred Heart!

By Thy pierced Side in which we wish to take refuge during life, at the hour of death, and for all eternity,

Convert all sinners, O Sacred Heart!

If you feel remorse of conscience, if those Hands wounded by your half-heartedness touch you, yield to His loving call.

* * *

In a spirit of penitent love kiss with fervent love the Savior's Feet!

With that cruel nail Jesus rooted and nailed Himself to our land of exile where He was born. With these wounds He repairs the awful abuse of Christian liberty, for the prodigals of His fold, and most especially for those slipping fast into the abyss of sensuality and impurity.

Yes, He repairs for the frightful neo-paganism of modern families, for the incredible relaxation of morals, and in a special way for the social, dreadful plague of birth control and the ruinous scandal of divorce.

Like Mary Magdalen, tearfully kissing those adorable Feet, let us implore mercy:

For those who traffic in public sins, in the depravity of morals and the perversion of consciences, my Jesus, mercy!

For perverters, who through the press and bad literature, enrich themselves while leading souls to eternal damnation, my Jesus, mercy!

For those who make a real sacrilegious profession of exciting evil passion through corrupt theaters, licentious shows, and the profanation of art, my Jesus, mercy!

For those weak souls who, in defiance of Thy Law and the remorse of conscience, cooperate in the social scandal of luxury, of immoral fashions and the indecent stage, my Jesus, mercy!

For the great number of those who falsifying their conscience and their Christian sense, see no grave danger in the social revolt against Thy Holy Commandments, my Jesus, mercy!

For those who by their position, Jesus, should spare Thee the bitterness of these insults and who are not opposed to them through timidity or because they wish selfish transactions with the world, my Jesus, mercy!

263

The thirst for His Father's glory and for souls has exhausted Jesus' Precious Blood.

"Father, into Thy Hands I commend My Spirit" He cries out. And Jesus breathed His last!

One hour later the soldier Longinus approaches and thrusts the lance into Jesus' side! His Sacred Heart is pierced through!

Listen: that lance is the sin of ingratitude.

In that solemn hour Our Lady could have said the same words that Jesus, centuries after, will pronounce before the bewildered eyes of St. Margaret Mary, "Behold the Heart that has loved men so much!"

Alas! the Lover Jesus is not loved in return. "They repay me," He said to St. Margaret Mary, "with coldness, indifference and ingratitude, especially in the Sacrament of My love." This is indeed very sad but unhappily it is only too true!

For instance, the gift of God, The Holy Sacrifice of the Mass is not thoroughly appreciated. We would sacrifice everything and rush to see an extraordinary being coming from outer space and landing on our earth; and the Creator of the stars and the Son of God is daily immolating Himself at the altar, and we remain cold, indifferent. Even Holy Communion itself is not always fruitful because we are lacking due generous dispositions.

The forsaken Tabernacle is very often a lonely prison. Jesus is left alone with angels. But the Eucharist was not created for angels but for us His children. "What else could I have done? What else could I give to win your hearts, to melt the ice of indifference, to kindle the fire of love in your souls?"

Oh, adorable Master, my beloved Savior, my God and my all, allow me to make a bold but legitimate statement. Yes, allow me to give you an answer in the name of this loving "little flock."

Jesus, you reproached your Apostle Thomas for his lack of faith; to cure him and to conquer him You said: "Come and put your hands into the wounds of My feet and hands. Come and put your hands in the wound of My side!" Jesus, adorable Master, You transformed your Apostle Thomas when you allowed him to enter into that sanctuary to feel the beatings of Your Heart. Jesus, Jesus, do the same with us. With the lance we have opened wide and deep the wound of your side. We, not the lance have pierced your Sacred Heart. Permit us then, give us the right, to put not only our hands but our very souls, our hearts into that precious, delightful, saving Wound. But, oh, beloved Master, please, close that wound behind us, and keep us captive in that heavenly prison with all those we love. For your glory keep us there in time and for eternity!

FINAL PRAYER

Remember Thy Promises, O Divine Heart!

Have pity, sweet Jesus! Remember Thou hast promised victory to the armies which fight under the standard of Thy Sacred Heart!

Remember Thy Promises, O Divine Heart!

Have pity, sweet Jesus! Remember Thou hast promised peace to the homes which lovingly enthrone the image of Thy Sacred Heart.

Remember Thy Promises, O Divine Heart!

Have pity, sweet Jesus! Remember Thou hast promised to soothe the pains of afflicted souls who seek consolation in Thy Sacred Heart.

Remember Thy Promises, O Divine Heart!

Have pity, sweet Jesus! Remember Thou hast promised to melt the ice of indifference by firing the world with the burning love of Thy Sacred Heart.

Remember Thy Promises, O Divine Heart!

THE HOLY EUCHARIST

*Glory be to the Father and to the Son and to the Holy
Ghost ...*
We love Thee Jesus because Thou art Jesus!
Most Sacred Heart of Jesus, Thy Kingdom come!
We want Jesus to reign over us!

Close to St. John the beloved apostle, like him leaning
our hearts on the Sacred Heart, let us in spirit assist at the
Last Supper. In the Tabernacle He is the same living, loving
Master, Jesus Son of God, Jesus Son of Mary, gentle, sad, as
appealing as He was on Holy Thursday. "Take," He says,
"eat ... and drink ... for this Eucharistic Banquet is the
greatest gift of my Sacred Heart. Take and keep in this
Eucharistic Sacrifice and Sacrament the treasure of My own
Sacred Heart — yours forever!"

Ah! is this not what St. Paul calls the *stultitia* ... "the
foolishness" of Christ, of Jesus' love?

Yes, "foolishness" because the Lord knew in advance what
Calvary and the altar would mean for Him.

Yes, while celebrating His first Mass on Holy Thursday
He saw throughout the centuries the army of ungrateful children. He saw the army of His mortal enemies, but He saw
you too, the little flock of His friends, making reparation this
evening, offering Him the Chalice of your consolation.

Overwhelmed by such a miracle of love let us say together:
Blessed be Jesus in the most holy Sacrament of the altar!
(5 times)

(*Here make a personal intimate consecration to the Sacred
Heart. This is His own request. Include in it the members
of your family.*)

Oh, wonder of wonders! In order to perpetuate the startling miracle of the Eucharist, during the Last Supper Thou
hast created, oh Jesus, another Christ.

Yes, Thou didst create that marvel the priesthood. Since

then, we Catholic priests reproduce at the Altar the prodigy of the Last Supper. Invested with Thy power we offer to the Blessed Trinity the Oblation of Holy Thursday, we renew the Sacrifice of Calvary.

Dear friends, always remember the priest is far greater, more richly blessed than the angels. The priesthood is the greatest honor bestowed upon mankind. We belong to Christ's royal dynasty!

Here let us ask for priestly vocations in your Catholic families:

Multiply Thy apostles, oh Sacred Heart! (3 times)

Bless our Christian homes with vocations, oh Sacred Heart!
(3 times)

Give us saintly priests, oh Sacred Heart! (3 times)

We Catholics possess a still greater gift, the Holy Father, the vicar of Jesus Christ.

Our visible Jesus, His face, His countenance: the Pope.
Jesus' audible voice: the Pope!
Jesus' positive word: the Pope!
Jesus' genuine teaching: the Pope!
Jesus' infallible authority: the Pope!

We thank Thee, Jesus, for the gift of the Pope! (3 times)

We praise Thee, Jesus, for the grace of priesthood!
(3 times)

(Three Hail Marys for the Pope and for the clergy.)

Now let us follow the Lord Jesus from the Cenacle to Gethsemane.

Oh! the awful vision of horror and crime that like a hurricane struck Jesus' soul in the Garden of Olives.

So cruel is His agony that His veins burst asunder ... He is sweating blood.

One of the most deadly arrows piercing His Sacred Heart was the vision of unfaithful and ungrateful friends.

"Didst Thou see us amongst that crowd, Lord?"

Oh! the countless multitude of false friends, of traitors who for money and for creatures, for a brilliant position, for pleasure, or for ambition, betray Thee, Jesus! They belong to the dynasty of Judas!

Forgive them, Jesus, we'll pay their ransom. (5 times)

(Two promises here in the name of the Sacred Heart to pay the ransom of your loved ones:)

One more Mass, one more Communion during the week for sinners, for those who never go. Don't refuse that joy, that glory to the Sacred Heart. And once a month one hour of Night Adoration in your home! If you actually saw Jesus covered with wounds, bathed in His Blood, in agony, would you dare refuse Him this consolation?

May He say to you this evening, "I looked for consolation and I found it. I bless you because you have been generous enough to watch one hour with Me!"

I know you are generous and responsive, then let us ask without delay the reward promised to loving friends:

"Jesus, Jesus, when we are in agony give us your promised consolation, oh Sacred Heart!"

"Jesus, Jesus, when we are in agony give us your promised peace, oh Sacred Heart!"

"Jesus, Jesus, when we are in agony give us your promised mercy, oh Sacred Heart!"

* * *

Judas approaches, and with a perfidious kiss betrays his Master, his Savior, his Lord, his God!

Jesus surrenders. Look at Him stretching out His adorable hands to be tightly bound — and that to give us Christians freedom!

From one in the morning until 5... He remains a King of shame, King of a sacrilegious comedy, crowned with thorns, covered with the mantle of ignominy; He the Son of God; He the splendor of the Father; He the Judge of the living and the dead.

With loving indignation let us make reparation for that crime:

"King of sorrows crowned with thorns, have mercy on us!"
"King of justice crowned with thorns, have mercy on us!"
"King of wisdom crowned with thorns, have mercy on us!"
"King of truth crowned with thorns, have mercy on us!"
"King of love crowned with thorns, have mercy on us!"

Now listen with deep emotion: what I've quoted from the Gospel was the crime of Holy Thursday night twenty centuries ago. But unhappily it is also the crime of our own days.

The anti-Christian forces are waging a world wide war of hatred against God.

To make up for those who try to dethrone the Beloved Master, let us say:
"We adore Thee, Crucified Master!"
"We glorify Thee, Crucified Savior!"
"We love Thee, Crucified King!"

Still better than your prayer of love and reparation is your apostolate. Catholic actionists, legionaries of Mary, sodalists, promise to crown Jesus with souls; promise to be apostles of the Sacred Heart.
"We'll be Thy faithful friends, oh Sacred Heart!" (3 times)
"We'll be Thy soldiers, oh Christ the King!" (3 times)

⁂

Contemplate now the King of Kings before the tribunal of the wicked ... the sentence is an iniquitous "Tolle!" away with Him ... we don't want Him to reign over us.

His crime? He has loved us as only God can love! "Away with Him! Away with Him!"

Once again that sentence was pronounced by Pilate and ratified by the mob, 20 centuries ago.

Alas, that sentence of death against Christ and His Church is a storm of satanic fury constantly dashing against Calvary; constantly storming Christ's Kingship on earth today worse than on Good Friday.

A few years ago the whole world, and the Pope first, protested vigorously against a cruel persecution of the Jewish people. But tell me, dear friends, where have you heard of such a unanimous and strong protest against the awful and long persecution of Catholics in Ireland? Against the satanic persecution of Catholics by the Communists? Against the shameful persecution of Catholics in Mexico?

A worldwide plot of silence and sometimes abominable approval covered up these countless attempts against the rights of Jesus Christ. That is to say: pity and tears and help for all the victims excepting the divine Victim.

No pity, no tears for Jesus Christ; no protesting against the official Neros in history who everywhere have crucified Him. Jesus Christ is not allowed to appear in public. He is tolerated to reign in Churches but not in public institutions:

• not at home: godless families, crime of birth control and divorce;

• not in the school: godless neutral schools;

• not in society: when sin is pleasure it is no longer sin, say the worldly.

• not in national life: godless nations and godless states, excepting your dear America where officially the Holy Name of God is often pronounced. May He bless your country!

You easily understand now why the world seems a tremendous volcano in eruption belching forth fire and hatred.

Does this mean that we are lost, without any hope? No, a thousand times no!

Jesus solemnly affirmed: "I promise I will reign through My Heart," and He added explicitly, "in spite of My enemies!"

Leo XIII said officially: "The modern banner leading the Church to victory is the Sacred Heart."

And Pius XI has affirmed: "The hour of the Sacred Heart has come and that hour is the greatest hope of the Church and Society!"

In a spirit of loving reparation, while the anti-christian army cries out with fury as on Good Friday, "Away with Him. We want Him not," we, the friends of the Sacred Heart, we His soldiers and apostles, will answer that blasphemy with a prayer of atonement:

270

Come, reign over us, King of souls! (3 times)
Come, reign over us, King of families! (3 times)
Come, reign over us, King of society! (3 times)
Come, reign over us, King of nations! (3 times)

And through Thy reign, oh Christ the King, give to this topsy-turvy world true Christian, social justice and Thy peace-divine, unshakable!

Most Sacred Heart of Jesus, Thy Kingdom come!

Chapter 26

IN THE SANCTUARY OF THE HOME[1]

MANY YEARS AGO I launched my first appeal to generous souls to watch one hour at night in the home in reparation to the Sacred Heart for the sins of families. My invitation was intended for a chosen few — faithful friends of the Sacred Heart — the "little flock" of adorers who, once a month would offer consolation to the Master during the hours of the night, when He is so outraged and insulted by the sins of His so-called "friends."

The response to the first appeal was overwhelming: a veritable Palm Sunday of Hosannas to the King, rising from thousands and thousands of family sanctuaries all over the world, sanctuaries wherein an army of Night Adorers is watching during the night in a spirit of love, of social reparation and apostolate. Truly, we may say an army of *perpetual adorers* who, "from the rising of the sun until the going down thereof," in union with the priests offering the Holy Sacrifice of the Mass, are making reparation for the sins of men.

Here in this great country, the number of Night Adorers is already well over the four hundred thousand mark, and perhaps even higher than we realize, for there are many who sacrifice an hour of their sleep each month and even more often, whose names are known only to the Sacred Heart.

If, twenty years ago, I was convinced of the necessity and importance of penance in the sanctuary of the home itself, I am now convinced more than ever. The attack on the home, the last line of defense of Christian civilization, has been

---

1 While in the United States, Father Mateo issued a new call
for Night Adorers directed to American Catholics.

intensified, and pagan ways and pagan customs have invaded the homes that should be other Nazareths, to such an extent that many — far too many — superficial Catholic families are lifting their voices with those of the enemies of Christ: "We will not have this man reign over us!" If reparation is not made by penance for this modern betrayal, *in the home itself*, then we may expect and fear the swift punishment of a merciful but just God avenging the sacrilegious violation of a sanctuary consecrated by the Incarnation and Birth of His own divine Son.

I say that I am more than ever convinced of the necessity of penance in the home itself. Naturally I praise and admire the great effort being made on all sides to develop the Eucharistic spirit in the church, and while I heartily applaud this splendid Christian idea, I must say that I cling more strongly still to the no less high ideal cf Eucharistic adoration *in the home*. Those really acquainted with the spirit of reparation of our crusade and its transcendent importance in the home, will readily understand the "why" of this preference on my part for the *Eucharistic adoration within the family circle*. Not every one is able to make the hour of Eucharistic adoration in the church, particularly at night. Must they be deprived, then, of the honor and privilege of consoling the Divine Prisoner, alone and forsaken in so many tabernacles? By no means! In the *sanctuary of their own homes*, let them prostrate themselves in spirit before the tabernacle, and in union with the priests who at that moment, in some part of the world, are offering the Sacrifice of Calvary to the Triune God, let them adore, praise, petition and atone in the name of their own and other families who offend and sadden the Sacred Heart by their daily denial of His rights as King. I think there is no stronger, no better way to stress the beauty and necessity of family prayer, of penance and Eucharistic spirit, than by developing this threefold spirit in the home where the Sacred Heart has been *enthroned*[2] in spirit and in

2 It is to be noted that it is not necessary to have the *Enthronement* in order to become a Night Adorer. Nor is it *obligatory* to make Night Adoration if you have had the Enthronement.

truth. I would even dare affirm that the truest Catholic families are those that have understood the beauty and the duty of offering the homage of prayer and penance in the sanctuary of the home, where the family lives, struggles and where we die.

Once more then, Christian fathers and mothers, sons and daughters — all you who love the Sacred Heart, priests and sisters as well as the laity — once more I appeal to you in His Name and for His outraged honor and glory, to make reparation in a spirit of generous love and penance, for the fatal modern social apostasy of the home.

Will you not offer to watch one hour once a month with the adorable Master during His mortal agony? Is it asking too much of you to sacrifice one hour of your sleep once a month to console the sorrowful Heart of the King, when so many are devoting hours and even entire nights to sins which afflict and insult Him? Is not this the least we can offer? Prove that you are His faithful friends!

I have never been disappointed in American Catholics, and I am convinced that I will not be disappointed now. Many more will join the thousands already giving consolation to the King, as did the angel in the Garden of Olives. But — and this is most important — only generous and fervent souls are wanted, not those who think to console Him by night and insult Him by day, or those who try to make up in one hour for the offenses they have committed during the rest of the month. And this is particularly true of those so-called Christian women, who by their pagan attitude especially as regards dress, are piercing the Hearts of Christ and His Blessed Mother.

I am appealing to a select few now, as I appealed before. It is not the crowds of Palm Sunday we want, but the little band of faithful friends who stood by the Cross of Jesus as He died amid the taunts and insults of His own people. To them I stretch out my hands, pleading in the name of the Divine Outcast . . . What is your answer?

* * *

274

From the Vatican, April 4th, 1929.

Most Reverend Father,

The Sovereign Pontiff gladly received the letters in which so many Bishops give their approbation to the work of Nocturnal Adoration. These letters, coming from you as a homage, on behalf of all the Night Adorers and on the occasion of His jubilee, have given Him the greatest pleasure.

His Holiness cordially thanks you for this fresh testimony of the veneration felt for His Sacred Person. He sees in it, yet another mark of the zeal for souls which animates you, and of your devotedness to the social duty of making reparation for the many outrages offered to Our Lord, who loves men so much, and yet, is not loved in return.

The Sovereign Pontiff, having noted with great satisfaction the good results of this apostleship, blesses it wholeheartedly. In the belief that it will help much towards enabling many souls to live in true accord with the teaching of the Holy Gospels, He sends, as a pledge of His Fatherly interest, to you and to *all Nocturnal Adorers, a special Apostolic Blessing*.

Accept, most Reverend Father, the assurance of my own devotedness in your regard.

(*Signed*) CARD. GASPARRI.

FURTHER INSTRUCTIONS

The following simple remarks will help our crusade to keep up faithfully the enthusiasm which marked its origin and even intensify the flame of love that gave it birth.

1) I have never written on the subject of Night Adoration in the Home without recommending to our promoters to recruit only among the best Catholics. I repeat this because it is most important. Enthusiasm must never cause us to forget that we are not looking for numbers, but for hearts "of gold." I say of gold, not of silver, gilt, still less of gilded straw. Choose carefully, this is an altar-offering, it must be as worthy as possible of the Sacred Heart. We need a select group of sincerely pious souls, joyful in sacrifice because

275

they love Jesus Crucified, souls that understand immolation, penance and the redeeming value of a love that is as strong as death; a chosen few with a high standard of morality and shrinking with horror from all guilty compromise with worldliness, dangerous amusements and occasions of sin. Frivolity and reparation cannot go hand in hand, so be scrupulously careful in choosing these "living Night Lamps."

2) It would be a source of great spiritual profit and edification if, at least twice a year, a meeting of Adorers could be held in church. On this occasion, a zealous priest should preach about the great and beautiful duty of reparation and recite a public act of reparation to the Blessed Sacrament before giving Benediction. In the United States, Canada, Italy and elsewhere, this initiative has given most consoling results. I have myself presided over many splendid meetings of Adorers and was deeply moved thereby.

While kneeling silently before Jesus in the Host and steeping our souls in the true spirit of this beautiful devotion, it will stimulate us to think that, if careless Catholics are innumerable, yet Jesus has many faithful friends ready to make reparation.

3) One day the last hour will come — that hour of peace and merciful justice, when the King of Love will call His fervent Night Adorers to the eternal marriage feast. Therefore I ask:

(a) That the death of each Night Adorer should be made known to the local or National Center, for we intend to celebrate once or twice a month a Mass for deceased members. Thus we shall repay their fidelity in the name of the Heart of Jesus and with nothing less than His own Precious Blood offered on the Altar.

(b) The promoter, or family of the deceased, should endeavor to find, as soon as possible, another Adorer to take the vacant post at the same hour and on the same night. We are happy to note that this has often been done without our having proposed it. This proves to what an extent we can trust souls formed at the school of the Heart of Jesus.

I recommend to our fervent Adorers always to pray for the following intentions during their hour's watch:

For our Holy Father the Pope, who greatly needs his children's prayers.

For the clergy, the special friends of Jesus — His priests.

For the prodigal sons, the poor sinners of the family, whom we shall save by this penance and prayer.

For those who are in their last agony and perhaps will appear before the tribunal of the Sovereign Judge before the end of the hour's watch. By imploring mercy for them we, too, shall obtain mercy.

Let us make reparation for the insults offered to the Most Holy Sacrament of the Altar, insults far more frequent than we can imagine. Remember how our Lord Himself asked Saint Margaret Mary for this Eucharistic reparation.

Lastly, pray fervently that the Heart of Jesus may reign over society, not only by a silent, rather timid triumph, but as King and Master, as divine Lawgiver, in social and national life. Let us do all in our power to build up His reign. Dear Night Adorers, make straight His path! Cut out for Him a road to victory! Forward! May His Kingdom come.

One final thought. If Jesus has promised to repay by a heaven of delights one cup of cold water given in His Name, what does He reserve for faithful Adorers who offer Him the chalice of love and reparation? If the reward of eternal life is promised to those who have visited the poor, consoled them in their sadness and given them food and drink, what reward will not Jesus give to the faithful friends who watch with Him at night to make amends for sin?

Relying on His divine promise, I venture to assert that the names of Night Adorers have already been faithfully inscribed in the Book of Life, the Heart of Jesus, whence they will never be effaced.

APPENDICES

Appendix 1

HOW TO ENTHRONE THE SACRED HEART

1. *Why prepare for the Enthronement?*

For the same reason you prepare for a birthday, or for the arrival of a distinguished guest! But the Enthronement is more important than these. By it you are inviting to your home the King of Kings, a Divine Guest, Whose birthday is celebrated by the entire world. The coming of Jesus to your home is worthy then of a fitting preparation.

2. *How prepare?*

a. *By reading.* Learn more about the Enthronement by reading one of the pamphlets or books listed below. For pamphlets we suggest: *The Enthronement of the Sacred Heart in the Home*, 64 pages. *Favors from the King*, by Fr. Mateo, gives examples of blessings from the Enthronement, 80 pages. For a complete manual read: *Enthronement of the Sacred Heart*, by Fr. Francis Larkin, SS.CC., 416 pages. All may be ordered from the National Enthronement Center, Washington 17, D.C.

b. *By prayer.* We suggest a triduum — the three days preceding the day of your Enthronement right in your own home. The prayers in this triduum were composed to help you. In them you will find the main ideas of the Enthronement: Jesus our King, our Brother and our Friend, sharing our everyday family life; also the Biblical texts on which these ideas are based. We suggest members of the family take turns reading these texts.

c. *By Mass and Communion.* It would be good if at least one member of the family could go to Mass and receive Communion during the triduum. But at least on the day of the ceremony the entire family should make every effort to receive Communion together, in honor of the Sacred Heart of Jesus.

d. *By setting up a "throne"* in the living room in a conspicuous place. A fireplace mantle is ideal. Otherwise use a table fixed up like an altar. Place a box or books in the center on which to enthrone the image of the Sacred Heart. Cover it with a white cloth and decorate the "throne" with flowers and candles. (They need not be blessed). In another part of the room place the statue or picture of the Sacred Heart on a small table with Holy Water. Here it will be blessed and then carried by the head of the house to the "throne."

Note: If you use a picture to be hung on the wall, in order to bring out the idea of a shrine, place a wall bracket below the picture on which flowers and candles may be placed. This shelf may also be used for a statue. It is important to emphasize the throne aspect of your enthroned Sacred Heart image. Otherwise it will be "just another picture or statue."

e. *Invite guests.* Obtain ceremonials for each person present, and an Enthronement certificate which will be signed at the end of the ceremony. (Ceremonials and certificates may be obtained from your local center or directly from the National Center). Prepare to serve refreshments.

Note: While it is fitting that your home be neat and clean on the day of your Enthronement, it is not necessary to repaint your home, get new furniture, or otherwise go to great expense. But we do suggest the members of the family be clothed in their Sunday-best, as befitting the Divine Guest Who honors the family by His presence. Let mother and girls be modestly dressed and the men-folk with coats and ties. When the priest arrives all should rise to greet him, and if necessary, he should be introduced to the guests. If you wish, the ceremony may be preceded by the liturgical blessing of the home. In this case, let the father escort the priest through the house with a lighted candle, accompanied or not, by the immediate members of the family, as you see fit (It is

well to tell the priest in advance you want your home blessed,
so he may bring his ritual. Be sure to have Holy Water.)

f. *Invite a priest to preside.* If for any reason you are
unable to have a priest present, you may have the ceremony
without him. In this case have your picture or statue blessed
in advance. The father, mother or other member of the family
may lead the prayers. Instead of the talk, the 12 Promises
could be read.

TRIDUUM OF PRAYERS
IN PREPARATION FOR THE ENTHRONEMENT

THE FIRST DAY:

TO THE HEART OF OUR KING, "JESUS OF BETHLEHEM."

1. The father or mother announces: "The third joyful mystery, the Birth of Jesus in the stable at Bethlehem. In this
mystery we will see Jesus being adored as King, by His
parents, the shepherds and the Three Kings." One of the
children (or parent) reads a passage from the New Testa-
ment:

Now in the sixth month the angel Gabriel was sent from
God to a town of Galilee called Nazareth to a virgin betrothed to a man named Joseph, of the house of David, and
the virgin's name was Mary. And when the angel had come
to her, he said, "Hail, full of grace, the Lord is with thee.
Blessed art thou among women." When she had heard him
she was troubled at his word, and kept pondering what manner of greeting this might be.

And the angel said to her, "Do not be afraid, Mary, for
thou hast found grace with God. Behold, thou shalt conceive
in thy womb and shalt bring forth a son; and thou shalt call
his name Jesus. He shall be great and shall be called the
Son of the Most High; and the Lord God will give Him the
throne of David his father, and he shall be *king* over the
house of Jacob forever; and of his kingdom there shall be no
end." . . .

But Mary said, "Behold the handmaid of the Lord; be

283

it done to me according to thy word." And the angel departed from her . . . (Luke 1: 26-38)

And Joseph also went from Galilee out of the town of Nazareth into Judea to the town of David, which is called Bethlehem — because he was of the house and family of David — to register, together with Mary his espoused wife, who was with child. And it came to pass while they were there, that the days for her to be delivered were fulfilled. And she brought forth her firstborn son, and wrapped him in swaddling clothes, and laid him in a manger, because there was no room for them in the inn.

And there were shepherds in the same district living in the fields and keeping watch over their flock by night. And behold, an angel of the Lord stood by them and the glory of God shone round about them, and they feared exceedingly.

And the angel said to them, "Do not be afraid, for behold, I bring you good news of great joy which shall be to all the people; for today in the town of David a *Savior* has been born to you, who is *Christ the Lord*. And this shall be a sign to you: "You will find an infant wrapped in swaddling clothes and lying in a manger." And suddenly there was with the angel a multitude of the heavenly host praising God and saying, "Glory to God in the highest, and on earth peace among men of good will." . . .

So they went with haste, and they found Mary and Joseph, and the babe lying in the manger. And when they had seen, they understood what had been told them concerning this child. And all who heard marvelled at the things told them by the shepherds. But Mary kept in mind all these things, pondering them in her heart. And the shepherds returned, glorifying and praising God for all that they had heard and seen, even as it was spoken to them. (Luke: 1-20)

Now when Jesus was born in Bethlehem of Judea, in the days of king Herod, behold, Magi came from the East to Jerusalem, saying, "Where is he that is born *king* of the Jews? For we have seen his star, in the East *and have come to worship Him.*" . . .

And behold, the star that they had seen in the East went before them, until it came and stood over the place where the child was. And when they saw the star they rejoiced exceedingly. And entering the house, they found the child with Mary, his mother, and falling down *they worshipped him*. And opening their treasures they offered him gifts of gold, frankincense and myrrh. And being warned in a dream not to return to Herod, they went back to their own country by another way. (Matt. 2: 1-21)

2. One decade of the Rosary:

(1 Our Father, 10 Hail Marys)°

3. Prayer.

LET US PRAY

Sacred Heart of Jesus, we salute You, for You are the King of Kings, the Ruler of families and nations. But sad to say in many nations You have been dethroned and Your rights rejected. This is mainly because You were first dethroned in many families of which nations are composed.

Loving Master, we want to make up for this insult to Your divine Majesty by lovingly enthroning You as King of our family. Like Mary and Joseph, like the shepherds and the three Kings, we want to give You a royal welcome as they did when they adored You in Your humble home at Bethlehem.

Like them, we have no royal throne to offer You, but we can and we will offer something even more pleasing to You. In our home Your throne will be a living throne — the loyal hearts of the members of this family; Your royal crown, our acts of love.

O Mary, Queen of our home, by Your loving submission to the will of God in all things, obtain for us the grace never to sadden the Heart of our King by willful disobedience to His commandments or to those of His Church. May it be said of each of us what the Gospel says of Jesus, "He was subject to them."

---

* *Note:* If you so desire, after the Rosary you may add the beautiful Litany of the Sacred Heart, which will be found on page 293.

Good St. Joseph, guardian of our family, help us to make our Enthronement the beginning of a new life of love in our home. Through the presence of the Sacred Heart of Jesus in our family circle, and through your powerful intercession, may we receive the grace to know our King more personally, love Him more ardently and thus serve Him more faithfully. Amen.

INDULGENCED PRAYER TO BE SAID EACH DAY

O Christ Jesus, I acknowledge Thee to be King of the universe; all that hath been made is created by Thee. Exercise over me all Thy sovereign rights. I hereby renew the promises of my baptism, renouncing Satan and all his pomps and works, and I engage myself to lead henceforth a truly Christian life. And in an especial manner do I undertake to bring about the triumph of the rights of God and Thy Church, so far as in me lies. Divine Heart of Jesus, I offer Thee my poor actions to obtain the acknowledgment by every heart of Thy sacred kingly power. In such wise may the kingdom of Thy peace be firmly established throughout all the earth.

Most Sacred Heart of Jesus, Thy Kingdom come through Mary!

Sacred Heart of Jesus, protect our families!

Immaculate Heart of Mary, Queen of heaven and of our home, pray for us.

St. Joseph, friend of the Sacred Heart, pray for us!

St. Michael, first champion of the Kingship of Christ, pray for us!

Guardian Angels of our family, pray for us!

HYMN

(Here all stand and sing "To Jesus Heart All Burning.")

1. To Jesus Heart all burning, with fervent love for men.
   My heart with fondest yearning shall raise the joyful
       strain:

   CHORUS: While ages course along, blest be with loudest
       song,
   The Sacred Heart of Jesus, by every heart and tongue.
                                                    (repeat)

2. O Heart for me on fire, with love no man can speak.
   My yet untold desire, God gives me for Thy sake.

                                                    (Chorus)

END: All make the sign of the Cross: "In the name of the
Father, and of the Son, and of the Holy Ghost. Amen.

THE SECOND DAY:

TO THE HEART OF OUR BROTHER, "JESUS OF NAZARETH"

1. The father or mother announces: "The fifth joyful mystery, The Finding of the Child Jesus in the Temple and His
Return to Nazareth. In this mystery we will think of Jesus
the son of God living an ordinary life in the little home at
Nazareth with Mary and Joseph."

Bible reading:

And the child grew and became strong. He was full of
wisdom and the grace of God was upon him.

And his parents were wont to go every year to Jerusalem
at the Feast of the Passover. And when he was twelve years
old, they went up to Jerusalem according to the custom of
the feast. And after they had fulfilled the days, when they
were returning, the boy Jesus remained in Jerusalem, and his
parents did not know it. But thinking that he was in the cara-
van, they had come a day's journey before it occurred to them

to look for him among their relatives and acquaintances. And not finding him, they returned to Jerusalem in search of him.

And it came to pass after three days, that they found him in the temple, sitting in the midst of the teachers, listening to them and asking them questions. And all who were listening to him were amazed at his understanding and his answers. And when they saw him, they were astonished. And his mother said to him, Son, why hast thou done so to us? Behold, in sorrow thy father and I have been seeking thee."

And he said to them, "How is it that you sought me? Did you not know that I must be about my Father's business?" And they did not understand the word that he spoke to them.

And he went down with them and came to Nazareth, and was subject to them; and his mother kept all these things carefully in her heart. And Jesus advanced in wisdom and age and grace before God and men." (Luke 2: 40-52)

 2. One decade of the Rosary:
  (1 Our Father, 10 Hail Marys)*
 3. Prayer.

LET US PRAY

Dear Jesus, Son of God, when we call You, "Brother," we speak the truth for You are indeed just that. St. John told us so when in his Gospel he wrote: "But to as many as received him, he gave the power of becoming sons of God." Therefore we are Your adopted brothers and co-heirs of Heaven. But since You are a King, we too, have the privilege of being members of a royal family, as were Mary and Joseph.

How honored will we be to have our Brother-King come to dwell in our humble home in order to share our joys and sorrows! Once You are enthroned in our family, we will understand as never before the meaning of these words, "And the Word was made flesh and dwelt among us." No longer need we envy Mary and Joseph at Nazareth, for Your abiding presence in our home will make our family another Nazareth wherein we will vie with one another in giving You proofs

---

 * The Litany of the Sacred Heart may be added.

of our love. We will do this especially by the practice of family charity, trying to love each other as You have loved us.

O Mary, Queen of Nazareth, Mother of Jesus, obtain for us the grace to appreciate the presence of Your Divine Son enthroned in our home. Grant us a greater love for Jesus ever present in the Blessed Sacrament, a deeper love for Holy Mass, a more ardent longing to unite ourselves as often as possible with our loving Savior in Holy Communion.

Good St. Joseph, you were privileged to share the joys and sorrows of your foster-son at Nazareth. Teach us how to share our every-day joys and sorrows with our Brother, Jesus, here on earth, so that one day our entire family may join you and Mary in sharing the joys of Heaven where we will see our King and Brother face to face, and with you love, adore, thank, and praise Him for all eternity. Amen.

Here repeat the prayer, "O CHRIST JESUS..." from the first day.

Eucharistic Heart of Jesus, Thy Kingdom come in our home!

Our Lady of the Blessed Sacrament, pray for us!

O St. Joseph, foster-father of our Lord Jesus Christ and true spouse of Mary the virgin, pray for us!

Saints Joachim and Anne, parents of the Blessed Virgin Mary, pray for us!

Guardian Angels of our family, pray for us!

HYMN
(To Our Lady, or "To Jesus Heart All Burning.")

THE THIRD DAY:

TO THE HEART OF OUR FRIEND, "JESUS OF BETHANY"

1. The father or mother announces: "The first glorious mystery, The Resurrection. In this mystery we will think of Jesus rising in triumph from the tomb and we will hear Him promising Martha and Mary that their brother also will rise again."

Bible reading:

Now it came to pass as they were on their journey, that he entered a certain village; and a woman named Martha welcomed him to her house. And she had a sister called Mary, who also seated herself at the Lord's feet, and listened to his word..." (Luke 10: 38-42)

Now a certain man was sick, Lazarus of Bethany, the village of Mary and her sister Martha. Now it was Mary who anointed the Lord with ointment, and wiped his feet dry with her hair, whose brother Lazarus was sick. The sisters therefore sent to him, saying, "Lord, behold, he whom thou lovest is sick."

But when Jesus heard this, he said to them, "This sickness is not unto death, but for the glory of God, that through it the Son of God may be glorified." Now Jesus loved Martha and her sister Mary, and Lazarus. So when he heard that he was sick, he remained two more days in the same place. Then afterwards he said to his disciples, "Let us go again into Judea."

So then Jesus said to them plainly, "Lazarus is dead: and I rejoice on your account that I was not there, that you may believe. But let us go to him." Thomas, who is called the Twin, said therefore to his fellow-disciples, "Let us also go, that we may die with him."

Jesus, therefore, came and found him already four days in the tomb. Now Bethany was close to Jerusalem, some fifteen stadia distant. And many of the Jews had come to Martha and Mary, to comfort them on account of their brother. When, therefore, Martha heard that Jesus was coming, she went to meet him. But Mary remained at home.

Martha therefore said to Jesus, "Lord, if thou hadst been here my brother would not have died. But even now I know that whatever thou shalt ask of God, God will give it to thee."...

Jesus said to her, "Thy brother shall rise." Martha said to him, "I know that he will rise at the resurrection, on the last day." Jesus said to her, "I am the resurrection, and the life; he who believes in me, shall never die. Dost thou believe this?" She said to him, "Yes, Lord, I believe that thou art the Christ, the Son of God, who hast come into the world."

And when she had said this, she went away and quietly called Mary her sister, saying, "The Master is here and calls thee." As soon as she heard this, she rose quickly and came to him, for Jesus had not yet come into the village but was still at the place where Martha had met him.

When, therefore, the Jews, who were with her in the house and were comforting her, saw Mary rise up quickly and go out, they followed her, saying, "She is going to the tomb to weep there."

When, therefore, Mary came where Jesus was, and saw him, she fell at his feet, and said to him, "Lord, if thou hadst been here, my brother would not have died." When, therefore, Jesus saw her weeping, and the Jews who had come with her weeping, he groaned in spirit and was troubled, and said, "Where have you laid him?" They said to him, "Lord, come and see." And Jesus wept. The Jews therefore said, "See how he loved him." (John 11: 1-7)

2. One decade of the Rosary:
   (1 Our Father, 10 Hail Marys)*
3. Prayer.

LET US PRAY

"My delights are to be with the children of men." These words of the Book of Proverbs were certainly spoken about You, dear Jesus, Who came down to share our exile here below. You delight in being with us because we need You and You are our best Friend. You love all without exception: saints and sinners, the rich and the poor, the learned and the uneducated. You love all races, all peoples, but above all you love all families. You proved that love by spending thirty years in your home at Nazareth, and during Your public life many times You accepted invitations to visit families; You even told Zaccheus the sinner that "I must stay in thy house today."

---

* The Litany of the Sacred Heart may be said here.

But there was one family for whom You had a special love, that of Lazarus, Martha and Mary. How many times did You not stay in that beloved family at Bethany! It was there You found rest and solace after the fatigue of Your labors and the insulting attacks of Your enemies. At Bethany You were always received as a royal Guest, but also You were treated as a Brother and a Friend.

Dear Jesus, once You are enthroned in our home, we too, want to be Your true friends. We want You to feel at home with us. We will try to console You for those who do not love You. We will serve You like Martha; listen to You like Mary and thank You as did Lazarus. We feel confident that You will richly bless our family as You did this Family and all those families who invited You to their homes.

And if there are in our homes prodigal sons, lost sheep, sinners dead to the life of grace, we know that You will say to them as You did to Zaccheus, "Today salvation has come to this house." You will be to them a loving Father, a Good Shepherd, a divine Physician, for You are "the Resurrection and the Life."

O Mary, Mother of our best Friend, St. Joseph our patron, obtain for us the grace to make our home a true Bethany of the Sacred Heart. May our friendship with Jesus be loving, loyal, and lasting. May our daily living with our King and our Guest bring about a closer union of hearts, of minds and wills so that our entire family united with the Heart of Jesus here on earth, may remain united with Him and the Father and the Holy Spirit in our true home, Heaven, for all eternity! Amen.

Here repeat the prayer, "O CHRIST JESUS . . ." from the first day.

Heart of Jesus, King, Brother and Friend of our family, we welcome You to our home. Thy Kingdom come!

Our Lady of the Sacred Heart, pray for us!

St. Joseph, Model and Patron of lovers of the Sacred Heart, pray for us!

Saints Lazarus, Martha and Mary, pray for us!

Guardian Angels of our family, pray for us!

O Jesus, the Friend of little children, bless the little children of the whole world.

"Holy God We Praise Thy Name"

1. Holy God we praise Thy name. Lord of all we bow before
    Thee.
    All on earth Thy sceptre claim. All in Heaven above adore
    Thee.

    Chorus: Infinite Thy vast domain, everlasting, is Thy
    reign. (repeat)

2. Hark! The loud celestial hymn, angel choirs above are
    raising.
    Cherubim and Seraphim, in unceasing chorus praising.

    Chorus: Fill the Heavens with sweet accord,
    Holy, Holy, Holy Lord. (repeat)

LITANY OF THE SACRED HEART
(If so desired this Litany may be said each day after the Rosary.)

Lord, have mercy on us. Christ, have mercy on us.
  Lord, have mercy on us.
Christ, hear us. Christ, graciously hear us.
God, the Father of heaven,*
God the Son, Redeemer of the world,
God the Holy Ghost,
Holy Trinity, one God,
Heart of Jesus, Son of the eternal Father,
Heart of Jesus, formed by the Holy Ghost in the
  womb of the Virgin Mother,*
Heart of Jesus, substantially united to the Word of God,
Heart of Jesus, of infinite majesty.
Heart of Jesus, sacred temple of God,

* Have mercy on us.

Heart of Jesus, tabernacle of the Most High.*

Heart of Jesus, house of God and gate of heaven,

Heart of Jesus, burning furnace of charity,

Heart of Jesus, abode of justice and love,

Heart of Jesus, full of goodness and love,

Heart of Jesus, abyss of all virtues,

Heart of Jesus, most worthy of all praise,

Heart of Jesus, king and center of all hearts,

Heart of Jesus, in whom are all the treasures of
wisdom and knowledge,

Heart of Jesus, in whom dwells the fulness of divinity,

Heart of Jesus, in whom the Father was well pleased,

Heart of Jesus, of whose fulness we have all received,

Heart of Jesus, desire of the everlasting hills,

Heart of Jesus, patient and most merciful,

Heart of Jesus, enriching all who invoke thee,

Heart of Jesus, fountain of life and holiness,

Heart of Jesus, propitiation for our sins,

Heart of Jesus, loaded down with opprobrium,

Heart of Jesus, bruised for our offences,

Heart of Jesus, obedient unto death,

Heart of Jesus, pierced with a lance,

Heart of Jesus, source of all consolation,

Heart of Jesus, our life and resurrection,

Heart of Jesus, our peace and reconciliation,

Heart of Jesus, victim for sin,

Heart of Jesus, salvation of those who trust in Thee,

Heart of Jesus, hope of those who die in Thee,

Heart of Jesus, delight of all the saints.

Lamb of God, Who takest away the sins of the world,
spare us, O Lord.

Lamb of God, Who takest away the sins of the world,
graciously hear us, O Lord.

Lamb of God, Who takest away the sins of the world,
have mercy on us.

    V. Jesus, meek and humble of Heart,

    R. Make our hearts like unto Thine.

---

* Have mercy on us.

LET US PRAY

O Almighty and eternal God, look upon the Heart of Thy dearly beloved Son, and upon the praise and satisfaction He offers Thee in the name of sinners and for those who seek Thy mercy; be Thou appeased, and grant us pardon in the name of the same Jesus Christ, Thy Son, Who liveth and reigneth with Thee, in the unity of the Holy Ghost, world without end. Amen.

Appendix 2

THE CEREMONIAL *

1. The ceremony begins with the family gathering around the table holding the Sacred Heart image. This table is in another part of the room or in another room, some distance from the home altar where the image will be enthroned, to allow for a procession.
2. If a priest presides he begins with *the blessing of the image*.

Priest: Our help is in the name of the Lord.
All: Who made heaven and earth.
Priest: The Lord be with you.
All: And with your spirit.

Priest: Let us pray: Almighty, everlasting God, You approve the painting and sculpturing of the images of Your saints, so that as often as we gaze upon them we are reminded to imitate their deeds and sanctity: in Your kindness we implore You to bless † and sanctify † this image made in honor and in memory of the most Sacred Heart of Your only begotten Son, our Lord Jesus Christ; and grant that whosoever in its presence humbly strives to serve and honor the Sacred Heart of Your only begotten Son, may obtain through His merits and intercession grace in this life and everlasting glory in the world to come. Amen.

---

* For sample copies of updated, Scripture-oriented ceremonial, or combined Enthronement-Mass in the Home Ritual, please write to the: National Enthronement Center, Washington, D.C. 20017. Send self-addressed stamped envelope or 12¢ in stamps.

(The priest here sprinkles the image with Holy Water.)

[If the **Enthronement Record** is used it should be started and the instructions of the narrator followed.]

3. The father, accompanied by his wife and children (or, in his absence, the wife or other representative of the family), slowly carries the image to the altar where it is enthroned.

4. All recite the *Apostles' Creed* as an act of faith and reparation.

I believe in God, * the Father Almighty, * Creator of heaven and earth; * and in Jesus Christ, * His only Son, * our Lord; * Who was conceived by the Holy Spirit, * born of the Virgin Mary, * suffered under Pontius Pilate, * was crucified; * died, and was buried. * He descended into hell; * the third day He arose again from the dead; * He ascended into heaven, * sits at the right hand of God, the Father Almighty; * from there He shall come * to judge the living and the dead. * I believe in the Holy Spirit, * the holy Catholic Church, * the communion of Saints, * the forgiveness of sins, * the resurrection of the body, * and life everlasting. * Amen.

5. All sit down. (If the record is used, it may be interrupted at this point for a Scripture reading. Suggested are: Luke 19:1-10 or Luke 10:38-42 or Luke 1:26-33. Then follows a homily by the priest if he presides — or use the recorded talk.)

6. All kneel and say in unison

THE ACT OF CONSECRATION OF THE FAMILY

O Sacred Heart of Jesus, * who made known to St. Margaret Mary your great desire to reign over Christian families, * we are gathered here today * to proclaim your complete domination over our family. From now on we promise to lead a Christlike life: we will strive to develop in our home * all the virtues which bring with them the peace that you promised. And we will not compromise with the spirit of secularism * which you have so strongly denounced.

297

You will rule over our minds through our deep and living faith. You will be King of our hearts by our generous love for you; and we will cultivate this love by the frequent reception of you in Holy Communion.

Divine Heart of Jesus, * preside over our family gatherings; bless all our family undertakings, both spiritual and temporal. Sanctify our joys and comfort us in our sorrows. And if any member of our family should have the misfortune to offend you seriously, * remind him, O Sacred Heart of Jesus, * of your infinite love and mercy for the penitent sinner.

And when the hour of separation comes, * when death brings its sorrows into our family, * whether we go or whether we stay, * we will humbly accept your divine will. And at the same time we will console and comfort ourselves with the thought * that the time will come when our whole family will be united lovingly with you in heaven forever. There we shall sing a hymn of praise * to the infinite mercy and love of your Sacred Heart.

We ask the Immaculate Heart of Mary and our glorious protector, St. Joseph, * to offer you this family consecration of ours. May the memory of this consecration be with us always.

Glory to the divine Heart of Jesus, our King and our Father! Praise to the Divine Heart of Jesus that brought us salvation. To it be honor and glory forever. Amen.

7. One Our Father, Hail Mary, Glory be — for all absent members of the family, living and dead. (If so desired the "Prayer of the Faithful" may be added. If the priest presides he leads these prayers. Otherwise, the father. Or they may be said by five different persons.)

PRAYER OF THE FAITHFUL

That the loving Heart of Jesus become in truth the King, Brother and Friend of this consecrated family and of all here present, let us pray to the Lord. — (*All*: Lord have mercy!)

That the members of this family prove their love by generous obedience to God and His representatives: to parents and priests, to the Bishop and our Holy Father the Pope, let us pray to the Lord. — (*All*: Lord have mercy!)

That this family practice true Christian charity at home and with all neighbors, relatives, friends and enemies, regardless of race or color, let us pray to the Lord. — (*All*: Lord have mercy!)

That this dedicated family become outstanding in this parish by fidelity to family prayer, by love for the Eucharist, and by apostolic activities, let us pray to the Lord. — (*All*: Lord have mercy!)

That this consecrated family, by its love for chastity, modesty, and purity, console the Hearts of Jesus and Mary and make reparation for the breakdown of morality, especially in Christian families, let us pray to the Lord. — (*All*: Lord have mercy!)

(It is suggested that each member of the family, or one of the parents, add personal petitions to the above whenever these prayers are said. Daily use is suggested.)

PRAYER OF THANKSGIVING

O divine Heart of Jesus, who said to Zacheus, * "Today I must abide in your home," * we thank you for your great mercy in choosing our family from so many others * to receive the gift of your presence and of your love * and to make of this home a "domestic church" * wherein you will receive love, reparation, and consolation for the ingratitude of men.

Unworthy though we be, * we thank you for the honor you have bestowed upon us * by coming to preside over our home. Gratefully we adore you, * overjoyed to see you sharing with us our work, * our family problems, * and the joys of the members of this portion of the people of God.

We thank you for dwelling with us. From now on may this home be for you another Bethany * where you will always find yourself among friends.

Stay with us, Lord, * for as in Nazareth's lowly home, * we too have a tender love for the Virgin Mary, your mother, * whom you gave us to be our mother. Dispel from our hearts through your holy presence * all sorrow and discouragement. O most faithful Friend, * if you had been here in time of sorrow * the consoling balm of your peace would have healed those hidden wounds * which are known to you alone.

Stay with us, * for perhaps the darkness of trial is about to come upon us. Stay with us, for the night is coming on! The world strives to envelop us in the shadows of unbelief, * but we want to be faithful to you, * who alone are the Way, the Truth, and the Life. O divine Jesus, let your words to Zacheus be fulfilled in our family, * "Today salvation has come to this home."

Yes, dear Lord, take up your abode with us * so that we may live in your presence and grow in your love. You alone are King and you alone will we serve.

May your triumphant Heart, O Jesus, * be forever loved blessed, and glorified in this home! Most Sacred Heart of Jesus, Thy kingdom come! Amen.

8. *All stand.* (In honor of the Immaculate Heart of Mary, Queen and Mother of the Church and of the home, recite the following prayer.)

HAIL, HOLY QUEEN

Hail, Holy Queen, * Mother of mercy, * our life, * our sweetness, * and our hope! * To thee do we cry, * poor banished children of Eve; * to thee do we send up our sighs, * mourning and weeping in this valley of tears. * Turn then, * most gracious advocate, * thine eyes of mercy toward us, * and after this our exile, * show unto us the blessed fruit of thy womb, Jesus. * O clement, * O loving, * O sweet Virgin Mary.

V. — Pray for us, O holy Mother of God.

R. — That we may be made worthy of the promises of Christ.

9. *Leader*: Immaculate Heart of Mary, (*All*: pray for us!)
3 times
Leader: St. Joseph, (*All*: pray for us!)

Leader: St. Margaret Mary, (*All*: pray for us!)
All: Glory to the most Sacred Heart of Jesus forever and ever. Amen.

10. If a priest is present he gives his blessing. (If not, all bless themselves.)

11. Then the family (and the priest) sign the certificate of the Enthronement. It should be framed and hung near the Sacred Heart shrine.

KEEP YOUR ENTHRONEMENT ALIVE!

You have invited Christ into your home and you promised to share your family life with Him. Here is how you can do this.

1. Say the renewal prayer daily, before leaving the dinner table. Of course you can say it before your Sacred Heart shrine as well. But say it.

2. On certain occasions gather around your Sacred Heart shrine for a more formal renewal of the family consecration. For this purpose you may use either the Act of Renewal (beginning: "Most kind Jesus, humbly kneeling at Thy feet") or the Act of Consecration used on the day of your Enthronement. Both prayers are contained in the Enthronement Ceremonial.

Suggested occasions for this more solemn renewal are: First Fridays, birthdays, wedding anniversaries, day of Baptism, Baptismal anniversaries, First Communion, departure from home, Thanksgiving Day, family reunions, Christmas, New Year's Eve. (Many families make a Family Holy Hour from 11 p.m. to midnight New Year's Eve; why not yours?)

3. On the anniversary of your Enthronement we suggest you repeat the entire ceremony. Also when you move into a new home. In this way you give a new token of your love for the Sacred Heart and ask for His continued blessings. No obligation, of course, but love is given freely.

4. Since one of the purposes of the Enthronement in your home is to bring the family closer to Jesus in the Eucharist, at least one member should try to represent the family

at daily Holy Mass. Sunday — or at least monthly — should be "Family Communion Day," if at all possible.

Remember our Lord's words: *"I say to you further, that if two of you shall agree on earth about anything at all for which they ask, it shall be done for them by My Father in heaven. For where two or three are gathered together for My sake, there I am in the midst of them."* — *Mt.* 18:19-20.

Encourage daily reading from the Gospels, where you learn how much the Sacred Heart of Jesus loves you and your family This is another way to *keep Christ present in your home.*

DAILY RENEWAL

(We suggest you say the renewal prayer before the evening meal at table. The prayer below may be used to renew your "covenant" with our Lord on First Fridays, birthdays, etc. Of course, it may also be said daily.)

Most kind Jesus, humbly kneeling at Thy feet, we renew the consecration of our family to Thy divine Heart. Be Thou our King forever! In Thee we have full and entire confidence. May Thy spirit penetrate our thoughts, our desires, our words and our deeds. Bless our undertakings, share in our joys, in our trials and in our daily labors. Grant us to know Thee better, to love Thee more, to serve Thee without faltering.

By the Immaculate Heart of Mary, Queen of Peace, set up Thy kingdom in our country. Enter closely into the midst of our families and make them Thine own through the solemn Enthronement of Thy Sacred Heart, so that soon one cry may resound from home to home: "May the triumphant Heart of Jesus be everywhere loved, blessed and glorified forever! Honor and glory to the Sacred Hearts of Jesus and Mary.

"Sacred Heart of Jesus, protect our families."

(Say one Our Father, Hail Mary, Glory be for the intentions of the Holy Father.)

Most Sacred Heart of Jesus, Thy Kingdom come! Immaculate Heart of Mary, pray for our family! St. Joseph, friend of the Sacred Heart, pray for us! Our Patron Saints and Guardian Angels, pray for us!

(The *parents may now bless their children*. Make the sign of the cross on their foreheads and say, "May the blessing of almighty God, the Father, the Son and the Holy Spirit, descend upon you and remain forever. Amen.")

Appendix 3

NIGHT ADORATION — HOW IT WORKS

Spirit

Night Adoration in the home is made in a spirit of reparation, especially for the sins of pride and sensuality of so many so-called "Christian" families, most of which are committed during the night. Since sins are being committed every hour of the day and night, reparation should also be perpetual. Therefore, night adoration in the home is organized in such a way that at every hour of the night throughout the year, reparation is being made by the sacrifice of an hour of sleep, offered to the Sacred Heart as an act of homage and love during His mystical agony.

Regulations

1) The night adorer promises to make one hour of adoration once a month during the night. The night begins at 9 p.m. and ends with the hour from 5-6 a.m. Adoration made at any other time is meritorious but is not sufficient to gain the indulgences.

2) As an act of generosity, night adorers are encouraged to leave the choice of their date and hour of adoration to the director, but they are perfectly free to choose their own date and hour for any reasonable motive. Any date and hour of the month may be selected, either a fixed date, such as the 15th of the month or a movable date such as the First Friday.

3) In order to keep accurate records and to maintain continuous nights of adoration, deaths and withdrawals of members, as well as changes of address, should be made known to the promoter or to the center where your name is registered.

4) It is not necessary to renew the enrollment each year. Once enrolled, you continue to be a member until death or voluntary withdrawal.

5) The promise you make does not bind under pain of sin, even venial. Father Mateo started it as an act of loving homage and reparation to the Sacred Heart. Accordingly, its success and duration will depend upon the extent of the faithfulness and generosity of the members. This fidelity will be proved when through sickness or otherwise prevented you make your hour of adoration some other night. It is not necessary to notify the director of *temporary* change of date or hour.

Conditions for Membership

1) To become a member of the League, one's name should be inscribed at a local center or at the National Center. This may be done through a promoter or directly by mail. There is no charge for inscription. A small donation will be welcome to cover cost of membership card, postage, etc.

2) To be a true member of the League, the night adorer should pledge himself to give the example of a true Christian life which does not contradict the spirit of reparation, particularly by conforming to Catholic standards of decency in dress, reading, recreation, language and morals.

Individuals

As stated above, individuals are free to select any date and hour. However, they may try to organize *groups* of adorers, arranging the hours in such a way that a complete night is filled. This is being done on a wide scale. It is an incentive to the individual to know that his hour of adoration is one of a series that is continuing through the night. Let it be clearly understood, however, that it is not *necessary* to form a group but that the individual is free to make a separate hour at any time selected. *Let the individual adorer "pay the ransom" for his relatives and friends.*

Families

In large families the adoration may be arranged in such

a way that each member of the family watches in turn before a picture of the Sacred Heart. This is already being done in many families in the United States. If the Sacred Heart has been *enthroned* in the home, then the adoration should take place before the enthroned image of the Sacred Heart, around which lighted candles and flowers have been placed, whenever this is possible. (This is not essential.) The hours are assigned to each member of the family by the father or mother. If the family is large enough (nine members) then the adoration may begin at 9 and continue to 6; in smaller families, it may begin at 9 and continue until all members have made their adoration. At the end of each hour the next adorer is called by the preceding one. If it is not practical to make the adoration successively as described above, then the entire family may make it together at one determined hour. Again the father and mother may desire to make it alone or even one member of the family. The family is free to arrange this matter according to circumstances. If the family makes adoration at the same hour, then the father or mother might lead the prayers and the others join in the responses, as is done during the Holy Hour in church. This will make the hour pass quickly and pleasantly, especially for the children. *Let one family "pay the ransom" for other families.*

Parishes

It should be the goal of those promoting night adoration in the parish to have perpetual adoration.* This means that eventually at every hour of the night from 9 to 6, for every night of the month, some member of the parish is making adoration in his own home. To make this possible the immediate aim should be to fill as many nights as possible, using

---

* Note: We speak here of "home" adoration, not of adoration before the Blessed Sacrament. We encourage the latter wholeheartedly, but where it cannot be made, the adoration can be made in the home. The indulgences for home adoration can be gained only when the adoration is made in the home between 9 p.m. and 6 a.m. Other indulgences are attached to adoration before the Blessed Sacrament.

a chart for this purpose, which will enable the priest or promoter in charge to see at a glance what hours are taken and which ones are open. In this way when a person applies for an hour, leaving the choice to the priest or promoter, then the gaps may be filled up. Thus night by night the month will be filled, and consequently the entire year, as the monthly adoration is repeated for the twelve months of the year. As soon as an adorer's name is withdrawn for any reason another name should be assigned to his hour. In some parishes, night adoration is 100% perfect. What an avalanche of graces is going to descend on those parishes in which so many fervent parishioners *are "paying the ransom" for other less fervent parishioners!*

Schools, Societies, etc.

Catholic schools, societies, etc. may also aim at perpetual adoration within their own groups. Thus a school may strive to have enough pupils making adoration so that every night of the month is taken. The same is true of Catholic societies and groups, many of which are city wide as far as membership is concerned.

Priests

It is not necessary for priests to send in a specific date and hour to become members of the League. It is sufficient that they be enrolled at an authorized center. They may of course, select a fixed date and hour, if they so desire, or have one assigned to them. However, due to the fact that a priest's time is not always his own, he is free to change his date and hour according to circumstances. *Let priests "pay the ransom" for other priests.*

Religious

Individual religious may enroll, or entire communities. In the latter case, the arrangement and assignment of the hours of adoration are left up to the religious superior. In a religious house where nocturnal adoration in the chapel already exists, in order to gain the indulgences and share in the merits of the League, it is sufficient that the names of the religious be sent to a center for enrollment. This is also true in the case of those who make the "Holy Hour" as a group in the chapel. It is not necessary to make night adoration in the chapel, but it may be made in one's room or cell. This is especially true when adoration in the chapel might disturb the rest of the community. The superior may change the hours of adoration for any reasonable motive, as may the individual religious. It goes without saying that religious should consult their superiors and spiritual directors before undertaking this work of reparation. *Let religious "pay the ransom" for other religious.*

Seminarians

What has been said of religious applies also to seminarians. Hundreds of seminarians are making night adoration, *"paying the ransom" for other seminarians.*

Nurses

Nurses may make their hour of adoration while on night duty, even while watching beside the bed of a patient. Many outstanding conversions have resulted from this practice; one nurse *"paid the ransom" for a lost sheep who returned to the fold at the last moment.*

Sick and Aged

The sick and aged are permitted to make their hour of adoration in bed, if they are unable to get up. They need have no scruples of conscience about this, but let them offer their sufferings to the Sacred Heart, *"paying the ransom" for sinners.*

Night Workers

Night workers find it difficult to make their hour of adoration at night. There are several possible solutions. They may make their adoration *before* they go to work, especially if they are working on a late shift; or they may make their hour *after* they return from an earlier shift; or (as some are doing) they may make their hour during the "lunch hour," in the factory itself, if they find that conditions warrant it. Let them

308

find a secluded corner and offer up their hour in reparation for their fellow-workers, *"paying the ransom" in the very place, where, perhaps, many sins are being committed.* Night adoration may be made anywhere, provided there is no irreverence intended.

General Observations

Father Mateo strongly urges the night adorers to begin their hour of adoration by uniting themselves in spirit with the priests who at that moment are offering the Holy Sacrifice of the Mass in some part of the world. Let them "pray the Mass" by using their missals and reciting the Canon of the Mass with the priest. It is also suggested that the night adorer obtain a copy of the booklet NIGHT ADORATION IN THE HOME written by Father Mateo especially for the hour of adoration in the home. To vary the prayers Father Mateo has written a series of 21 Holy Hours for every month of the year and special occasions. *These books may be obtained from your promoter, local center or from the National Enthronement Center, Washington, D.C. 20017.*

Night Adoration is distinct from the work of the Enthronement, although a logical sequence of the former. Therefore one can be a night adorer without having one's home enthroned, even though all night adorers are strongly urged to enthrone the Sacred Heart as King of their family in reparation for His dethronement by so many modern "Christian" families. For information regarding the Enthronement, contact the nearest center of the work, or write directly to the National Center.

Indulgences

By decree of April 27, 1929, the Very Reverend Father General of the Franciscan Fathers affiliated the League of Night Adoration to this order, and granted all night adorers participation in its merits. On the 17th of May, 1929, the League of Night Adoration was affiliated 'to the Franciscan Confraternity of Nocturnal Reparation in Italy. This was ratified by the Sacred Congregation of the Council by a rescript of April 14, 1930. By virtue of this affiliation, the members of the League can gain the following indulgences. *Note* — To gain these indulgences it is necessary that the name of the night adorer be inscribed at a duly authorized center; that the adoration be made between the hours of 9 and 6, according to the legal time in your locality.

1) *A Plenary Indulgence* on the ordinary conditions (confession, communion, visit to a church or public oratory, prayers for the Holy Father's intentions):

(a) On the day of their admission as members of the League. (This means the day they hand in their enrollment to a promoter or send it to a center. Promoters must send in the names to a center.)

(b) Every time members make their hour of adoration according to the regulations given above.

2) *A Plenary Indulgence* at the hour of death if the members, having received the sacraments of penance and Holy Eucharist, or at least, being contrite, invoke the Holy Name of Jesus, if possible with their lips or at least in their heart, and patiently accept death as coming from the hand of God and as the wages of sin.

3) *Partial Indulgence* of 7 years for every extra hour of adoration made with a contrite heart.

Appendix 4

THE POPES SPEAK — PAPAL APPROVAL

LETTER OF HIS HOLINESS BENEDICT XV

To our Beloved Son Mateo Crawley-Boevey
Priest of the Congregation of the Sacred Hearts of Jesus
and Mary

Beloved Son, Health and Apostolic Benediction.

We have read your letter with interest and likewise the documents that accompanied it. From them We have learned of the diligence and zeal with which for many years you have devoted yourself to the work of consecrating families to the Most Sacred Heart of Jesus, in such a way that while His image is installed in the principal place in the home as on a throne, Our Divine Savior Jesus Christ is seen to reign at each Catholic hearth.

Our Predecessor, Leo XIII, of happy memory had already consecrated the entire human race to the divine Heart, and his noteworthy Encyclical Annum Sacrum on this subject is well known. Notwithstanding that general and collective consecration, however, the devotion as applied to each family in particular is not without its purpose. On the contrary, it is perfectly in accord with the former, and can only contribute to the religious aim of that Pontiff. For what concerns each one in particular, affects us more deeply than the interests we share with others. Therefore We rejoice at the thought that your work has borne abundant fruit in this direction, and We exhort you to persevere with diligence in the apostolate which you have begun.

Nothing, as a matter of fact, is more suitable to the needs of the present day than your enterprise. To pervert, both in private and in public life, the concept of morality engendered and fostered by the Church, and, after having almost effaced the last vestige of Christian wisdom and decency, to lead human society back to the miserable institutions of paganism, such is the plan which too many are trying to realize today. Would that their efforts were fruitless! Moreover, the attacks of the wicked are directed primarily against the family. For, containing within itself as it does the principles and, as it were, the germ of all human society, they clearly see that the change, or rather, the corruption, which they are trying to bring about in human society, will necessarily follow, once the corruption of the family itself has been accomplished. Hence divorce laws are introduced to put an end to the stability of marriage; children are forced to follow an official teaching for the most part estranged from religion, thus eliminating the authority of parents in a matter of the highest importance; moreover, countenance is given to the spread of a shameful course of selfish indulgence which contravenes the laws of nature, and striking a blow at the human race at its very source, stains the sanctity of marriage with impure practices.

You do well, then, dear Son, while taking up the cause of human society, to arouse and propagate above all things a Christian spirit in the home by setting up in each family the reign of the love of Jesus Christ. And in doing this you are but obeying our Divine Lord Himself, who promised to shower His blessings upon the homes wherein an image of His Heart should be exposed and devoutly honored.

It is assuredly, therefore, a holy and salutary work to secure for our beloved Redeemer such worship and honor. But that is not everything. It is of the utmost importance to know Christ, to know His doctrine, His life, His passion, His glory. For to follow Him does not consist in allowing ourselves to be swayed by a superficial religious sentiment that easily moves weak and tender hearts to tears, but leaves vices intact. To follow Christ is to be permeated with a lively and

312

constant faith, which not only acts upon the mind and heart, but likewise governs and directs our conduct. Moreover the real reason why Jesus is neglected by so many and but little loved by others, is to be found in the fact that He is almost entirely unknown to the former and not known sufficiently by the latter. Continue therefore, beloved Son, in your efforts to enkindle in Catholic homes the flames of love for the Most Sacred Heart of Jesus: but likewise and before all else, and this is Our wish, endeavor to make this love result from a knowledge of Christ the Lord, and from a greater and deeper understanding of the truths and laws which He Himself has given us.

For Our part, in order to encourage the piety of the faithful in this matter, we extend to all families of the Catholic world that consecrate themselves to the Most Sacred Heart of Jesus, all those spiritual favors which Our predecessor, Pius X, of happy memory, granted with Pontifical liberality, in 1913, at the instance of the Bishops of Chile to the families of that Republic consecrated to the Sacred Heart.

As a pledge of divine favors and as a mark of Our paternal goodwill, We impart to you affectionately, beloved Son, the Apostolic Blessing.

Given at St. Peter's, Rome this 27th day of April, 1915, in the first year of Our Pontificate.

BENEDICT PP., XV

LETTER OF HIS HOLINESS PIUS XI

To Our Beloved Son, Fr. Mateo Crawley-Boevey.

PIUS XI, PP.

Beloved Son, Health and the Apostolic Benediction.

It will soon be your happiness to renew the holy memory of that day on which, twenty-five years ago, you offered for the first time the Holy Sacrifice to God and promised to work for the salvation of souls and His own Divine Glory. And, in fact, how absorbed you have been by these resolves, during the years gone by, is easily seen by the manner in which you have spread filial love everywhere to the August Heart of Jesus not only by consecrating families to this worship, but seeing to it that Christ the Lord should have, as King, the place of honor in every home.

We therefore seize this favorable opportunity to manifest Our personal good-will to you. We join Our late Predecessors in showering praise upon you, and very willingly share with you the joy of this happy occasion.

We pray God may keep you in His graciousness for long days to come to carry out even more devotedly your original enterprise, and with an ever-expanding love to the Most Holy Eucharist; for if ever before, it is now, in the great upheaval of all things, a most pressing need, that the Lord Jesus, the King of Peace, Who is alone the Way, the Truth and the Life, should rule the social life of men.

As a forecast of Heavenly gifts and from the depths of Our heart, We grant you, beloved Son, and all belonging to you, the Apostolic Blessing.

Given at St. Peter's, Rome, this 15th day of the month of December, 1923, in the second year of Our Pontificate.

PIUS PP., XI

Very affectionately in the Lord, under Our own hand.

LETTER OF POPE PIUS XII

To our Beloved Son Mateo Crawley-Boevey,
Priest of the Congregation of the Sacred Hearts of Jesus and Mary.

Beloved Son, Health and Apostolic Benediction.

Now that fifty years soon will have elapsed, since that day on which, endowed with the sacerdotal dignity, you offered the Holy Sacrifice for the first time, We do not wish you to be deprived of the felicitations and good wishes of

314

Our Paternal Heart. All the more so, since We have learned that you are presently confined to a hospital, not so much by reason of declining years, but rather because of serious infirmities, and thus are unable to labor with that zealous ardor which was your wont, for the Consecration of Catholic families to the Most Tender Heart of Jesus.

Nevertheless, what you are unable to do by apostolic labors, by apostolic journeys and preachings, you can accomplish undoubtedly by ardent prayers addressed to God, and by sufferings and afflictions cheerfully accepted in a spirit of reparation. That you are doing this with a humble and willing heart We do not doubt, and while We desire to console you in your present illness, yet We also express the wish in your behalf that your strength be restored as soon as possible and that once more you may be permitted to strive earnestly to obtain for this salutary enterprise an ever increasing success.

This undertaking corresponds to Our most cherished desires, as it did to those of Our Predecessors. We long for the return to the private life of men and the public life of peoples of the love of Jesus Christ, which springs from this Divine Heart. In this way alone will it be possible to console the many who are afflicted and in misery, to strengthen the many who are weak and wavering, to arouse effectively the many who are negligent and lukewarm, and finally to induce everyone to the fervent practice of that Christian virtue which gave to the primitive Church its greatest glory, that of sanctity and martyrdom.

Let the Divine Redeemer reign once more in civil society and in family life, by His Law and His Love, and then without any doubt will be rooted out entirely those vices which are the source of human unhappiness and human misery; then without any doubt discord will disappear; then justice — but true justice — will solidify the foundations of human society, and that true liberty "wherewith Christ has made us free" (Gal. 4: 31), will enhance the dignity of citizens and will make them brothers.

However, there is one thing We desire in a special way

— and which is moreover the principal goal in the Work which you have propagated so long and so diligently — namely, that Christian families consecrate themselves to the Sacred Heart "in such a way that His image being installed in the place of honor in the home, as on a throne, Christ the Lord is seen to reign truly within the Catholic family." (Bened. XV, Epis. *Libenter tuas* d.d. xxvii Apr. MCMXV; A.A.S. vol. vii, p. 203). This Consecration is not a useless and empty ceremony, but requires of everyone that their lives be in harmony with Christian precepts, that they burn with an ardent love for the Holy Eucharist, and that they share in the Heavenly Banquet as often as possible; and that they strive by humble prayers addressed to God, and by works of holy penance to provide by all means in their power not only for their own salvation but also for the salvation of others.

These, dear Son, are Our wishes and desires which it pleases Us to express to you on the occasion of the Fiftieth Anniversary of your priesthood which you are soon to celebrate, and the fulfillment of which we entrust to the Divine Goodness and Mercy. But in the meantime, as a proof of Our paternal good will and as a pledge of heavenly graces, We impart to you affectionately in the Lord, the Apostolic Blessing.

Given at Rome, at St. Peter's, the second day of the month of July, in the year nineteen hundred and forty-eight, the tenth of Our Pontificate.

PIUS XII, POPE

LETTER OF HIS HOLINESS PAUL VI

(A letter from His Eminence, Amleto Cardinal Cicognani, Secretary of State, written in the name of His Holiness, Pope Paul VI, on the occasion of the 60th anniversary of the founding of the Enthronement of the Sacred Heart of Jesus in the home.)

To the Reverend Francis Larkin, SS.CC.

Reverend and dear Father,

The knowledge that the crusade for the consecration of

families to the Most Sacred Heart of Jesus, "king and center of all hearts," is shortly to celebrate its sixtieth anniversary of foundation, has filled the heart of the Sovereign Pontiff with sentiments of paternal pleasure, warm comfort and lively hope.

The late Father Mateo Crawley-Boevey, illustrious son of your Congregation and modern apostle of devotion to the Sacred Heart, founded this movement at Paray-le-Monial on August 24, 1907, beside the tomb of Saint Margaret Mary Alacoque, and proceeded to spread it throughout the entire Catholic world, to make more visible and efficacious the Kingdom of the divine Savior in the family.

Such consecration is not an entirely new devotion. Rather is it the full flowering of that piety towards the Sacred Heart promoted by Saint Margaret Mary and approved by the Apostolic See. Moreover, it may be considered a concrete and more specific application of the consecration of the human race to the Heart of Jesus, which was performed by order of Pope Leo XIII in June of the Holy Year 1900.

It is not surprising, therefore, that the Roman Pontiffs have approved and encouraged this salutary undertaking, ever since Saint Pius X received Father Mateo in Audience in June, 1907. Still valid today are the words of praise which Pope Benedict XV addressed to the zealous founder on April 27, 1915: "You do well, beloved son, to take up the cause of human society, by first stirring up and spreading the Christian spirit in families and homes, and by establishing in the center of our families the love of Jesus Christ to reign and rule therein. You thus obey Jesus Christ Himself, since He promised to pour forth His benefits upon those houses where the image of His Heart would be exposed and venerated. To give Our beloved Redeemer such cult and honor is indeed to perform a holy and salutary work" (A.A.S., VII, 1915, p. 204).

Where, in fact, apart from churches and oratories, is the divine Heart of Jesus more fittingly adored than in the sanctuary of the family? From His pierced side on the Cross, together with the other Sacraments, there also flowed the "great Sacrament" (Eph. 5:32) of Matrimony, from which conjugal love derives its holiness, its stability and its sublime dignity. Consequently we may truly say that the Christian family is rooted in the very depths of the Sacred Heart of Christ the King, whence the Church Herself was born.

This Kingship of God in the home reminds Christian spouses that true conjugal love is taken up into the divine Love, is sustained and enriched by the redemptive grace of Christ. They are in this way enabled to fulfill worthily their high mission as fathers and mothers, able to educate their children religiously, and even ready to give some of them joyously to the Lord, to be consecrated to His service and that of their neighbor in the priesthood or in the religious life (Second Vatican Council: Pastoral Constitution *Gaudium et Spes*, No. 48).

Hence it is evident that the cult of the Sacred Heart of Jesus, King and Friend of the family, does not end with family consecration or with nocturnal adoration. It demands, moreover, as Pope Pius XII wrote to Father Mateo, "that each must conform his own life to Christian precepts; must burn with ardent love for the Blessed Eucharist, and partake of the divine Banquet as often as possible; must strive, through humble prayer to God and through holy penance, to obtain by every means in his power not only his own salvation, but also the redemption of others" (Letter of July 2, 1948).

If it is thus nourished by liturgical worship, especially in the Holy Sacrifice of the Mass, personal and family devotion to the Sacred Heart will never become "a sterile and ephemeral sentimentality, or a sort of vain credulity" (Dogmatic Constitution: *Lumen gentium*, No. 67), but rather a witness to the true faith, to sincere love and to a generous spirit of reparation, attaining even to the apostolate of suffering, according to the example of our Savior Who, on the Cross, "loved the Church and gave Himself up for her" (Eph. 5:25).

The Holy Father is confident that the devotion to the Most Sacred Heart of Jesus, so wisely and zealously promoted by your Congregation, will ever contribute to the progress of strong Christian piety, according to the wishes of the Second Vatican Council which He Himself renewed in His Apostolic Letter *Investigabiles divitas Christi* (February 6, 1965; A.A.S., LVII, 1965, p. 300). In that prayerful hope, He lovingly imparts to all the promoters of this pious practice, and to all those families consecrated to Jesus Christ, the King of Love, His Paternal Apostolic Blessing.

With my personal felicitations and good wishes, I remain

Sincerely yours in Christ,
Amleto Card. Cicognani.

(Vatican City, March 13, 1967)